THE SUCCESS TRIP

THE
SUCCESS TRIP

How They Made It
How They Feel About It

ROSS FIRESTONE

P⋎P

A Playboy Press Book

Copyright © 1976 by Ross Firestone.

FIRST EDITION

Playboy and Rabbit Head design are trademarks of Playboy, 919 North Michigan Avenue, Chicago, Illinois 60611 (U.S.A.), Reg. U.S. Pat. Off., marca registrada, marque déposée.

Library of Congress Cataloging in Publication Data

Firestone, Ross.
      The success trip—how they made it, how they feel about it.

      Includes index.
      1. Success—Biography. I. Title.
HF5386.F4154 650'.1'0922 [B] 76–15224
ISBN 0–87223–451–7

FOR
My Mother and Father

Contents

Preface

This book explores the diverse, sometimes contradictory realities of success in present-day America through the words and perceptions of thirty-four people who have experienced it in their own lives.

In choosing the people to interview for the book, I looked for men and women somewhere near the top of their professions who would, I felt, have something to say about success and be willing to say it. I spent an hour or so with each of them, taping their responses to a series of questions that required them to sum up their personal experiences of such matters as ambition, wealth, power, fame, work, luck, fulfillment, failure, and the gain and the loss, the pleasures and perils encountered along the way. I edited the transcripts to make them read as smoothly and concisely as possible without distorting individual patterns of thought and expression, then asked each contributor to check my final draft to make sure he or she was represented fairly.

The more interviews I compiled, the more I was struck by the drastically different ways success is experienced and perceived. It is far from always the same, even though it may sometimes look that way to those of us who haven't gotten close enough to get the feel of it. Whatever success is—and I think we better leave it undefined—it is a good bit less simple or uniform than either its boosters or detractors would have us believe with their rather too certain generalities.

I thought it important to have the structure of this book reflect the complexities and ambiguities I found. Accordingly, I have organized it not as a series of self-contained interviews but as a kind of mosaic of contrasting responses to the various aspects of success most everyone I talked to has had to come to terms with.

Each chapter juxtaposes a number of different answers to the same basic questions. The questions themselves are indicated by the chapter titles. Through this juxtaposition, what one person has to say is in effect made to comment on someone else's perspective, usually to modify or oppose it but sometimes, when the same points were stressed by a number of contributors, to reinforce it or develop it more fully. The contents of each interview may appear in half a dozen or more places, and should you wish to follow any of them through from beginning to end, I have provided an index to make that possible.

In telling us their feelings about success, the men and women in this book inevitably also reveal something more about themselves as people—the childhoods that shaped them, their expectations, dreams and fears, the ways they related to the world around them, what they consider important and unimportant, what gets them off about their lives and what doesn't. Success isn't something one usually talks about in public, and in consenting to answer my questions they have also consented to let us see some of the private person usually obscured behind the more public self. I thank them for their generosity.

I would also like to thank some of the many others who have helped bring this book into being: Bill Adler, Gloria Adler, Zohn Artman, Marion Billings, Bob Cato, Alan Douglas, Ed Eckstine, Levi Fears, Gail Firestone, Robert Gardner, Shep Gordon, Norman Gorin, Bert Greene, Connie Harper, Barbara Hohol, Janice Jakubisin, Stanley Kay, Ed Kuhn, Peter Levinson, Sandy Manley, Mandi Newall, Marilyn O'Brien, Richard Rubinstein, Bruce Savan, Ken Schaffer, Irvin Shapiro, Ilene Shifrin, Glen Simoes, Nat Sobel, Wayne Smith, Lynne Volkman and Basil Winston.

The Contributors

Auto racer **MARIO ANDRETTI** has won the Indianapolis 500, the United States Auto Club National Title and many other major racing competitions.

ROCKY AOKI is founder and president of the Benihana of Tokyo restaurants.

Actress **ELIZABETH ASHLEY** was acclaimed for her recent stage performances in *Cat on a Hot Tin Roof* and *The Skin of Our Teeth*.

Trial lawyer **F. LEE BAILEY** has defended such clients as Sam Sheppard, the Boston Strangler, Captain Ernest Medina and Patty Hearst. His books include *The Defense Never Rests* and *For the Defense*.

JOAN GANZ COONEY is the creator of *Sesame Street* and president of the Children's Television Workshop.

ALICE COOPER is a rock superstar.

Sportscaster **HOWARD COSELL** is the voice of *Monday Night Football* and author of *Cosell* and *Like It Is*.

CLIVE DAVIS is president of Arista Records. His book *Clive: Inside the Record Business* recounts his years as head of Columbia Records.

Copywriter **JERRY DELLA FEMINA** has his own advertising agency in New York. He is the author of *From Those Wonderful Folks Who Gave You Pearl Harbor: Front Line Dispatches From the Advertising War*.

JOHN DIEBOLD pioneered both the practical application of computer technology and the understanding of its social impact. He is president of the Diebold Group, the international management consultant firm.

Psychologist and sex researcher **ALBERT ELLIS** is founder of the Institute for Rational Living in New York. His many books include *Sex Without Guilt, Humanistic Psychotherapy* and *The New Sex and the Single Man.*

JOE EULA does fashion illustration, stages shows, paints, designs sets and costumes for ballet and theater, and is consultant to Halston and *Vogue* magazine.

EILEEN FORD runs the prestigious Ford Model Agency with her husband Jerry. She is the author of *Eileen Ford's Book of Model Beauty* and *Eileen Ford's Secrets of the Model's World.*

Biographer **GEROLD FRANK** has written such books as *I'll Cry Tomorrow, Too Much Too Soon, Beloved Infidel, Zsa Zsa, The Boston Strangler, The Deed, An American Death* and *Judy.*

WILLIAM GAINES publishes *Mad* magazine.

Graphics artist and designer **MILTON GLASER** is a founder of the Push Pin Studio design group and cofounder and design director of *New York* magazine.

AL GOLDSTEIN publishes *Screw* magazine.

BILL GRAHAM is a music impresario and concert producer. His Fillmore auditoriums in San Francisco and New York set the standards for the production of rock concerts.

Photographer **MILTON H. GREENE** has taken pictures for many national magazines and advertisements. His work is frequently exhibited in galleries and museums.

JACK HALEY JR. is president of the 20th Century-Fox television division. He produced, wrote and directed the film *That's Entertainment!*

Fashion designer **HALSTON** has twice received the Coty American Fashion Critics highest award for his great influence on contemporary American dress.

GEOFFREY HOLDER dances, choreographs, acts and paints, and directed the award-winning Broadway musical *The Wiz.*

REVEREND IKE (Frederick J. Eikerenkoetter) is one of America's most popular mass evangelists. He is founder and president of the United Church, Science of Living Institute in New York.

Composer **QUINCY JONES** writes and arranges music for films and television and his own recordings and concert appearances.

MURRAY KEMPTON has written political and social commentary for the *New York Post,* the *New Republic, Esquire,* the *New York Review of Books* and PLAYBOY. His books include *America Comes of Middle Age* and *The Briar Patch.*

DON KING promotes Muhammad Ali's fights throughout the world and other major sports events.

ALEXIS LICHINE is a grower and merchant of wines and author of *Wines of France* and *Alexis Lichine's New Encyclopedia of Wines & Spirits.*

Astronaut **EDGAR D. MITCHELL** was the sixth man to walk on the moon. Since retiring from the space program in 1972, he has devoted himself to the research of human consciousness.

GEORGE PLIMPTON edits *The Paris Review* and writes about sports. His books include *Paper Lion, Mad Ducks and Bears* and *One for the Record.*

REX REED writes about film for the *Chicago Tribune–New York News* syndicate newspapers and *Vogue* magazine. He is the author of *Do You Sleep in the Nude?, People Are Crazy Here* and other books.

Jazz great **BUDDY RICH** plays drums and leads a big band.

BRUNO SANMARTINO is the professional heavyweight wrestling champion of the world.

Filmmaker **MARTIN SCORSESE** directed *Mean Streets, Alice Doesn't Live Here Any More* and *Taxi Driver.*

MIKE WALLACE is a correspondent for CBS television news and appears regularly on *60 Minutes.*

Part One

HOW THEY MADE IT

MIKE WALLACE

I suppose in subtle ways it was made apparent by my family that they would be happy if I were "successful." Success, as I remember it, meant material success as I was growing up. Not that I came from a poor family, we were middle class, middle income. But inasmuch as both of my parents were immigrants and I was the first generation to follow—I was one of four children in my family—success meant economic security. The men who had "succeeded" had businesses, supported their families, sent their kids to camp in the summer, had money in the bank; they were the examples held up to us as something to shoot at. And I reacted as I might very well have been expected to react: I tried. I tried to do that.

JERRY DELLA FEMINA

Success was truly the only idea. I had the advantage of coming from a rather modest background, kind of an Italian semi-ghetto. Until I was twenty-five I never earned more than ninety bucks a week and I had a family with kids and everything else. And so I was not just a failure but a nose-rubbed-into-it kind of failure, which made the taste of any kind of success even so much better. I mean, I wasn't someone who said, "Gee, I want to be a success because Dad sent me to Harvard and therefore I have to succeed." No, it was, "Hey, I want to get out of this fuckin' neighborhood, I want to make some money and I want *everything.*" That was part of a dream, and I guess if you lived in a neighborhood like mine, without it you're dead 'cause that's what keeps you going.

So it was very important that I do something. It wasn't laid on me, but parents don't have to talk. They can just be there. My mother keeps every clipping, every story, every everything. Yeah, my success is very important to her. What happens with Italians is they equate success with respect. It's the same word. When an Italian says he wants to be a success, he means he wants to be respected. It's always outer-directed. They want the other people, everyone around them, to feel that about them. So I could say that success/respect was the theme of the neighborhood. And more than anyone else, I wanted it and I wouldn't stop until I got it.

But there are successes and successes. Some guy could say, "Hey, I want to be a fireman." Because that's what the neighborhood dream was: I want to be a fireman, I want to be a policeman, I want to be a numbers runner. But I didn't just want to be a nice family man who goes to work at nine o'clock in the morning and comes home at five and earns a decent living for his family, and then they shovel the dirt over the body and say, "Well, he was a nice man." That was not my concept of success. That's the only thing that was different about me from the rest of the people in that neighborhood. Me, I wanted to taste everything, see everything, do everything. I can remember when I was very, very broke, really broke, I guess I was about nineteen. I was just about to get married and was making forty or fifty dollars a week, and I would go into very expensive restaurants to eat and drag my friends along on the theory that some day I'm going to be able to afford great restaurants and I want to practice for them now. I remember blowing a couple of salaries practicing for success. That's how much I wanted it. I wanted even to prepare for it.

EILEEN FORD

I don't think my family ever put any emphasis at all on my being successful. They were extremely comfortable financially, and therefore I never had any sense of needing to do anything.

I had as much money as I wanted. I had a car when I was sixteen. The one thing I needed to do was bring home a good report card. I would have just been killed for goofing around. I didn't have an A average or anything like that, but if I had a bad average I would have been grounded, that would have been it, and I would never have wanted to risk ruining my social life.

So I never thought about being successful. I never had any doubts about myself. I think that a lot of people are driven by fear of lack of success. Me, I was loved. I was the only daughter. Everybody was wonderful. I had a great life. But it never occurred to me that I wouldn't be successful at whatever I did because I'd never been unsuccessful. It's not that I was highly motivated. "Motivate" is a very poor word to use with me. I just do things. Ah, but I'm fiercely proud. Maybe it's just my ego. I wouldn't want anybody to say that I'd done a bad job at something, because it'd kill me. I guess it goes back to the old report card.

REX REED

Nobody ever even mentioned success. That word never came up in my family. There was no pressure at all to do anything more than be a functioning member of society, which, given my own particular working class background, meant having enough money to marry some nice girl and make a down payment on an Amana freezer and live a nice life in a house with an electric kitchen. None of that ever interested me particularly. In the back of my mind was always the possibility of something else. And somehow I just always knew that I would be a success. The alternative never occurred to me.

I always knew that I would leave the South and go to New York. I guess for about ten minutes I considered going to Hollywood and becoming a movie star, but I was always a much better writer. I had been writing since the age of ten, I guess, and was considered fairly precocious. And I was very impressed by the success of other people. I was never content to settle for local success. When I majored in journalism and started getting job offers from the local newspaper and various local employers, I knew that was not enough, that there was something else out there and I was good enough to achieve it, so that's what I aimed for.

MURRAY KEMPTON

I remember my mother saying, "I hope you'll be a success." I don't know what she meant by it. I suppose to have some money. I think that's how success was thought of, at least in my family, which was kind of out of it in some curious way. It's a pompous thing to say, but they were more downward mobile than upward mobile. The last half of the nineteenth century was a time of disaster for both sides of my family. My mother was from West Virginia, and the loss of the Civil War had been pretty serious to everybody. My father's family was from Philadelphia, and they had gone from rags to rags in one generation. My grandfather had had money long before he went broke for his daughters to marry rich men, but his son had married my mother and then he died. So we were very much the poor relations, and my mother always worked.

I don't really know what her notion of success would have been, but as she said, she wanted me to be successful. How did I respond to that? With the expectation of failure. How do you ever respond to that? I took it for granted I was unworthy. I don't know what my own notion of success was at that time. I probably would have thought that if I had what I have now that would be a great success, but I had a more limited view of the world than I have now. I think that's one of the real problems. You don't know much about the world, so neither success nor failure seems to be that important. Maybe what's wrong is that people are not taught what constitutes success.

F. LEE BAILEY

Success was a somewhat cloudy perception when I was a boy and could be demonstrated only in competitive sports or competition in the classroom. But I would say that the idea was present to a very strong degree, just the notion that, you know, you ought to do your best, you ought to at least want to be number one in the class, whether you are or not. I was once castigated before the whole student body for going from number twenty-nine in the class to number ten through one series of midterm examinations as a good example of someone who wasn't trying very hard. I think I usually got either Cs or As but not many Bs. It would depend on interest. If the course was uninteresting I must confess I didn't put much effort into it. I guess I sort of expected to be successful. I did not expect to be looking up from the bottom of the barrel. On the other hand, I probably expected no more than to be a member of a certain recognized group that was at least doing a competent job.

WILLIAM GAINES

I don't recall that success was made at all important to me when I was growing up, and I never expected to be a success. I expected to be a failure. I was kind of inept, I never did anything well. I was never good in athletics. I was never good with my hands. I could never fix things like my friends. And I guess mostly it was because my father gave me the idea that I was an idiot and I kind of acted the way I was expected to act.

ALBERT ELLIS

Success as a young boy meant you were a great athlete, that's what it normally meant. My brother and I used to make up the usual fantasies when we were young. I was only six or seven at the time. We'd fantasize that the Babe Ruths and the Lou Gehrigs were our friends, and we were also the friends of the movie stars. We were equal with them. And we had women around, but they were the women in the movies. We probably really didn't think of screwing them or anything, but they were our sidekicks, just as Tom Mix in the movies had a sidekick. So we used the popular heroes, mainly athletes and cowboys and rarely captains of industry, maybe an occasional millionaire or general, a Rockefeller or a General Pershing. But I'd say our heroes were more masculine and chauvinist than anything else.

It was mainly the masculine prowess kind of thing, the ego horseshit. I accepted all that as a young boy, but by the time I got to college I understood it for what it was, horseshit of the worst sort. I despised the competitive things that went on in college, especially the fights between the classes. We had tugs-of-war, and I thought they were idiotic. In high school I devoutly went to see the football and baseball games, but by college I had given it all up. I realized that cheering for our team to win was really dull and boring and not in the least "masculine."

JOAN GANZ COONEY

I don't think I thought of women having careers, but there was a great deal of talk around our house about working after you finished college. And it was always *"after* you finished college." That was not a negotiation between my parents and the three children, nor did it ever cross our minds to negotiate it. We were the products of the forties and early fifties and there was no dropping out. You went to college if you were of the upper middle class. Or got married. Girls were allowed to leave college and get married, but it would have been unthinkable to leave college and go to work as a secretary for a year, for example, and just say, "I'm going to take a year off."

So I knew I would work after I got out of college if I weren't married, and I assumed I would do something like teach or be a secretary. This is when I was a little kid. I remember saying to my mother, "I think I'll be a secretary," and her saying, "Oh, surely you can think of something more imaginative than that." And I felt so put down because I didn't know what all those things meant. She had been a secretary before she got married, so I just assumed that's what I would be.

But in college I majored in education, still on the assumption that I would marry young, which I did not do. One's parents kept saying things like, "Now if you're widowed at an early age, teaching is a marvelous thing to have." So I majored in education and went to Washington for a year and worked for the government as a clerk-typist, and then went back out to Phoenix and worked as a reporter for the *Arizona Republic* for a year, and then came to New York and began publicizing television shows for NBC.

I was highly motivated to succeed but only in very short-term ways. I never said I will someday be successful or famous or any of those things. My conscious thought was an extremely conservative of-the-day kind of thinking about the role of women. And they *were* allowed to work after they finished college at jobs that men approved of, meaning as assistants-to or as publicists for TV shows, as long as they weren't the most important shows in the house. I think I was constantly wanting approval. I mean, I really accepted my assigned role, but I wanted to do my assigned role excellently. I was always driven to succeed in whatever the assignment was. It took a long psychoanalysis in my twenties to get me to understand that I didn't have to accept the role assigned me as a woman, but all through my twenties and much of my thirties I still did accept it.

BRUNO SANMARTINO

When I came over to the United States from Italy I was very, very grateful just to be here, but I guess I was also pretty ambitious. I was going to get married, I was going to have children. And call it ego if you want, but I wanted to be a man in the sense that I wanted to be a good provider. I didn't want to get married and have to see what I saw in my youth with my mom and dad, because it couldn't be helped, where it was, "Hey, here's twenty-five bucks, you gotta buy food for the week." I wanted to be able to be somebody. Not to become a millionaire, that's the least interest in my life, but not to have to worry if I feel like eating a steak or to be able to send my kids to school if they want to go and have the ability. I have a brother who's a genius. This guy's brain is unbelievable, yet he didn't have the opportunity to go to college when he was young. Now he's going to college on his own at night because he works during the day. He's gotten a master's degree and he's going for his doctor's. I wanted to give my kids the opportunity to do it in their youth, if they have it, if this is what they choose. My father wouldn't have deprived me or my brother or sister of anything, but he had no choice. He just had no means.

But I didn't even start thinking about success until after the time we left Italy and came to the United States after the Second World War ended. During the war, who thought of anything past tomorrow? That's all you wanted, to reach tomorrow, to survive.

I was just a kid, about seven or eight years old, the terrible night it started, but I remember it very, very clearly, like a bad dream. It was the middle of winter and we were all sleeping, and suddenly we were awakened by these enormous noises like nothing you ever heard before. There was a lot of commotion, and then I remember my uncle pounding on the door. What was happening was that a lot of German SS troops in armored trucks and jeeps had moved into our little village. It was terrifying. I'm sure you're familiar with the SS. They were pretty coldhearted people. Some of us were able to grab a blanket or some clothing to put on our bodies, and we ran away and made it. But a lot of people didn't make it. They were just shot and butchered.

Everybody who was able to get out just scattered in different directions. About forty of us made it to the top of this mountain, about a day-and-a-half climb, and we hid there for almost a year. The men cut up some timber and made Indian-type tepees for shelter, but of course they didn't have any equipment to really do the job right, and there was very little protection from the hard weather. Some of the old people just couldn't survive it. Some of the very young died too. Had it gone on any longer I probably would have gone next because I came down with pneumonia and there was no medication or doctors or anything like that. It was pretty bad.

If you looked at my mother, all you would see would be a very plain little old lady from the other side, but to me she is the greatest woman in the world. I can't imagine many women doing what she did. My father had come to the United States before the war to earn some money so he could better himself back in Italy, so my mother was alone with six small children that were too young to take care of themselves. There was no food to eat, so she would climb back down this mountain at night and sneak past the Germans and when no one was looking steal some food from the cellar of our home, some potatoes or corn, anything she could get her hands on that would keep us alive. There were days in between her trips when we had to live on snow. You just stuffed yourself with it until you were no longer so hungry.

My mother was close to fifty years old when this terrible ordeal took place. She wasn't young, but she did everything she could for our survival. The Germans captured her a couple of times while she was trying to get us food. Once they put her on this open truck with other people who had been captured. Where they were transporting them only God knows. They had barbed wire all around the truck to keep the people from getting out, but because of us kids nothing would hold her back and she pushed and scratched and threw herself past the barbed wire and escaped. They shot their rifles at her, and she still has the bullet holes in her shoulder from where she was hit. If you had seen her, how ripped up and bleeding she was. But it seemed like there was nothing in the world that could stop her.

The Germans finally discovered where we were hiding, and two of them came up there with their tommy guns and lined up all of us who were left, some twenty or thirty people, I'm not sure. They were going to kill us all. By this time I had lost a sister and two brothers. Only three of us children were still alive, and while the Germans were lining us up, she held us and tried to comfort us to take any fear out of us. She kept saying, "Don't be afraid because pretty soon there's going to be no more starving, no more cold, no more of this. We're going to be in heaven with God where everything is going to be beautiful." She kept talking to us like this until we were no longer scared, and everything was fine because, you know, you believe your mother. She was completely unconcerned about herself. Her whole concern was for her children. What finally saved us was that three or four of the men who had been out someplace came back and saw what was happening, and got those two Germans from behind with their knives and killed them. Had they returned a couple of minutes later we would have all been gone. But of course we were kids then, and you have to grow older before you can fully understand what it was all about. That's why I've never had as much appreciation of my mother as I do today. There's nothing in this world I wouldn't do for her, and I just wish she were a little bit younger so she could enjoy some of the good things that have happened to me. She lived a very hard life, as did my father.

But anyway, we finally survived all this, and when the Germans were driven out of our village we came back. The sad part was that the war hadn't really ended for us. The bombings had stopped, but our homes were all destroyed and there were bodies of dead English and German soldiers all over the place and a lot of people were getting sick and dying from diseases. So the hell wasn't over yet.

In 1947 the immigration quotas opened up for us and we were able to come here to the United States. But as I told you, I had come down with pneumonia when we were hiding in the mountain and wasn't healthy enough to pass the physical, so I kept my whole family back, which was a real heartbreak. The next time an opening came was in 1951. This time I was pretty well okay and a year and a half later we finally immigrated to America. To me, when we landed here it was truly like coming to heaven and I mean that from the bottom of my heart. My father was a poor man, we had nothing. But my brother and I were young and we went to work, doing construction, cutting people's lawns, driving trucks. I did anything and everything, but so help me God, whatever it was I did it with great joy because I was here. That's the greatest gift I ever received in my life.

BILL GRAHAM

We all have our reasons why we started to do what we did. I didn't want to live at home so I started to wash dishes. I wanted to go to school so I started driving a cab. I was an orphan when I came to the States and I lived with foster parents and started working when I was very young. It's no great story. Everybody else has done it. But from the very first day I said that the one thing I'm going to do is have dollars, I have to have income to pay my way. Daddy isn't going to do it for me, and it's not such a terrible thing. I've never known what it was like to have hand-me-downs because my father died when I was two days old and that was it.

So from the very beginning whatever the job was, there was always the awareness that I needed it. There was also the awareness that I wanted it. But I never really looked too much for material things, and whenever I wanted something, really wanted it, it usually seemed within reach, it wasn't that far away. It wasn't the sailboat at the age of twenty. And when I wanted it, I didn't give a fuck. I wouldn't kill for it. I wouldn't steal. Well, I sort of borrowed here and there from the A&P, a little candy, and when I worked at Grossinger's, maybe a little silverware and that kind of stuff. I'm talking about when I was eighteen, nineteen years old.

I don't remember too many things about that time, but I have one strong recollection of what success meant to me then. I was a mambo-nik, one of the few really fanatical maniac white kids who were into that then. There were maybe twenty-five of us. I'd go to Brooklyn for Tito Puente and back to Manhattan for Machito and then up to the mountains for someone else. We were crazy. And one day I was walking past a men's store on Fifth Avenue and I saw this pointy pair of black shoes in the window. I mean they were Ricardo Montalban, you just saw his name on them. Or Fernando Lamas. And I had to have them. I remember I walked in and said, "Do you have those shoes in twelve EE?" and the guy gave me a look that said, "Why do you even bother to ask me? You know you can't afford them." You know: "Puleeze!" And he said, "Do you want to look at them?" I said, "I want to *buy* them. Do you have my size?" The guy thought he was wasting his time, but I guess there's a law saying he has to show them to you. They were thirty-five bucks in 1958, '59. I loved those shoes and wanted them, and I thought it was a great accomplishment that I was able to buy what I wanted. To this day I have them. To this day I still wear them. They're very symbolic to me because they're something that I loved and wanted and was able to get. I've worn through maybe three sets of heels, but they're still there. That was a very big successful thing to me.

QUINCY JONES

I guess success is made to seem important to everybody, especially when you come from a trip where your family's scuffling. That's the way out, man, and I was lucky enough to get into it at an early age. I just liked to work, and at eleven years old I was running a cleaners. The guy would send the clothes out to be cleaned and we would do the pressing at his place, and after a while I got interested in it and learned how to press and because he had a lot of other jobs he just turned the whole shop over to me. I was about eleven and I'd sit down there and put the rag on my head, press all the stuff up and eat sweet rolls, man. Then I'd put the papers on it and deliver it.

I always used to plunge into everything I'd do and I guess that's the whole point—to get an attitude from the beginning of plunging in and giving it all you've got, whatever it is. The same principle applies in whatever you do. And I was lucky that I always saw the difference between the hunt and the kill. I always knew that if you kept the focal point on the kill of success you really wouldn't get too much done, so I always found a way to enjoy the hunt. If I knew I had to walk across the park, I'd say to myself, I know where it is and I know I'm going to get there, but I might as well enjoy the pond and the birds and the trees along the way. You've got to enjoy what the trip is about because the success in itself as a final goal is really a false value.

I didn't know that as much then as I do now, but I always found out if I worked hard and came home tired that I felt good inside and the reward took care of itself. It just happened to be commensurate with that effort. I think it would have been a different trip if there'd been no effort at all and the same reward came. I don't think it would have meant the same thing to me. I wouldn't have grooved with it as much. Oh, sure, sometimes there was a lot of effort and no reward, but generally it worked out.

EDGAR D. MITCHELL

I grew up with a notion of personal responsibility, the idea that you shouldn't be afraid to work hard and that you better not expect anything to be handed to you. You should go out and do it for yourself, whatever it is. It was something that came from my entire family, both parents and grandparents. We had several family businesses when I was a boy—ranching, farming, farm machinery dealerships, what they now call the agribusiness. I participated in them when I was young, and though they were always offered to me for later, there was no real push to stick with them and I didn't. The only really strong push was, whatever you do, do it well and be as good at it as you can be. The pressure wasn't to become wealthy or successful but more to achieve all that you can achieve within your capabilities. I was allowed to know fairly early that I had considerable capability and that the family would be pretty disappointed if I didn't rise to it.

I guess I took those lessons to heart. I never became very concerned about the drive for money or power or any of those things that are normally termed "success." I was more concerned with doing things that interested me and with using my talents to do the very best I could and to just go like hell. Yeah, I worked my tail off.

DON KING

I've always had the aspiration to try to do something, not knowing what that something would be. I've always really wanted to work at whatever I do, and it's just been a continuing process of moving ahead and getting it together. My mother instilled in us a certain dignity and pride. You know, try to be able to do for yourself and don't shirk work, and that gave me some good early motivation. And I've always had confidence in myself. I feel that I'm very good at whatever I do, so I've never really had any type of insecurity feelings about any endeavor that I would pursue. This stems all the way back to the hard-core ghetto when you really didn't have nothing to go with but you take that nothing to nothing and make something out of it. So that's always been there.

I've always been like a hustler. My father got killed in a steel accident in 1941, ironically enough on December seventh, the day the Japanese bombed Pearl Harbor, and that left us with a family of six and no father. And then they give you the ten-thousand-dollar double indemnity, what I call the tragedy money, and that's supposed to take care of everything. It's supposed to take care of the comfort of a father. It's supposed to take care of all your bills. It's supposed to give you life infinitely. It's really ludicrous. But anyway, having a frugal-minded mother, she used the tragedy money to move us out to a little better neighborhood to give us a little bit more chance for expansion, but that ten thousand dollars was gone in a second and we had to hustle in order to survive.

So I've always been around people that were oriented toward money. I used to call myself a money getter. Where others could sing or dance or box, I could plant a money tree and then have a real bumper crop. This is the kind of spiel I used to go through when I was in the ghetto, and I became a hustler extraordinaire. When other little boys, my white counterparts, maybe were thinking about going to Harvard and Yale and Princeton and becoming lawyers or bankers, I was thinking about becoming a policy operator. I wanted me a policy bank because this was the only thing I had ever seen that demonstrated any type of security so that a man could do what he wanted. I used to watch the policy bookies and they could buy whatever they wanted to.

And when I grew up, my wish was granted to me. I ended up with a policy house and I did very well with it. It was a situation where what one visualizes from childhood, that image is what you have. I was a good hustler, and my whole world existed within the confines of the ghetto. I never sought to go out of it, so therefore I didn't have no problems, you know? I never realized the real vulnerability and unpredictability of black life in white America till I went to jail.

I was always a guy who desired knowledge and wisdom. I had an avid desire to learn, but the more I got involved with one thing or another, the less time I had to read. I started out in the hustling field because I wanted to go to school. If my parents ever had the money to send me to school, I probably would have been a lawyer today. My brother, who was a numbers runner working for a bookie, didn't believe in giving me the money, but he did give me the opportunity to earn it for myself by working for him. I did very well, I must have multiplied what he gave me to start out with two and a half times, and it wasn't very long before I'm two inches from home, I'm ready to go off to school in the next couple of weeks. Then unfortunately I inadvertently left a lady's policy slip in one of those flower pots they used to have on the outside of the window, which is where we would hide our business from the vice squad, and as you would know it, the slip hit. This means I have to pay her, and the hit is enough to take the whole tuition. But my brother made me fulfill my obligation, which taught me a good lesson about how important it is to always keep your word because your money comes and goes, but your word follows you forever.

So I had to use my own money to pay the lady and that put me back in the numbers field to try to recoup. I started all over again and did so well that I thought I could quit for a while and get the bookie to loan me the money for school. I felt he really wanted to see me go to school. The people in the community felt I had the intellect to do it. But I found out that because people feel this way, it doesn't mean anything. You know, they're not gonna take the initiative and action to make it possible. So a lot of lessons were learned. But when I went back I decided I wasn't going to go into the business with that bookie any more. I figured I could get the same kind of backing he had and go into business for myself and then I'd have enough money to go to school and do whatever I wanted. I decided that I would lay off the big bets and hold the little bets myself. And that's what I did and I was so successful at it that the bookie and my brother and everybody else ended up working for me because I persevered so hard. But in the meantime school had been sidetracked.

Later on in 1961, some ten or twelve years later, I did get to college for a while. I did one year in Western Reserve to see if I could do it. I'm sitting there with seventeen- and eighteen-year-olds doing their thing, and here I am, thirty-some years old. I'm like an old man in the classroom, but I can't let them outdo me. So even though I had to run my business, I put in the extra hours to get my studies in, and I came out of the year with a three point average, which was really exciting to me because there wasn't too many in there that much better. Later on when I was in prison I worked right straight through in a program run by Ohio University in Athens, and I did superior the whole time. It was a little harder to concentrate in there than on the street because your mind wanders. You can never really understand what it means to be immobilized behind bars, it is so dehumanizing and mentally subjugating. But during this period I had to do a great deal of reassessment and reevaluation of all situations to find a course of direction I really wanted to pursue, and I found it in reading and sharing with all those philosophers of old. It was quite difficult, but I really enjoyed that.

MILTON GLASER

Success was certainly an issue when I was growing up, though it was really bonded to the notion of accomplishment. It *was* important to accomplish. The Jewish Middle European ethic was very heavily involved with that notion, and if it wasn't made explicit it certainly was something just below the surface. It's curious, I was talking to a friend yesterday who grew up in the same neighborhood as I did, a very interesting neighborhood in the Bronx called the Coops, a cooperative building mostly inhabited by Russian and Middle European immigrants working in the garment area, generally intellectuals with a very strong sense of the need for education and continuity in the family. We were just talking about it. Ninety-eight percent of the kids went to college. And this guy was mentioning where some of the people ended up. It was astonishing. One kid whose mother owned the newsstand on the corner, a guy named Anatole Beck, who was a pain in the ass in those days, turned out to be the first or second leading mathematician in the world. And he just ran down this list, a litany of people from the neighborhood in terms of where they are. Obviously the context of that particular situation produced a generation that was very success- or accomplishment-oriented.

The Coops was a center of Communist activities in the United States during the 1930s, a high degree of social consciousness of one kind or another and also ideological conviction, but one of the by-products was the development of a generation of young people who were in fact very success-oriented. So it didn't seem to me that there was any other way to be. Right? I mean, that was the way it worked—you did it, you grew up and you became successful. You tried very hard and you worked and persevered and made a name for yourself and tried to be better than your father. The idiom is not an unfamiliar one. So even beyond the context of my immediate family, it was an ethical situation that existed in that particular community. And it has been borne out, I think, if you really follow through on the people that came out of that. My friend was just going through the list: "This guy is a president of a university and this guy's running a school, this guy's the leading physicist on the West Coast, this guy . . ." Astonishing, really astonishing. All the guys who were hanging around the candy store.

REVEREND IKE

My mother demanded excellence from me. She was a school-teacher and her mother was a schoolteacher. I lived with both of them after my mother left my father. Her three sisters and her brother also taught school at some point, and I went to college before I was old enough even to go to grade school. I remember attending college classes with both my mother and my grand-mother. They would teach in the winter and go back to college in the summer to keep up their standards and so on, so I was around perhaps a different class of black people, especially for that day. It was sort of an elite type of situation, and my mother demanded excellence of me. In school I better do my work better than anyone else, you know. And of course, your mother being the teacher, she's there to know what you're doing. It put a certain amount of pressure on me, but I do not think it was overbearing because whenever I excelled she always gloated over me and praised me, and naturally that helped to cater to my elephantiasis of the ego.

So I did expect to be successful and I was very highly moti-vated to succeed. My mother's idea was that I'd finish high school, go off to college and then become a teacher. And when I became interested in preaching she said, "Well, you can preach too, but teach to make a living so you won't have to depend on the people."

I try to give people a philosophy to live by that will make life meaningful and help them meet the challenges of life with solu-tions, and I've always been put in the position where I've had to get solutions. Even when I was in school the kids would come to me for counseling when they had a problem and so would the teachers. Instead of playing ball with the other kids at recess, there was always a flock of kids following me, and whenever they had problems they would come to me. So I was always on the spot.

I preached my first sermon at the age of fourteen and the next day I met with the first person I ever counseled officially, a man who had a marriage problem, so I had to have an answer. I got into the money thing so heavily, as they say, because when I started counseling people and they began to hear me on the radio and to write to me and come to me, the number one problem was always money. And so I had to either say like the rest of the preachers, "Hey, be good. Serve the Lord. Stay in your place. And when you die you'll get your pie in the sky by and by," or I had to go back to that same Bible and say, "Hey, look, it says, 'The Lord is my Shepherd, I shall not want.' " So I really believe that God does want you to have what you want. God does want your needs to be supplied. And I've always had to find solutions, yes.

AL GOLDSTEIN

The idea of success was almost all-pervasive when I was growing up. It was a total feeling that either you made it or you didn't. I know I quickly got into a world of fantasy and created a fictional character who was both a magnificent ballplayer and owned a department store like Macy's. I still remember his name: Allen Green. I grew up in a lower-class slum in Williamsburg, Brooklyn, like so many other people. I'm almost your standardized neurotic Jew. I mean, we're just stamped out. If the machine ever breaks down, America's not gonna have any more weird eccentrics to preoccupy itself with. Anyway, I remember if I was reading or had friends, my father would always say, "What good are they?" Everything was very pragmatic in terms of money.

I thought I rebelled against my father's values, and now it frightens me how much I'm like him. The cliché about the apple not falling far from the tree is so true. All the things I found despicable I am. I mean, I fight them and there's a constant battle. But I have difficulty relaxing. I'm unable to. I drive to do everything, to control everything. What is it, type A behavior? I realize I'm a heart attack, that's gotta be. Or a psychopathic killer. It's one or the other. But I can't let things be. I bug my wife. I bug my employees. I drive myself. And it's that kind of craziness my father had that I used to hate. I said, "I'm different. I'm an English major in college. I'm not that way. I think of the spirit and beauty and sensitivity." Well, I still have that, but it's constantly at war with our balance sheet, with getting the circulation up, with survival itself because of the nature of my particular business.

JACK HALEY JR.

I was lucky because something got lodged in my genes. When my father was five years old, he went to a Nativity show in a church basement and when he saw a kid his own age blow his lines, he said, "I could have done that better," and from then on he was determined to be a performer. And early on, I guess from around eleven or twelve, I knew I wanted to be a director, I knew I wanted to be behind that camera. I'm not sure why I didn't want to be in front of it like my father. Part of it is that I'm not that extroverted a person, that's just my nature. My mother was in the Ziegfeld Follies and my "aunts" and "uncles" were people like George Burns and Gracie Allen and Jack and Mary Benny, so I've known performers all my life. But I don't know, something turned me off of it and I'm not sure exactly what it was. Perhaps I sensed there was more security behind the camera than in front of it.

I grew up with Bing Crosby's kids. Gary was one of my closest companions, and I noticed how he suffered from the success of his father, so outrageously so that maybe that had something to do with it. I remember he and I going out one night with no dates. "Let's just go have dinner, fool around," he said. We went to about four or five places, and each place some drunk would come up and start annoying him: "Aw, yer Bing Crosby's kid, huh?" This was right at the time when Gary got his gold record for "Sam's Song." And he kept saying to me, "See? I haven't had a drink. I'm minding my own business." We finally ended up in a joint where somebody started a fight. We tried to get the hell out of a back door and somebody threw a girl down the stairs on top of us and she broke her arm and the ambulance came. And in the midst of this chaos Gary turned to me and said, "See? I'm tellin' ya." People tend to measure the children of a famous show business mother or father in terms of their parents if they choose to follow the same path. They seem to expect a lot more out of you. Not that being someone's son or daughter doesn't give you some helpful credentials, much to the contrary of the rumor. My God, I could always get in to see anybody. The door was always open. I mean, you had to deliver, but they would look at you a lot less critically. You had them half won over before you even began your pitch.

I stayed with a good friend of mine when I was going to high school in New York for a while, William Gargan's son Leslie, and I remember kidding around one night when we were walking home from a movie. We were all charged up from the picture, and I said, "Leslie, we can really score. We know so much. We can really score well in this business. And by God, I'm gonna . . ." I just had that feeling, that really good feeling, that I was going to do terrific in show business. We both still remember that night. He was so impressed, you know, that instead of worrying about my homework I was thinking that far ahead. It just hit me that, sure, it seems though there's a logic here and I seem suited for this profession and I seem to understand it, I think I can deal with it. And I guess that's pretty unusual at that age, to have that kind of vision. I think it is enormously helpful. I pointed to the RCA Building and said, "Hell, we could *own* that building!" Very romantic and very juvenile, but I had this strange feeling of confidence and I never lost it. Also, I had great security at home. Great love. I was well aware of not only my father's success in the business but also his financial success. I didn't really have to worry about the future, you know. In case I failed, I had a fallback position. I could always go to work for him in his real estate office or something. It was just the opposite from those people who had such miserable home lives and wanted to get out so bad that they just clawed their way to the top. I feel I've been so enormously lucky every step of the way.

When I was eleven or twelve we lived in New York for almost

two years, and I discovered the Museum of Modern Art on the next block. I used to go to the film library there and look at the old movies. There wasn't any television then. The museum's program changed every two or three days, but that wasn't fast enough for me. I "discovered" silent movies. Chaplin, Keaton, Pickford, Fairbanks, D. W. Griffith—I absorbed their work like a sponge. My father used to say I was the only kid in Beverly Hills who knew who John Bunny was. When we moved back to California I talked my parents into buying a movie projector for the house, and I'd constantly get them to rent 16 mm films. We'd get the old Frankenstein movies, and I'd invite the whole neighborhood over. So I immersed myself in what was then *the* medium. Broadway was fun, but it was the same show over and over again every night. I'd been on radio when I was seven so that wasn't terribly mysterious, but the other part, film, was engrossing and interesting and fascinating to me. I was really like a UN observer from the time I was a kid. Backstage. On sets. I was six years old when I was on the set of *The Wizard of Oz* looking at all those little Munchkins who were the same size I was. It was really far out. That's probably when it dawned on me, hey, this is a *good deal* here. And Judy Garland was dismissing my governess and insisting that I have tea with her in her dressing room like I was a little toy doll, and it was great fun. So I've been immersed in it. You know, other people will say that they think they'll be an artist, a doctor, a lawyer, or something when they're sixteen. They're off to a late start compared to me.

JOE EULA

I was a hustler from the age of nine. I used to sell newspapers. You realize that you want something and to fill that need you must go out and get it. It's too bad you can't steal. They made that dumb law. I wasn't sure where I was going when I started out. It was very vague, just a thought. I knew it had to do with art and with fashion. Fashion was the quickest way to make a buck. I took a look at what everyone else was doing in art school and said, "Well, that's exactly what I *don't* want to do." I checked out the newspaper and magazine ads and billboards and said,

"Okay, what's the way that will make you happy with all of this?"
It really didn't satisfy me, so I started thinking about my own way
of approaching it. That was the beginning. In six months I was
out workin'. I haven't stopped since.

GEOFFREY HOLDER

Success for me came very early. I've been dancing since I was
seven and painting since I was fifteen. And how I began painting
was I stole paints from my brother Boscoe. I was living in Trinidad, I was a little boy of fifteen, and one day Boscoe went out
into town shopping and I was home sick, and I remember being
very bored, like all kids are bored, and I stole his paints and
began painting like mad. Like every child, I used to draw on the
back of my school books, and so I tried to paint and I got very
turned on, and when Boscoe came back he freaked out and ran
me around the room for stealing his paints.

This was during the war, in 1945, and you couldn't get Winsor
Newton paints and any of that shit because they came from
England. And what happened is, after scolding me for stealing
his paints, Boscoe looked at my paintings and did a double take.
"They're not bad, you know. But don't steal my paints anymore." I had taken his paintings down from the walls and put
mine up. So he called a man who was in charge of the public
library and said, "Come see what Geoffrey's doing." And the
man saw my paintings and loved them and said, "Why don't you
hang these paintings at the library for the weekend. They will
encourage the youth of Trinidad to be in the arts." Well, it was
a big success. A man bought three of them, and I made a vow
that I would always have an art exhibit every year. So that to me
was the beginning of my success. My head has been quite large
ever since.

Everybody needs to have their head get large because as you
grow up it gets knocked down to size. You have to have that
layer, that thick layer under your stomach to know that you *are*
and you *can* and you *will*. It happened to me at the age of fifteen.
After that everything was anticlimactic. Everything else was just
another job. It's like when I left Trinidad in 1952 with a dance

company of thirty to represent my country at a Caribbean festival in San Juan, Puerto Rico. The opening night I cried after the performance. This was my first real opening night, and you need only one opening night in your life. The rest is work. Backstage of *The Wiz,* opening night I was cool as a cucumber because I do not create for critics. Everyone was worried about what Clive Barnes would say and what would this one say, but I couldn't care less. Not that I felt satisfied, but because I did the best that I could. That's all you can hope to do if you are honest about your work. You do the best you can under the circumstances. What else?

BUDDY RICH

At nineteen or twenty, which was really the beginning of my second career, you don't think in terms of success. You just think about getting one job and then another job and then another job. I had so much fun playing with the various bands—Artie Shaw, Tommy Dorsey, Bunny Berigan—that each time I got a job, I suppose, that would be success. My first career was as a kid in vaudeville, working in an act with my parents. I was Traps the Drum Wonder. And then when they got out of the act I continued to work and that's what I know.

I worked from the time I was very, very small until today, and the only thing that's changed is that I don't wear a sailor suit anymore.

MARTIN SCORSESE

I always dreamed about films when I was a kid even though I was involved in other things. I was going to be a priest for a while and then a painter, but still deep down I was thinking about what comes with film recognition, whether as an actor or something else. I didn't know what a director was at the time. I'm talking about when I was seven years old, eight years old, that kind of thing. I used to go to movies all the time. I had asthma and my father wouldn't let me play any sports, so he used to take me to the movies. I used to make up my own films in my head and imagine I was an actor in them. A little later when I was about nine I would draw my own storyboards, and then when I was fifteen I got more sophisticated and got into 8mm very briefly for about a year. I guess success really meant recognition for me, for your work or for yourself as a person.

But I didn't really expect to be a filmmaker. I really expected to be a priest. From public school I was put into parochial school and I was fascinated by the religion. The main thing about the priesthood was being a force in helping and shaping people in the society. I think it's a physical thing. If you saw *Mean Streets,* the line is, "You don't make up for your sins in the church. You make up for them in the streets." It was almost like becoming a social worker for me. Of course, there was also the glory that went with it.

But when I got out of high school I couldn't make it into Fordham because my scholastic record wasn't too good, so I went to NYU and they had film courses there. I figured if I couldn't get into the priesthood I had always liked film, so I became a film student and from the very first class I was really taken with it. This was around 1958, '59, '60, and it happened to be the best time to be a film student. It was the time of the New Wave and the New American Cinema with Shirley Clarke and John Cassavetes. Cassavetes showed us in *Shadows* that you could just pick up a camera and shoot in the streets at a very low budget. He proved that, and that's what we did.

MARIO ANDRETTI

My twin brother Aldo and I shared the same dreams about becoming auto racers when we came over to this country with our parents in 1955. We were fifteen years old, and we discovered that not too far from our home some sort of automobile racing activity was taking place. It was modified stock car and jalopy racing, quite different from what we knew in Italy. That sort of thing doesn't exist there. But still, it was motor racing. The cars, with their big wheels and everything, looked very exciting. And the other appealing thing was that it looked like it wasn't going to take a very sophisticated approach to get involved. Even as youngsters, we could really look into this thing seriously and realistically become racers. On a local level, but obviously you've got to start somewhere. So we went to work after school for an uncle of ours and tried to put a few dollars together. And by the time we were eighteen, in 1958, we got seven partners and went out and bought engines and all the other pertinent things and put together a stock car. And that's how we got involved.

My brother and I would flip a coin and if he won the first toss he got to drive the first race and then we would alternate. And it was one of those things: Aldo won the very first race and I won the second and he won the third. We didn't know what the hell to do with our success. All of a sudden we realized that we put together a pretty good car. I must say it wasn't just by accident. We had a lot of good information from down South. Marshall Teague was one of the best stock car drivers of that era, and when he was killed his widow had a lot of notes and information for sale, and we bought into some of them. So we really had a lot of valid information for how to do it. Because mechanically, I can't take much credit for being a genius, that's for sure, but we did put together something I guess pretty decent. But then again, we were inexperienced, and we started crashing and all the other normal things, so we realized that it wasn't always going to be that easy.

One unfortunate thing happened at the end of the season, in the very last race. My brother was running a qualifying event in Hatfield, Pennsylvania, and he flipped a car violently and was hurt very badly, seriously hurt. He had a concussion and was in the hospital in a coma for about a month. And if you can believe this, my parents didn't even know we were racing. At no time did my dad ever accept the idea that we wanted to be race drivers. He just didn't understand this sport and didn't want to understand it. He probably never even read a magazine about it. To him it seemed almost like a disgrace because of the breakneck part about it. He wanted us to follow up on our formal education, to take up another, as he would say, more sane career. But that was to no avail. And of course after Aldo was hurt, you know, I went through the pain of facing him, but thank goodness he recovered one hundred percent. It was like a miracle. He started racing again a year later, but he never really regained his reflexes. He got married at a very young age, and that also slowed down his progress because of his obvious responsibilities.

I was luckier. I kept on. And it was just a matter of exposing yourself and more or less establishing a reputation that would get you rides with people in different ranks. It's like going to school. You know, you just progress from stepping stone to stepping stone. And my goals were always very ambitious. My goal was always right at the top. Like you can be a janitor and say, "Some day I'm gonna be the president of this company." Well, I started down at a local level. You can't say at an *amateur* level because I always got paid for racing. In a rough way this was still professionalism. But I said, "Indianapolis, the national championship, this is my goal and I'm going to reach that somehow." And when you set your sights that high, there's going to be a lot of hard work in between. That's the thing that sometimes makes me cringe about a lot of youngsters. They'll write and ask me, "What's the easy way to get this? What's the easy way to get that? What's the easy way to break into Indianapolis?" But that's like you're in kindergarten and all of a sudden you want to be a senior in college. You cannot skip the in-betweens. And there've been many cases where wealthy people would try to buy their way into this thing, but with competitive sports you don't really buy your way into anything because when the chips are down, it's you who's got to do it, and you've either got it or you don't. You know, all the bankroll in the world is not going to back you up when you've got to play the game.

So when you reach the top step by step, you feel, well, you've done your apprenticeship so at least you can say you've earned it. And one thing I can very proudly say is that I feel I've earned it every inch of the way and it wasn't easy. That's why I appreciate it. I have always appreciated it.

QUINCY JONES

I've got to knock wood that everything happened on a steadily ascending basis and there were no kinds of freakish phenomenal jolts in the beginning when everything gets all out of hand when you're nineteen or twenty-four. It was just always a constant growth. Touring with a band, records, arranging, musical direction, record executive, film scores—I don't know, it all just seemed like that was the way it was supposed to happen. I think a lot of it had to do with being lucky enough as a young cat to run into the right kinds of models. People like Clark Terry, who taught me how to play trumpet. Ray Charles, who I met when I was fourteen. Count Basie, Dizzy Gillespie, and Billy Eckstine, who I played with when I was about fifteen. My admiration for their talent was automatic, that goes without saying, but even more important was the way they were as human beings. They all had a sense of humor, man, and an incredible sense of reality about their own self-worth.

Somehow they put it in my head early that, man, in this business you're apt to be up or down from one day to the next and all you have to do is learn how to cushion the blows on the falls, on the low parts. The rest of it you can take for granted, you don't have to wallow in it. Because a lot of people don't know what success means, you know. Being a successful human being is the first goal. Lord knows, man, the bread and the position and the glamour of it are bullshit. That certainly came home to me when I had that operation last year and almost died. But those people I respected were always like that. They naturally were going to groove with the success when it came, but they also knew how to take the falls. And they had a very strong family sense. I remember Basie, about 1948, '49, when things were a little rough for him and he was kind of laying low with a six-piece band up in Seattle. Billy Eckstine was on top of the heap then —he had about fifteen gold records—and he said, "Come on, Basie, man, get your big band together. Come out on the road with me, man. I got it going." And you know, ten years later Basie's got a hit record and B's traveling with him. It was a family, man. They weren't cutting each other's throats. They had been up and down so many times they didn't get carried away with it, either one of them. And I said to myself, hey, man, I like that feeling. That's the way it ought to be. I still hang out with all those cats—we have been friends for so long—and it helps you keep your eyes open and your feet on the ground.

So it was a steady thing for me, man, a steady thing. Sometimes it would be hard as a bitch, but there was always something inside that would just never say it was impossible. I just omitted every negative from my vocabulary, no maybes or can'ts. And I learned from those guys that when you get knocked on your ass you get back up, man, and dust it off and hit it again. I didn't get into personal trips with "this guy is trying to annihilate me from life" if he didn't accept my thing. You just keep on stepping, man. Besides, there is always something there to let you know what you've got in you. It's just maybe that it hadn't all come together yet or maybe you didn't have enough experience or enough training or you were in the wrong place. Whatever. But there was something inside that said, "yes, yes, yes," all the time. And so I would take any kind of negative trip that would happen, be it the unemployment line or being hungry or out of a job, and not let it turn into despair or escapism or bitterness or anger, but try to transform it into a positive energy. You know, put some notes on the paper, man, do some more records. The number one problem was that I wanted to write for the movies ever since I was fifteen and they wouldn't let any blacks get into that. So that part didn't have too much tangible hope in it. It took me seventeen years to do the first one.

But you just go with the flow. You know what your soul's about, and you just try to grow and prepare yourself and learn and get experience. Just keep on stepping.

ALICE COOPER

I never had any models for what I was trying to do, but certain friends really did help me out. Tragically, some of them had to die, like Jim Morrison of the Doors, who was a very good friend of mine. What he taught me was the fact that you can't live your image off stage. See, he tried to be Jim Morrison all the time, and since he was the big guy then I figured Alice has got to do that too. Alice has got always to be drunk and crazy and everything like that. So I was drinking two bottles of whiskey a day with Jim, and we were just always plastered. I never took drugs, but was continually drinking. Until he died, and then I realized that if I was going to have to be Alice all the time it wasn't worth it because it was just too intense. When Jim died I wasn't shocked at all. I heard it on the news and it didn't even faze me because I knew it was going to happen.

After that I put a limit on how much I drink and said, "Okay, now I start divorcing myself from Alice by developing the idea that Alice is on stage and *I'm* off stage." I'd go out and buy the squarest clothes I could possibly find so off stage I didn't look anything like Alice. And it made the other character that much more intense. When I got back on stage, suddenly it was *Aargh!* My eyes were glaring. It's the classic Jekyll and Hyde. I just couldn't have maintained Alice off stage any longer. It was just getting too crazy.

EDGAR D. MITCHELL

To the extent that I have had models for what I've been trying to do in my life, they have always been men of integrity and high drive, perseverance and straightforwardness like Charles Lindbergh and, almost grudgingly, Harry Truman, people like that. I'd read those people's lives and say, "Gad, that's neat." They were confirming what I already thought, so they became part of my model.

CLIVE DAVIS

There are people who I admired in the record business, but I didn't know them well enough to pattern my own style after them. It wasn't as if I had grown up in the industry and had a chance to use someone as a model or an inspiration. I really had to feel my own way and establish my own niche in terms of what felt comfortable to me. I was probably more intent on doing it in a way that was comfortable to me than anything else.

MIKE WALLACE

I started out in radio back in college at the University of Michigan. At first I thought I wanted to be an English teacher, and then I went into the campus radio station and in effect never came out. I was simply fascinated by the whole process of radio. It also seemed to be a fairly quick passport to a comfortable income. I found that I had a certain facility, a certain capacity to be effective on the air. Things came easy. I really never had much of a struggle.

I started in 1939 in Grand Rapids, Michigan, as a radio announcer, went from there to Detroit a year later, and went from there to Chicago a year and a half after that, all with the predictable increases in salary. And then in late 1943 I went into the navy, and while I was in the navy I began to understand that just making money and just reading words on the air were not sufficiently satisfying. In a sense I began to change my notion of what "success" was. I determined that when I left the navy I was going to try to break out of the mold of simply being a performer and attempt to do something of my own—my own ideas, my own ingenuity, my own initiative. When I came back to Chicago in 1946 I returned to work for the Air Edition of the *Chicago Sun,* which by then had become the *Sun Times,* and I also began to do interview broadcasts. And that began to shape the career which I would eventually settle into: news and interviews.

I cannot say that I was single-minded about news and interviews and simply went on a predetermined path toward that. The lure of money kept intruding. There was a considerable amount of money to be made in radio and later in television, and because I was versatile I was offered opportunities. I would take them. So I would detour and then come back to the spine of news and interviews, and then detour off into something else and come back again. It wasn't really until I'd been in New York for four or five years, about 1955, 1956, that I settled into news and interviews, and for the last twenty years I've been doing that kind of work just about exclusively.

REX REED

I originally came to New York to be an actor, but I've never been very good at deprivation. I couldn't see myself living on peanut butter sandwiches when my stomach wanted steak. The financial motivation had a lot to do with becoming a writer. I was just getting paid more money to write than I was to act.

Strangely enough, I never had any doubts about being able to do that. I *knew* that I would become a writer. I didn't know exactly how because I didn't know anyone when I came to New York. I didn't have letters of introduction to producers, directors, editors of newspapers. I absolutely carved out everything for myself. No help from anybody. It was fairly easy because this is a city where talent is admired and respected, I think. I'm not saying it would have been as easy to be an actor, because there it doesn't matter so much how talented you are. It has a great deal to do with who you know. But as a writer, there is so much space to fill and so few talented people to fill it that if you have any style and individuality and flair, you will get a chance.

I started out working in public relations, which was a very smart thing to do. I recommend it to all aspiring writers because it's a good way to meet people. I found myself working for public relations firms that were handling restaurants and personalities, and part of my job was to sell them to the press. I knew secretly that I was a better writer than the members of the press I was having to deal with, so I was always embarrassed at having to ask them to do me a favor. I've never been good at that. I've never been good at selling myself. When I was a kid I couldn't sell Christmas cards or magazine subscriptions as class projects in school. My mother would have to order everything herself to fulfill my quota because I just couldn't go around knocking on doors and asking people to buy Christmas cards and *Popular Mechanics* when I didn't like them myself. So when I got to New York I was having to ask a lot of people whom I didn't really have any respect for to please come and eat at this restaurant and write something about it, and I just thought it was very demeaning.

I knew that I could do a better job than they could, and so through a rather long and complicated process of meeting peo-

ple and talking to people I eventually got a chance to do some
movie reviews for the gal who was the movie critic for *Cosmopolitan.* She said, "You write better than I do. Where have you been
all this time?" and I was given a few by-lines in *Cosmopolitan.*
Through that connection I met people at the *New York Times* and
started doing Sunday pieces there. That's really where my success began because very few people at that time in the gray *New
York Times* were writing anything with style. The public acceptance part of it and the celebrity part of it really came as a result
of the hard work I was doing. If I have any gripe at all it's that
sometimes the celebrity part of the success seems to overshadow
the hard work I do. Too many people think of me as a celebrity
instead of a hardworking good writer, and that always annoys
me.

HALSTON

I've always had success in a sort of popular sense of being
successful with friends, successful in my endeavors, successful in
whatever I wanted to do. Not that I think of it as the prime
interest in my life, not at all, but I guess I did expect to be
successful when I was just starting out, and I think I was right
for my time. When I first started in my business career of making
hats, it was sort of against the system and everybody felt that it
wasn't maybe quite the proper profession for a young man. I was
discouraged considerably from going into the fashion business,
especially into the hat world. It just wasn't popularly accepted
in the Midwest as being a serious profession. But I just did it
anyway because I wanted to do it.

I think that the secret of success is really being vocationally
placed and liking what you do. Then it doesn't become a chore
or a job or work or anything else. It becomes interesting and fun.
And from my very first experiment I was successful. The first
three hats I made—the only three hats I had made—were sold
to a major television star in Chicago, that's where I started. She
was Fran Allison, who was part of the *Kukla, Fran and Ollie* show.
Then she ordered three more things and brought in a friend
who ordered three things, and it was a success, as it were, from

that moment. And I've always enjoyed that till now. Of course, there are different levels of success. If you make three things and sell them, then maybe that's a successful experiment. And then you get up to ten or twelve things, and that's another level. And then you go into a more serious business world and sell hundreds of units. And then it goes on and on and on.

But I always knew that I was vocationally placed in what I was doing. I liked to make things. It was interesting and fun, and I would spend long hours doing it. There were a few maybe testy moments when one would ask, "Well, where is the future in this?" and so forth, but I always knew it would be good. I always knew that. I never had a problem. You know, people will say, "Well, all of a sudden you're such a big deal," and all that kind of thing, but it just isn't true. I've always had a successful business.

BILL GRAHAM

There were failures. I went to school and said, "Well, I want to earn a living, but I can't stand regimentation." I'd been in the army and there had been a lot of court-martials, a lot of bullshit. I said, "No, eventually I have to be the boss of a section of some kind because otherwise I'll be court-martialed in whatever I do. I'll be fired, I'll be put in jail. I don't want people snapping their fingers at me. I can't take orders too well." I don't know why I was like that, but I guess being on your own most of your life gives you that kind of independence. "Office management," I said. "I'll get a business education. This is what I want to do. I want to be an office manager. I want to be a statistician."

But how do you know something's not going to get you off until you do it? You've got to go in there and try. So I got a paymaster's job in the middle of nowhere, and once I got there and took a look at it I found that telling twenty men how to do the payroll wasn't what I thought it would be. I had thought if I sat behind a desk wearing a different suit every day, wow. Then when I was twenty-six I became regional office manager for Allis–Chalmers. I said, "This is it." And three months later: "This ain't it." Then I went into acting and I loved it. I wanted

to become a young character actor, and I felt that I really had
it. There aren't any actors who don't think they're good. Otherwise they wouldn't do it. Actors, writers, dancers, we all think so.
We all lie to ourselves, which is not too healthy. And I spent a
number of years at it: fencing, diction, the whole thing—Off
Broadway, Manhasset, Paris, traveling, failure, who am I? , what
am I?, nobody understands me.

I went to LA and tried to get it on in films. I did a lot of extra
work, walk-ons, stand-ins, and then I went to read for the second
lead in a series and I really thought I was going to get it. After
sixty or seventy guys auditioned they chopped it down to four,
and then a couple of weeks passed. I was a waiter all this time
in a French restaurant. Then they got it down to two, and they
had both of us read against the male lead. Everybody was convinced that I was going to get this part, but it turned out that
the lead had the final say and he gave it to the other guy. This
was a very emotional thing for me. I remember when my agent
came out of the studio waiting room with the bad news. I said,
"You got to tell me why!" and he said, "Let's go outside. If I
tell you here, you'll tear the building apart." He said, "You
know, Bill, in the past you've been too tall, too skinny, too New
York, too Jewish." I said, "What is it this time?" He said, "They
looked at your footage. You were brilliant. You were perfect.
You were really fine. But the lead thought your face was too
strong to play against him." I said, "I quit!" It was very difficult
for me because I had worked so hard at it.

So I gave up acting and went back to San Francisco and office
management at Allis–Chalmers. I was making about twenty-
eight a year but I still wasn't enjoying it and eventually I quit
again and went to work for a radical theater group for $125 a
month because I was still looking for whatever it was that would
give me what I wanted. Well, we did a few benefit concerts with
some of the local rock bands and I thought, gee, this is really
nice, and then I started producing rock concerts on my own at
the Fillmore auditorium. And that was it, I finally discovered the
thing I was good at that would also get me off. This was in 1964
when that whole rock music thing was just starting to happen in
San Francisco, so I sure was at the right place at the right time.
But I also found that I really had the talent for it. I knew how
to work with large groups of people backstage to get them to do
what had to be done. I had good original production ideas.

When a show ended at two o'clock in the morning, instead of turning on the house lights and letting a security cop blow his whistle—*Tweet!* Everybody out! —the way everyone else did it, I put slides on the screen and played a little Villa Lobos music or a little "Greensleaves" to see the audience out without bringing anyone down. At the beginning of the night I'd put a barrel of apples on the stage and do things like that so that the inhibited ones who were just coming there for the first time would feel relaxed.

I put together combinations of artists that no one ever thought of before—a blues or jazz or gospel group with a rock group, Voznesensky with the Jefferson Airplane, the Byrds and two LeRoi Jones plays, a group called Love with the Staple Singers and Roland Kirk, the Grateful Dead and Miles Davis. And it was such a turn-on to get the people who came there for the rock to get hip to these other things, that was mind-boggling to me. You know, it wasn't like saying, "If you think this is a good egg cream, check this egg cream." I mean, this was Miles Davis. This was Chuck Berry. This was Mavis Staples. This was LeRoi Jones. These were giants. And I would never take shit from anybody. Never! "You deal acid in my building, asshole, I'll stick it up your fucking nose! You got that?" I used to get creamed for that—"Aw, you fuckin' rip-off!"—because I had strong beliefs, and I still do. So I was able to work instinctively and creatively and it came off.

I always had known that I had something to give, I always knew I had the talent, but I never knew how the talent was going to manifest itself. As an office manager? No. As a character actor? No. I don't think I would ever have been able to do what I did in any other field of endeavor. I don't think there was any other job in the world in which I could have proven those abilities, and the fact that I finally was able to has been a great source of happiness to me.

MURRAY KEMPTON

A lot of what framed my particular age group, the Nixon generation, was the Depression and the Second World War. In the Depression the help-wanted ads were all for salesmen. Everybody in the whole country was out selling from door to door. I mean, the symbol of the Depression was the Fuller Brush man. He was the most successful of all the salesmen. And so there just weren't any jobs. There were a few labor union jobs, but even that booming industry, by the time I got out of college, had already passed from the era of organizing where they'd hire anybody to the era of stewardship where there were certain basic requirements. There were only a few newspaper jobs and publicity jobs of various kinds, so getting on a newspaper was the height of my ambition. My notion of success was to be on a newspaper, you know, at thirty, thirty-five dollars a week. That would have been my idea of an elite something.

I had just gotten a job on the *New York Post* when the war came along. Then you were away for three years or so and you came back and were about twenty-eight, twenty-nine years old and were desperately anxious to make good, to make a place for yourself after those lost years. And we came back to a society in which somehow or other there'd been a change from production to distribution. When I was living in Princeton after the war there were just dozens of these guys who were in businesses that weren't really businesses. I mean, advertising is not a business. It's not a craft, particularly the way they did it because they were salesmen basically. A few of the more talented ones were copywriters, but most of them were account executives of one kind or another. And they had no function. They were not in jobs that were remotely interesting to them.

So I think that a tremendous amount of the success orientation of that time was simply to have a place in the world. It wasn't really to be president of the corporation. It was just to be *something*. If you look at Nixon's career, what did the son of a bitch ever do? He never did anything that could be thought of as doing something. And, heck, he was one of the craftsmen. He at least wrote his own speeches to a considerable extent, as awful as they were, and he is not untypical of that particular generation.

ROCKY AOKI

When I was a kid in Japan my father had a little money. He was a comedian and also had some small coffee shops. So we had a pleasant life when I was maybe nine or ten years old, and I didn't even think about money. Whenever I needed some, I would just pick up my father's bed, where he kept some bread, and take it and he never knew. So I never thought about working. But at some point I was dying to come here to the United States. Right after the war the GIs came to Japan and we kids dreamed about talking with them. They'd give us chewing gum and sometimes clothes to wear, so we were really fond of Americans. When I went to college I had a big chance to come to the United States to wrestle. Since then I've been living here.

I formed a rock 'n' roll group in high school called Ravi Sans and toured through all the American camps entertaining the GIs at night. The group hit very big in the Tokyo area and made a lot of money. And I used to write erotic books in Japanese—The Story of Everything—and sell them in my high school. That was my first job. I never wanted to work for anybody and I was looking for a fast buck. The main reason I came to the United States was because I'd heard it was the land of opportunity and I thought I could find something here. I didn't think I could find anything in Japan at that time because of the pressure young people got from older people. Because of the seniority system we couldn't express anything, we couldn't expand anything, we couldn't open anything up. The banks wouldn't give the younger people money. But here in this country it doesn't matter about age. It doesn't matter what kind of clothes you wear. If you have the right kind of credentials they'll lend you money without asking that many questions.

When I was studying in New York about eleven or twelve years ago I drove a Mr. Softee ice cream truck. I wasn't working for them but leased a truck for twenty-four dollars a day and bought my own ice cream mixture. And I checked around trying to figure out where I could make the best money. I did some small marketing research and found it was Harlem. So I was selling ice cream in Harlem from ten in the morning till four in the morning. I'd go to the same location at the same hour every day, even when it was raining, so I always found the same kids waiting for me. I made over ten thousand dollars in four and a half months selling ice cream in Harlem. Of course, I almost got killed a couple of times. You know, I'd get out of the truck and somebody would steal everything and try to knife me. I was taken to an empty building and cleaned out a few times. But Harlem was where I made money. I did so well because I gave my customers a lot of showmanship. I think you've got to have it with anything. Just selling ice cream by itself is nothing. I gave away little Japanese umbrellas and put Japanese music on the public address system of my truck. These little things helped me a great deal. Americans are always looking for something new and something extra. It's the same thing with my Benihana restaurants.

The concept of Benihana is from Japan. They had the same kind of restaurants in Japan but on a very small scale and without the showmanship. Because of the way people are here I decided to add the showmanship, and so we cook right in front of the customers. We have a course in Japan to train the chefs for that kind of performance. If we did it in Japan for the Japanese customer, people would laugh at me. People in Japan are still very conservative. They're not Americanized yet. But here, you give more showmanship, you get more customers. I used to work in my father's coffee houses in Japan, so I knew the restaurant business before I came here. I was a dishwasher to start with. And when I came to the United States and couldn't find a job, I washed dishes at night in the cafeteria where I went to school. I was taking hotel restaurant management, mainly because I don't like to study and thought it would be the easiest course. I also worked as an assistant chef, taking care of soups and things. When I was a student I had quite a few jobs. I was also a chauffeur for a limousine service for Japanese businessmen, so I got to know New York inside out. A lot of the customers would take me to restaurants because I spoke Japanese and they knew my father's name, so I got to know which restaurants were for rent and where it would make sense to open one up. It was like good marketing research without, you know, having marketing research. It worked out well for me.

ALICE COOPER

We came out at a time when I was going to rock concerts and saying, "Jeez, nobody's doing anything on stage, it's just not show biz." And I said, "Let's be as outrageous as possible, use as many props as possible, and then we will be an original." That was the idea, to become an original. So I was very conscious about what I was doing. I'd put myself in the audience's place and ask, "Now if I were paying six dollars what would I like to see?" And of course I'd love to see a fifteen-foot boa constrictor. Wouldn't you? And first I'd like to see this guy go up there and do his song and then hang himself. But on the level of theater it really worked. And that's what the business needed at that point.

When we were starving, people used to ask, "You guys, why don't you just quit?" And I'd answer, "Hey, listen, it's not even ego, it's the fact that I *know* that this is going to work." I could just see it. And I kept saying to myself, listen, I *know* the kids are going to be sensationalized by this and they're going to want to see it if they hear enough about it. That's why I worked so hard with the press. I wanted to make sure that before we even got to a city we were already hyped up to the level that "Wow, Alice is going to do this tonight and I can't wait to get there."

Building an image is so important. I would have been a great Madison Avenue cat because I know how to sell things. I don't know anything about business, but I know how to make people like things and that's the most important thing. I mean, I couldn't even write a check if I had to, that's how little I know about business, but if somebody brought me any band in this country right now, any band, I think I could make them a hit in four months if they just let me handle their image and their press. It sounds like a brag, but it's true. That's a thing I know I could do.

REVEREND IKE

Success defies reason. Invention always defies reason. So many times we try to confine ourselves to the intellect and we shouldn't. On a college campus the other day a young black girl from the state of Mississippi came up to me after one of the self-motivation lectures and said to me, "Reverend Ike, now you've talked about believing in ourselves and so on, but I don't have any money and that's a *fact.* Now how do I do something about that? It's a *fact* I don't have any money." I said, "Well, whenever you find yourself faced with a negative fact, treat it in a positive way. First of all, don't go around continuing to repeat that negative fact because as long as you continue to repeat that negative fact you are going to amplify it. If you don't have any money and that's a fact, I'm not going to argue with that fact. But go into the next level of consciousness, what I call the transliminal area of mind, and say, 'I *see* myself with all the money that I need.' " You see, there's no argument there. My intellect won't let me say I have a lot of money if it's a fact that I don't have money, because the intellect only works by reason. But in the transliminal I can see anything that I want. I can visualize whatever I want, and the reasoning mind is suspended.

BRUNO SANMARTINO

I always believed in myself as a wrestler. When I was working in construction, I trained every day, every day. I would even go up to the University of Pittsburgh and train with the college team. I was very young and maybe a little overconfident, call it what you will, but I felt that I had the ability to be the best. I never expressed this thought openly, but that's how I felt. I felt that all I needed was to be given an opportunity. And when the day came to try out, I guess that's when I did show a little cockiness about myself because I said to Rudy Miller, the man who was promoting wrestling in Pittsburgh, "I'd like to show you what I can do and I'm willing to show it to you against any professional you have." And he said, "You really think a lot of yourself, don't you?" But it wasn't really that. It was just that I was so anxious, I had such a strong desire for this, and that's the only way I knew to present myself. I had nobody speaking for me. So they tried me out with a couple of guys and they were very impressed and that was the beginning of it.

It took some time, naturally, before it began really working for me. It took about three years. Nothing comes overnight, you know. And there were lots of times I was very discouraged because I felt I was getting nowhere fast. People couldn't even pronounce my name. Today everybody seems to know my name because it's shoved down their throats so much, but in the beginning I was just a preliminary boy none of the promoters would give a chance to. They were only interested in the big attractions who the people would come to see and couldn't care less about someone just coming up.

One thing happened in New York that was a big break for me. Did you ever hear of the wrestler Haystack Calhoun? He's a huge, tremendous guy who weighs about six hundred pounds. Well, he was being interviewed on a show one time and somebody asked him, "Jeez, you weigh over six hundred pounds. Has anybody ever been able to pick you off your feet?" He says, "Nobody." That gave me an idea. I was twenty-two years old and had just won a world record in weight lifting and I thought, "Boy, nobody ever lifted this guy off his feet. If I ever get the chance to do it and I can, that's got to be a first and it's got to mean something to somebody, you know." So I was invited to be on this radio show and I had the fellow ask me that question. He says, "Haystack Calhoun claims that nobody has ever been able to lift him off his feet. Is there a wrestler who is able to do that?" And I said very cockily, "The reason Calhoun has never been lifted off his feet is because he's never wrestled me. If he ever wrestles me, I guarantee you he'll be lifted off his feet." Well, I didn't know what kind of rating this radio program had, but the darn thing was flooded with mail after this. People were writing, "If this guy can lift Calhoun, let's see him wrestle. Why doesn't he wrestle Calhoun?" So when this radio guy told me about all the mail I told him to tell his listeners to write directly to Madison Square Garden and to send all the mail he got over there too. And he did. So the Garden got very interested and they made the match. Me in the old Madison Square Garden. Me against Calhoun.

I was really happy about it, but then I started thinking about it too. It wasn't the six hundred pounds that worried me because I had lifted that kind of weight before. I had done a dead lift of over six hundred pounds. I had done a squat with way over six hundred pounds. And on the bench press I wasn't that far off. But this was all with Olympic barbells. Calhoun was a different ball game. This was a bulky, huge, colossal man carrying that kind of weight. So I started saying to myself, "Wow, I got my wish but now I've got to figure out where we go from here." Finally, I decided that I'm just going to go in there and I'll have to see when I'm in there what I can do and what I can't.

So I went into the ring. The place was jammed. Boy, the old Garden was sold out. Everybody wants to see whether this young guy from Italy could actually lift up Haystack Calhoun. Well, it was easy to move around him because he's so huge you can outmaneuver him easily. But when I tried to hook my hands around him to get the power to lift him I just couldn't do it, he was so big. I tried it this way, I tried it that way, but nothing worked. It got to where people were actually starting to laugh at me like I was making a complete ass of myself. The trouble was, no matter how good a wrestler you are, what do you do with a six-hundred-pound guy? People ask me whether Calhoun can wrestle, but that's not the point. The point is, what can a guy who *can* wrestle do with a guy like that? When he gets on his hands and knees, it's like trying to turn over an elephant, it's so ridiculous. But then he got a side headlock on me and took me down. He wasn't hurting me because of all his excess weight and he's not exceptionally strong for a man his size, and when I saw that big thigh of his and the way he was standing to balance himself it gave me an idea. I had very strong legs because I was a very heavy squatter, so I bearhugged his leg with my own and from that position I tilted him to me and got his legs straight up and got him up in the air.

When the people saw that it just wiped them out. I thought the Garden roof was going to fall in. And it was after that match that the people who couldn't pronounce my name would refer to me as the guy who lifted Haystack Calhoun. I became known as the guy who picked up Haystack Calhoun, and that helped a lot, it really helped. I went to Canada and became Canadian champion and from that I got a crack at Buddy Rogers in 1963 and that was it, here I am.

CLIVE DAVIS

I don't think that self-confidence has all that much to do with success. I don't know whether it's an asset or a liability. I've always operated on the theory that you've got to work hard to achieve anything and nothing happens either because you're confident or because you expect it to happen. So I've always run somewhat scared, even when I was in school. The idea is to have some inner standard of excellence that you follow. Even rising within the echelon structure of Columbia Records, it wasn't ambition. I mean, I was sort of happy doing what I did. It was purely fortuitous that all of a sudden the top job opened up and there was really no one around on the business side to fill it and I was considered sort of an acceptable unknown quantity. Being generally experienced, I was probably a good holding measure rather than someone about whom they could say, "Hey, he's got great creative instinct." Because I had never demonstrated creative instinct nor did I know that I had it, if I did have it. So I never prepared myself for that creative thing. Based on burning ambition, I didn't start to learn to read music and take lessons and say, "Hey, I'm going to be this and do that."

I think it's a certain standard of excellence that you work towards almost on an individual task basis that leads to a perspective of results after a period of time. Even in establishing this new record company, Arista, I was gratified that the industry expected it to do well, and now that it has done well, you know, with a lot of hits, everyone says, "Well, we *knew.*" Well, *I* didn't know. I knew that I didn't rely on my Columbia track record when I went out to a club or a loft at one in the morning and saw a group and said, "I want to sign you." That wasn't based on anything other than my ears. And you have to keep doing that day in and day out. Even within Columbia I had to do it over again two or three times as the scheme of music changed and as artists broke up and one or two died. So you just take each day and each artist as you see fit, hoping and trying to maintain your standard of quality. And then somehow when you look at it one day you can say, "Wow, we really do have a quality label!" Well, that's based on the accumulation of day-to-day results.

So I would say that it's a capacity for hard work, whatever

comes natural as far as instinct or ability, which is the major factor, coupled with a desire to excel. Probably not divorced from ambition—but in my case I think that's more unconscious than conscious. And with luck somewhere involved in there.

GEORGE PLIMPTON

Success involves such a tremendous amount of luck. In my own case I didn't really want to be a writer at all. I write slowly and unsurely: I doubted I could make a living at it. At college I was the editor of the *Harvard Lampoon,* but I always thought there were at least four or five other writers on the magazine with much more distinction and flair and style than I had. That's what I was going to be, an editor. Or, God help me, a producer. In other words, using and manipulating and fooling around with the results of other people's talents. An editor is in an enviable position because the work comes to him already done. He can take out his red pencil and he can change it around or mold it or suggest to the writer what should be done or if he finds it perfect give a great huzzah and print it. Whereas the writer has to sit down and punch at and thrash all this clay around until it turns into some recognizable sort of form. I started out in Paris editing *The Paris Review,* really thinking of it as something I might do for a couple of years as sort of a tutelage, then perhaps come back to New York and work for maybe *Harper's* or perhaps one of the Time-Life organizations. Writing was just something I did on the side without very much confidence. In fact, I still don't think of myself as a writer. I'm downstairs editing a magazine now *(The Paris Review),* not sitting at the typewriter writing.

And then of course I fell into this gimmick, this idea of participatory journalism—a terrible word, but I can't think of another one to describe it. It's not original. Paul Gallico did it years ago for the *Daily News.*

I wrote this book about playing last-string quarterback with the Detroit Lions football team, *Paper Lion,* and it happened to catch the public imagination. It came along at a time when people were curious about what was going on in football—it was beginning to absorb the national attention—and there weren't many other books around on the subject. So I was lucky. My book came along at just the right time. And I guess that turned me into a writer, whether I wanted to be one or not. I had absolutely no sense of direction about it, absolutely none.

Nobody thought *Paper Lion* was going to be successful. Books about sports had never gone anywhere in publishing. I think it went through eleven printings in three months, which is absurd. They'd always say, "Well, we'll print three thousand more and it'll stop." Well, they'd print three thousand and those would go, and then they'd print three thousand more. And finally, after I think the eleventh printing, they said, "Well, maybe we've got something here," and they printed ten thousand. And when those went they suddenly realized that they had an odd phenomenon on their hands. It was a great surprise to them, and it was a bit of a surprise to me.

JOAN GANZ COONEY

I wish I could tell you that the Children's Television Workshop and *Sesame Street* were thanks to my genius, but it really was a lucky break. I think that probably any successful career has X number of breaks in it, and maybe the difference between successful people and those who aren't superachievers is taking advantage of those breaks. But I had a friend, Lloyd Morrisett, who was then vice-president of the Carnegie Corporation, which was making grants in preschool education, and he knew I was doing documentaries up in Harlem on this very subject. It was pre–Head Start. Work was going on in New York with poor kids in the preschool years, and I was really into it and terribly interested in what was then called compensatory education. And so Lloyd asked me, knowing that I had majored in education in college, if I would have any interest in taking a two- or three-month leave from Channel 13 to talk to a lot of preschool educators and psychologists and people in children's television. I had never watched a children's TV show and did not have children of my own, but they wanted a very cold eye brought to the controversies that existed in preschool education and to some extent in children's programing.

So I did a report for Carnegie in which I noted—and it was *so* obvious, but it seemed like I had come up with some genius idea—that children liked commercials. Any parent you talked to said, "Well, what my kids really watch are commercials." I also noted that ninety percent of all American households had TV according to A.C. Nielsen. Everyone seemed to think that the poor didn't have television and this was just nonsense. And Nielsen was reporting that the average preschool child at the time—and this has since gone up—was watching twenty-seven hours a week. Well, somehow those three facts brought together with some recommendations were mind blowing, and they seem so obvious now. The upshot was the government liked the report and the Ford Foundation liked it, so Carnegie asked me if I would leave Channel 13 and come to work for them for a year to develop a really detailed proposal for the creation of the Children's Television Workshop. There was an hour-long daily program for children to be developed, and I was appointed executive director, and then CTW incorporated after we went on the air—that is, we became independent of NET—and I became president of the corporation.

But I was very lucky in staffing. It was the kind of effort that attracted the very best people. It was clearly serious in intent. It had a serious amount of money. I had made the point that what children really liked and what had the most impact—the commercials—were expensive and that the children couldn't be shortchanged if you wanted a serious educational effort mounted in their behalf. And it was to be autonomous. There would not be a network deciding how much money would be spent. When the network budget is divided up between news, public affairs and prime-time entertainment, well, children are always going to lose. So I think that was attractive to the people we wanted who were experienced in children's programing. And they got the idea right away that we weren't doing just your usual kiddies' program, that this was going to be something different, very sophisticated, very fast paced, and that we were going to work like the dickens to get every child in America watching it. Public TV was no longer going to be elitist, at least insofar as this show went. We spent a sizable amount of money in poverty areas, and of course we built very large audiences.

I had to spend a lot of time talking stations into putting *Sesame*

Street on the air in the morning because that's when their school schedule was on. That was the biggest problem we faced. I knew it had to be on twice a day and one of those times had to be in the morning because there was nothing on for children after *Captain Kangaroo* went off the air and I knew from Nielsen that little kids were at the set watching game shows and *I Love Lucy.* And I knew that if there was something really good for children on the air, their parents, rich or poor, would switch to it. Another thing we found out was that most homes had two sets, so there was no reason that the mother had to give up anything. But most mothers are doing housework at that time anyhow and are happy to have their children watching something they can trust. So I knew that would be the key to the success of the show, going up against no competition, and it did turn out that way.

HOWARD COSELL

I didn't know what I wanted to achieve when I was just starting out. I knew I didn't want to be a lawyer. I'd become a lawyer because I was a Jewish son of parents who wanted their son to be a lawyer. I knew I liked broadcasting and I still do. I love the industry because of its immediacy. You can cover a story and put it on the air immediately. I'm just born to report.

But I never wanted to be in sports. I was put in sports by accident. I tried to get out of sports seven or eight years ago, but I was stigmatized by then. I should have been in news, international and national. That's where I wanted to be. You see, basically my profession does not deal with truth. It's not allowed. Sport is sanctified. They play the game in St. Patrick's, at least as far as the great bulk of the sportswriters of America are concerned and also the sports announcers, because in most cases they need the approval of the owners and commissioners to be hired. And when they're on the local level they're even paid by the teams whose games they announce.

But that has never applied to me, and in my case I had the luck of timing. There's no question that I came along when the young people of this society were growing up far differently than my generation, and they had a sense of life and what was hap-

pening. They had the horrible unending war in Southeast Asia.
They had the narcotics addiction problems. They had the racial
anguish to deal with. They were circumscribed everywhere by
reality, so they weren't disposed to the notion that sport is
Camelot, that you go through a looking glass and there's a
whole pure world. And I told the truth about sport, and I think
the timing was right for me, especially in the age of Richard
Nixon.

F. LEE BAILEY

I would say my initial success came from two sources. First,
I had an inordinate opportunity to train, which my colleagues
absolutely missed. Before I went to law school I was a legal
officer in the military and was able to be involved in a lot of
litigation. I find now that having been to law school wouldn't
have changed things much. It's almost irrelevant to litigation.
And the other thing is to have gotten involved in a string of cases
which captured the attention of the press either before or right
after I got into them and which all hit almost simultaneously. It
was like a catapult. We defended Sam Sheppard, Dr. Coppolino,
the Boston Strangler, and the Plymouth Mail Robbery all in one
year, and because most of these cases turned out favorably in
one sense or another—they were all straight acquittals but the
Strangler—people got the notion, because people are very sim-
plistic, that if you hire this lawyer you will always win. I've had
to downgrade that notion substantially, saying that it's the evidence that determines the case and the lawyer can only help it
along. But this is the view that people have, and they come in
frequently looking for a miracle worker. We get bombarded with
cases from all over the world, not just the United States. People
from as far away as Germany, which has an entirely different
system of law, will write me, "Dear Super Lawyer, I have pleaded
guilty to seventeen murders. Please get me out of jail at once."

The very first case I ever tried when I got out of law school
—and the ink wasn't even dry on my license—was a first degree
murder case that was already on the front pages. The original
defense lawyer had a heart attack, and I happened to be the only

guy in town that knew anything about a lie detector, which had become a big issue. So I came in just to cross-examine the polygraph examiner and ended up finishing the case. The defendant was acquitted. The next week I had a front page case that I had taken as an investigator and was asked to try, a very bizarre rape case. So on a regional basis, right from the start I got an awful lot of cases. Before I was out of law school a year I took the Sheppard case, which didn't really go anywhere until four years after I'd been licensed, but when he was released it was the miracle of miracles, and so instead of just on a regional basis, pretty much New England, we began to get calls from all over the country on the theory that anybody that could get Sam Sheppard out must have a magic act somewhere. On a regional basis it got so bad that many of the people who asked us to defend them thought that I was fixing juries because I happened into a bunch of cases which could be won and were won. America thinks a win/loss record is the index to skill. Unfortunately, it's not.

MILTON GLASER

When I was in junior high school I had a very clear vision that I wanted to be the best commercial artist in the world. It was clear, whatever that meant at the time—and it was an innocent time—I really wanted to be the best in what I could be. I had chosen to be an applied artist. I just knew that I wanted to do something that had a problem at one end and a solution at the other. So I had some clarity around that issue although I never knew exactly what the form would be, or where the work would take me. I wanted to be a cartoonist then, and do comic strips basically.

I wasn't even conscious of the degree of difficulty, if there was any. I had early encouragement. After I got out of school and even at school—I went to Cooper Union—I was strongly encouraged in my talent. And ever since then it's just been a matter of moving with encouragement—from teachers, peers, clients, the world. I always knew that I wanted to be the best I could be. I always knew that the world's professional criteria for the graphic designer was very low, and I never used them for what mine should be. I never had the sense that they were a sufficient boundary for my own accomplishment. My own standards, I guess, were the history of the world, whatever occurred: Leonardo da Vinci, Michelangelo. . . . I mean, if you're going to shoot for something, you might as well shoot for the best that's ever been accomplished. And that was always my sense of it. It didn't seem to me appropriate to use the prevailing standards as a means of imitation or guide. I never did. I never do. My feeling about my work is that I'm at the beginning of it. I just feel for the first time that I'm beginning to understand what my profession is about.

JOHN DIEBOLD

I always tried to do what I was doing well and I always had a very positive view of things, so I guess I did expect to be successful though I never really thought much about it. From the time I was a youngster I wanted very much to be a doctor and do medical research, and that interest continued up to the point I went to college. At the time you could not go into medicine without having fluency in two languages, and so I switched to engineering, which only required one language. If it had not been for that I would have stayed with medicine. I knew that I could not handle the language requirement. My brother is fluent in nine languages, but I have a substantial problem. I made the switch to engineering because from a very early age I was also interested in the organization of businesses and factories, what was then called industrial management, industrial engineering. The idea of doing that on a consulting basis was with me virtually before I understood what consultants did. So there were two big career interests.

During the Second World War I was a merchant marine and trained at the Merchant Marine Academy, and the training included a lot of courses on gun control mechanisms. This is where much of the early work on computers originated, and I was fascinated right from that point. Since I had been interested earlier in the idea of factory organization, when I saw the gun control devices I immediately said, if you can do this with an antiaircraft gun, you can certainly control a lathe or a machine tool this way. When I got to Harvard Business School some years later I finally got the opportunity to do something about it, but, as I say, the idea came during the war.

After I finished graduate school I went to work for the oldest consulting firm in the country, Griffenhagen and Associates, for three hundred dollars a month. I was fired. I was working as Mr. Griffenhagen's assistant, and he allowed me to spend part of the time writing my first book, *Automation,* which was published in 1952. I was putting in very long hours as his assistant, in effect doing two full-time jobs, but after the first year he felt that I really should tend to business in a much more conventional way and that this whole field of computers and automation was going to be very interesting but it was not something that was serious. He fired me three times, and the third time I went away. The first two times I ignored his memoranda. He never fired me face to face, he always sent me a memorandum. Some years later when Mr. Griffenhagen wanted to retire, we bought the company.

When I left there were only a very small number of computers in the world. They were being used for engineering and scientific calculations but not yet for business purposes. I had not the slightest question about that happening, but it was early. I started my own business before the field even existed and had to hang on by the skin of my teeth. I was convinced that there would be a field, and then a field began.

I've always been interested in the next wave of things to come, and I felt that automation was very fundamental and would change an awful lot about society. I think that's happening, though there's a long way to go yet. But at any one moment people tend to see yesterday very clearly but don't believe tomorrow will be any different. They really don't. They think tomorrow will be the same as it was twenty years ago. It's very hard today to realize how long it took to get accepted any of the facts that are now taken for granted, that computers will be deeply enmeshed in normal day-to-day living and that they'll be very involved in altering the way people work and what they do. But in the beginning you had to argue and argue and argue about it, just as you do today to get people conscious that there will be changes in the 1980s.

I did a lot of writing and speaking to try to get my ideas across. Teddy Roosevelt said that American public opinion is a vast ocean and you do not stir it with a teaspoon, and I think that is correct. After doing it for a while, you begin to feel, well, anybody should understand this by now, everybody must have heard it, and that's always dangerous to assume because they haven't. But I think that perseverance is a very fundamental element in my nature, and it's very important when you're trying to start up something new. Almost everything I've done has involved trying to start new things, and starting new things have many similarities about them. One of them is that it is an uphill fight for much longer than one logically feels it should be. It takes a long time. But maybe to a fault, I always tend to approach things from the standpoint of a fairly long haul, and I think that's important if you want to initiate something. So you may have to just repeat and repeat yourself in order to get your ideas across. Sometimes I'd experience this as frustration, but more typically I would get bored. You make one speech saying that the sun was really going to rise in the morning and then you make a second and a third and a tenth and a twentieth and a thirtieth, and at some point you really grow tired of it. Staying with things can be a real problem. Occasionally I'll take one of the ideas of eight or ten years ago and put it out again and people will say, "Well, yes, that's very pertinent," but I got bored with it years ago and stopped using it then.

ALEXIS LICHINE

When I was separated from the army in 1946, I was told by people whose expertise was widely recognized in the liquor business that I would never be able to sell wines in the United States. "You're wasting your time," they told me. "You'll never be able to make Americans wine conscious. The American taste patterns are just too different." To a certain extent their judgment about the market was accurate. Before World War Two the drinking of wine was pretty much limited to a few moneyed people who learned what wines were like from their grandfathers. By and large, the wines of America were ice water, coffee, tea, milk and soft drinks. But I was determined to try. I felt sure there was a market for it, even though people far "wiser" than myself believed there wasn't. So I started, and believe me, it took a hell of a lot of work to get wines to where they are today. It was all upstream—up torrent, so to speak.

I was convinced that if and when an American was given the proper educational promptings, there would be a favorable response. Wine itself was complicated, less so today than it was then, and to be able to deal in it, one had to know it thoroughly. Wine was a very esoteric subject and no one knew how to approach such a broad topic: Thousands of labels existed, not with brand names, as Americans are accustomed to, but with geographic place names, none of which were familiar to the American public. Furthermore, all the people who were in the spirits business knew nothing about it, and, even though it was a cousin industry, never made the slightest efforts to find out. All the big distilling companies had made a failure of it. The only thing they knew from their bootlegging days was hard liquor. No one ever drank wine during Prohibition because you needed a compact form for transportation purposes and the only wine that could bear the huge bootleggers' prices was champagne. They still kept that same mentality even when they moved into legal sales after Repeal. All they knew was gin, whiskey, bourbon and rye, and those were products that were easy to sell because there were brands and you could advertise them. Wine is not sold as a branded product but by the name of the district where it is grown, and the better the wine the smaller the district and the less that is produced. So whenever one of the large distilling companies tried establishing a wine division it had difficulty finding the manpower to understand it, to define the way to market it.

But I was encouraged by the fact that whenever I talked to any given person, I could always interest him. I also felt that the war was bringing about an evolution in American taste. When I was in the army I had seen GIs being exposed for the first time to vino and vin ordinaire and they liked it. These millions of men would be coming home from Europe and I thought they would provide a base. Also, one could see the glimmer of a certain amount of postwar prosperity. Therefore I felt that there was room for one man who would dedicate his life to wines to create a market through his own immense efforts. Little did I know when I embarked upon it how much of an effort it would take. But, you know, when you have dedication as a base and a certain amount of encouragement along the way it's enough to sustain you. I knew that it would work, though I never thought it would take as long as it did.

I had no money at all when I came back out of the army. I came back absolutely empty-handed except for a few months' worth of severance pay and I had a mother and father to support. I had also married a French woman I met in Europe, a countess who was perhaps one of the most spoiled women on both sides of the Atlantic. She felt the United States was the land of plenty, and I recall looking into my pocketbook and seeing there wasn't much plenty to be found there. Her ideas were fast dissipated. But I got a job with Dr. Armand Hammer as import-export director for United Distillers of America. While we were overseas, Dr. Hammer was collecting distilleries one after the other and, being a very wily businessman, he accumulated a hell of a lot of them. He foresaw that there would be a shortage of whiskey when the war ended and also of industrial alcohol. So I sat on the seventy-some-odd floor of the Empire State Building with the great Hammer art collection—I remember there was a Frans Hals in my office—and started to slowly build up wines the way they should be built up. But Dr. Hammer did not understand wines. He did not have the patience to wait for me to build up a wine business for him, so we agreed to disagree and I went out on my own.

I went to several accounts I knew would be receptive to my supplying them with top wines. One was Antoine's in New Orleans. Another was Sherry Wines and Spirits, a retail store in New York. A third was the Waldorf Astoria. There were a few others. These places gave me a commitment, and I went to France to buy wines for them from the small estates in Burgundy and the châteaux in Bordeaux. This was sometime around 1948. Because I was underfinanced, I was not able to buy very much at one time, but with each dollar I obtained I'd return to France and buy some more. I just commuted back and forth. I had various shippers, and eventually I was able to establish my own brand name with them, "Selected by Alexis Lichine," which would go above the main château or estate label. So without even having a firm, little by little I began to establish a certain small, limited reputation. These were all top wines, better than anything else you could find in this country and at excellent prices because I was taking a very small markup and there were no middlemen.

But then I found that each time I would push the wines of some château in Bordeaux, the château would increase the prices on me. Not that one looks for gratitude in life, but there was very little appreciation of what to me was my hard work. So I decided I'd better get some vineyards of my own. By putting several shareholders together, I was able to acquire Château Cantenac-Prieuré, whose name I changed in 1953 to Prieuré-Lichine by applying to the Committee of Classified Growths. Then six months later I formed a syndicate with David Rockefeller and some others, all of whom subscribed small amounts, and purchased Château Lascombes and started my own company.

And to build it up I went about selling wines in the most unorthodox fashion. Typically, I could mention how I operated in San Antonio. I sold three large cellars—three hundred cases, four hundred cases, three hundred cases—to three wealthy men in San Antonio. I knew this was like setting up a cell because they introduced me to one of the most important restaurants in town and then to one of the better retailers, who, seeing one thousand cases of wine coming in right under his nose to three people in his own community, suddenly became interested in wines. And then the retailer and the restaurant put pressure on the local wholesaler, who was completely unknowledgeable. But since two of his good customers were so interested, he became interested too. Since the wholesaler didn't know how to sell wines, he gave me carte blanche to send him a small shipment. Then I had to tell him how to price them and how to sell them, and I had to go back out there and hold the hands of his salesmen and go around to give lectures to the women's clubs and go on radio and television and give interviews to the local newspapers. It would always cost me more than I could possibly make. And what happened in San Antonio happened all throughout the United States.

Few people have proselytized as much as I have throughout the country. I'd not only go to Omaha, Nebraska, but also to Lincoln. I not only went to Milwaukee, but also to Madison. Not only to St. Louis but also Kansas City. And little by little I'd dig up people in these towns who were interested in wines and they'd help me approach the stores, restaurants and hotels. Then I would work on the various retailers and restaurants and hotels and eventually find a wholesaler. I used that same process throughout the United States, and believe me, it took work, dedication, shoe leather, and a tremendous amount of will-power.

I remember as recently as 1959 going to a shop in Milwaukee where I spent two full days trying to sell them a forty-two-case assortment of wines to be imported from Europe. Two full days to sell them two cases of this, three cases of that, two cases of something else. And after the shipment arrived, they started to hesitate. They thought they'd have it on their hands forever. Even my own customers didn't believe in it. I had to really ram it down their throats. Well, they sold it all out in the first couple of weeks after they received it, and their next order was two hundred fifty cases, at which time I went out there again and gave talks in the store, met their customers and went around with them and put in cellars for them. Their next order was close to five hundred cases. Then it was one thousand cases. And today I suppose they must be doing twenty thousand cases a year, all from those original forty-two. And this was only seventeen years ago. Then because this retailer was selling wine, other people in the business took an interest. And when I went on radio and television, this was not only for Alexis Lichine wines, for French wines. It also rubbed off on Italian wines, Spanish wines, Portuguese wines, German wines, California wines—none of which I had. This is the process by which America became wine conscious.

I had to explain not only to the wholesalers and the retailers, but to the American public, the most elementary factors governing the production of wines—that the four most crucial elements are the soil, the grape variety, the vintage (the fluctuations in the weather in a given year), and the know-how of the individual grower. The tens of thousands of copies of my books, *Wines of France* and *Encyclopedia of Wines & Spirits*—a 900-page tome, twelve years in preparation, which capsulizes my experience of over three decades purchasing wines in the vineyards—were largely the textbooks for this effort.

The toughest but the most important part was the nonstop travel, covering all the bases. Sometimes I'd have to do two cities in a day, and you didn't have jet planes then. I remember a typical itinerary: I'd go from New York to Washington. From Washington to Cincinnati. From Cincinnati to Columbus. From Columbus I might go to Dayton by bus and then I would try to get some train to go up to Cleveland. There were no trains between Cleveland and Toledo, so I'd have to take a bus. From Toledo I'd take another bus to Detroit. From Detroit I'd fly to Chicago. From Chicago a train to Milwaukee. From Milwaukee a train or a plane to Minneapolis. From Minneapolis down to Omaha. From Omaha I'd go down to Kansas City. From Kansas City back to St. Louis, and then to some other circuits, through and back again. Then I'd head out for the West Coast. I'd be gone on these trips for four or five weeks, and this was time and time again. I covered the United States in length and in breadth.

I thought I'd never be able to do that again—but I've just returned from a month in France making the rounds of all the growers, tasting in cold cellars in the middle of January, from eight o'clock in the morning to midnight, driving over a thousand miles in several days in order to set up new sources of supply for Somerset Wines, which owns my name in the U.S., and for which I am now a director and consultant vice-president. And after that I jumped on a plane to begin the whole hopscotch all over again—lectures in Rochester, with over a thousand people crowded in one room for a wine tasting, and more of the same in Dallas, St. Louis, Boston and Chicago.

JACK HALEY JR.

I was approached by a couple of friends whom I had originally brought into David Wolper's organization who had gone out on their own and now headed up MGM's documentary TV division. They wanted to know would I do a television special with them on Hollywood musicals to be called *That's Entertainment.* The title was their idea. So I met with them a couple of times. They wanted to use footage from a lot of different studios—Warner Bros., RKO, MGM—and I told them, "You don't need all that.

It should come from one studio because that'll give you a point of view, a better story. You've got to keep it all Metro." They were dubious at first because they didn't really know the footage. That's why they asked me to come into it. They weren't musical buffs, but they knew I was and that I'd been through it ten years before when I was doing the *Hollywood and the Stars* series for television. One of the shows was "The Fabulous Musicals," and the only footage we couldn't get then was from MGM. I lusted after that material for ten years.

So I set up a meeting with Jim Aubrey at Metro and said to the guys, "Come with me. Let's go up and sell it to Jim as a feature." They said, "You're kidding. He'll never go for it," and I said, "Well, come on. We'll try." So we tried, and Aubrey kind of patted me on the head and said, "Look, we'll think about this later. Right now we need some help with the feature end of the studio. Would you like to be an executive here?" Well, I'd never tried that before. I'd done it in television but never with features, so I said, "Sure, what the hell. It's a new direction to go in life. I'm still young, so why not give it a shot?" So I became Director of Creative Affairs, in effect second in charge of production. After all the years of growing up in the business and being around it I thought I knew everything there was to know, but I soon realized I was learning a whole other end of things and I was really glad I had taken the job. Until you get on the other side of the desk, you have absolutely no knowledge of how pictures are put together and what distribution is all about and what packaging is in all its varied aspects. You may think you do, but you don't.

But I never let go of the idea for *That's Entertainment,* and I kept pestering and pestering MGM to let me do it. I'm sure part of the reason I took the gig in the first place was that I knew that's how I could get it done. I could just keep annoying them and whining, and finally they'd say, "Alright already, okay! Jesus!"

Eventually, I did get a little money to do a little development . . . a "sample" presentation. Sometimes I'd have to read as many as twenty or thirty scripts a week, but I'm a very fast reader and during lunches and in the evenings I'd screen all the old Metro musicals and start to bring the picture together in my mind. I couldn't afford to use the regular projection facilities, so

I rented a portable viewer and put it next to my desk. I viewed over two hundred MGM musicals on that little machine. Then I hired an assistant editor, and just the two of us worked on it for a while. And then I conned the lab into popping to do some tests, blowing this old film up into 70mm and trying to figure out how to make the black and white work with the color. I just kept plugging away. I got hold of Gene Kelly—a good friend I'd worked with before, I'm godfather to his daughter—and after he'd seen the assemblage, he agreed to do a voice-over narration. And about a year and a half after I started fiddling around with the footage, I finally brought the Metro people in and showed it to them, and they said, *"Why didn't you tell us this is what you meant!"* Then I was relieved of all my other responsibilities and concentrated on finishing up the picture, which took about another six months.

That's Entertainment just caught everybody by surprise. I was certainly the most enthusiastic person in the entire studio, but in my wildest imagination I thought that maybe it would do ten million dollars worldwide. They say it's going to do forty. And it's opened up so many other doors for me. Indirectly, that's how I got my present job as president of 20th Century-Fox television. My friends at Metro still call me one of two names, The Wizard of Was or The Phantom of the Vaults. I love old movies so much that my wife says that when I die she intends to bury me in a film can.

JERRY DELLA FEMINA

When I was twenty-five I was on my seventh year of looking for a job as a copywriter. I started in 1954. I got it in 1961. The country was in a boom, and I was in a depression. But I just methodically kept on looking and wouldn't stop till I found it. Now it wasn't that terrible because failure really isn't terrible if you can say to yourself, hey, I *know* I'm gonna be successful at what I want to do some day. Failure doesn't become a big hang-up then because it's only temporary. If failure is absolute, then it would be a disaster, but as long as it's only temporary you can just go on and achieve almost anything. Yeah, seven years went by, which made it awfully slow. But I wasn't running around saying, God, what's happening? I never blamed anyone for my failure. So I never give anyone else credit for my success.

I decided I wanted to be a copywriter when I was working as a messenger boy for the *New York Times.* I'd go up delivering copy to the different agencies and I'd always see a group of people with their legs up on the desk looking very comfortable and relaxed. I'd ask what they did, and somebody would say, "They're copywriters." Since I really didn't have enough money to go to college—I just went to Brooklyn College at night for a short while, then gave that up—I decided that that's what I wanted to be. I realized years later that the reason those people were sitting with their legs up on the desk was that they were paralyzed with fear and that in reality they had the worst jobs in the world. But I was just a kid and it seemed very glamorous and a lot of fun, and, gee, somebody pays you to think and to write. I didn't know if I could write or not, but at that point you think anyone can. So I decided I wanted to be a copywriter and started looking in 1954. In 1961 someone finally decided that that's what I was. After that, it was the easiest thing in the world. I *was* a copywriter. I discovered I had a flair or a nose or a talent for it. I liked it. It liked me. I saw I could do almost anything I touched.

Sure, I was surprised. I spent so many years saying to myself I could do it, it was shocking to find out I could. After seven years walking around saying, "Sure I can do it, sure I can do it if they only give me a chance," why wouldn't I be surprised when they gave me a chance and I could? It was a very natural, tremendous shock. But since then it's been a ball, it's been lovely.

BUDDY RICH

It's hard when you're doing it and it's easy when you've accomplished it, I suppose. You look back and you say, Jesus, that wasn't so hard, you know. So what the hell, so I sat in a cold bus. But when you're sitting in that cold bus, you say, "Fuck, what am I doing in this band, why am I on the road?" You know, you drive a bad car a couple hundred miles and you want to know why you're on the road, then all of a sudden you're there and there are three thousand people coming in from the snow to hear you play. That's pretty good. That's cool. I like applause. I'm not that kind of guy that it doesn't mean anything to. It means a lot to me. I love to hear the band break it up and I love to see people standing when they think they know what I've done. It's really great.

Every time I did something I always did it at the wrong time and it always turned out right. When I got my first job with Joe Marsala at the Hickory House, I had to go there three different weekends before he acknowledged the fact I was even in the room. I was eighteen years old, a kid, and he had big stars sitting in on those Sunday afternoon jam sessions. He had the best jazz people in the world and I was some bum from Brooklyn. But finally he let me sit in and he offered me the job that same night. So after that it was easy. I thought, you know, I got a job after only playing six minutes. Then I was offered a job with Bunny Berigan, and it wasn't a question of going up and auditioning and his saying, "Well, I'll call you." I was hired on the spot. And then I left Berigan's band because I was tired of the kind of work he was doing. I was on the band exactly six months, and out of the six months I did five months and two weeks of one-nighters. And not a very first-class bus. Then I went with Artie Shaw and from Artie Shaw I went to Tommy Dorsey. So it was never a question of a starving musician who finally gets a break. I got a break every time I went with somebody. And I always considered it an equal break for them when they hired me because I thought I was that good. So we both got a break.

I did two ridiculous things in my lifetime, really stupid things. Number one, I enlisted in the Marine Corps during the Second World War. That was probably *the* single most stupid thing that anybody could ever do. And the second stupid thing I did was to come out of the service and organize a big band in 1947, which was right at the beginning of the decline of the big bands. The war was over and people weren't going out to hear bands again and all that bullshit, so it was a fiasco and I lost all kinds of bread. And it was a dynamite band. It was the hippest band around. All the people who were on that band—Johnny Mandel, Tiny Kahn, Al Cohn, Zoot Sims—I mean I got some bitches, you know. So I was doing the right thing musically but I wasn't doing it at the right time. And then I went back with Harry James and that was a nice experience for almost six years. And then after six years I said, "Jesus Christ, man, you got to play something besides 'Sleepy Lagoon'!" I will admit that was the only time I started worrying about my playing because we were playing identical things night after night in the same slot, the same time, and you could just go up there and wind yourself up and know that the first tune was going to be "Don't Be That Way" and then on and on and on into the same set.

So in 1966 when everything was dead as far as big bands were concerned, I organized a big band because that's what I wanted to do. I wanted to hear what I could do with a new kind of big band, a kind of concert jazz band that would not play for dancing. And everybody in the world who knew anything about music said to me, "Man, a big band in these times? You've got to be crazy." So ten years later I'm still crazy with probably the best band I've ever had in my life. So, looking back, I didn't have such a bad time. I did a lot of dumb things, but that's cool.

MARTIN SCORSESE

It was always hard, always hard. It's always been a nightmare. It still is. It's the old story. You just move up to a different set of problems. The problems get worse sometimes. You start with a "success" in something in a certain way, you accrue certain things, you build up, and then you trade in old problems for new problems and those problems have to be dealt with. There's always somebody who says, "We want you to make a film. We're gonna tie up your arm. You have to do it with one arm and we're gonna pluck off one of your ears. But we want to do one of your pictures." How do you come to terms with that? You make the picture. And you try to peek through the blindfold.

JOE EULA

How did I do it? Like *that.* It was easy, very easy. I think it had to do with a goal that sure was way out of proportion. Way out of proportion. I don't believe in that one rung at a time stuff. That's a lot of crap. I never did it step by step by step. It always had to do with adventure, a total life-style, a challenge, with that crazy thing of throwing yourself into it like a kamikaze diver and you either come up smelling roses or you fail your ass off, but you've given your all.

MILTON H. GREENE

I never thought about success. I majored in art and came across photography as a hobby and became so involved in it that I went to work after school to learn and worked for nothing for a couple of years as an assistant to Maurice Bauman and Eliot Elisofon. And then as the years went on, before I knew it I was in business for myself, but I never thought about making it, becoming successful. I was just involved and interested in the work I was doing. After years of working in different places as an assistant and putting in all kinds of hours of the day and night, in 1940-something I got an offer from Macy's to open up a studio for them for two hundred dollars a week. I had been making $17.50, so that was an awful lot of money to me. It seems I was getting a bit of a reputation in the industry.

So I went to Bauman, the guy who taught me photography, 'cause I figured he wasn't making too much at the time and I said to him, "Why don't we open up Macy's studio together, and eventually we can leave them and go into our own business?" He liked the idea, and not long after that we did quit Macy's and open our own studio and for the first year things were very rough. I remember him saying to me, "Look, I'm ten years older than you, and I can't afford to do what you're doing." So I said, "Okay, we'll have a big party." I had to borrow money for the party, and I invited Buddy Rich and a lot of the other musicians I knew. Charlie Parker and Dizzy Gillespie and a lot of other people used to come to the studio to rehearse. So I had this big party and jam session and all the illustrators and advertising people were there and the next day I woke up with a hangover but everybody was calling for work. And from there on everything went uphill.

So it was something that just happened. I was working hard because I had to pay the rent and because I enjoyed it. I still enjoy it. There's no price on it. But then all of a sudden I was accused of being successful. People would start to say, "This is Milton Greene, the successful photographer." I found it embarrassing, that's why I say I was accused of being successful. I mean I know I'm good, but there's no such thing as the best. Every day I still work at improving whatever I do as much as I can.

And what is success? To be content with oneself. You could be a success at a dollar a week. I guess I do consider myself successful to the extent that I had to borrow money to go into business and I paid the money back, made money, loaned money, lost money and am still considered a good photographer and still work. I consider that successful compared to what I had. But I may end up dying in debt or considered no good. Who knows?

AL GOLDSTEIN

When Jim Buckley and I began to publish *Screw* we didn't have the slightest idea how hard it was to start your own business. I had absolutely no expertise. I had never been a publisher. Any number of things could have made it fail. About a year after *Screw* began I met a district attorney for lunch and asked him why he didn't arrest us earlier. He said, "We were afraid the publicity would help you." Well, he was wrong. If we had gotten busted with issue one or two, we wouldn't have come out with another one. We didn't have the money. We didn't have the sales so that dealers would have kept carrying the paper. By the time the first arrest took place nine months later we had money, we had some reputation, we had some support, and we could afford lawyers. So there were variables that I had no control over, that I didn't even know existed.

But Jim and I really believed in the paper. I mean I didn't care if I went to jail every day, the paper was going to come out. We did almost everything ourselves. We put the first five issues on the newsstands ourselves because no distributor would touch it. I went by subway and bicycle and taxicab and gave *Screw* to the news dealers. I didn't know it wasn't supposed to be done that way. We wrote everything. We typeset everything. Jim was a typesetter. And we made some terrible mistakes. I cannot believe some of the moves I made. I let myself be embezzled twice. I had to learn the hard way that so many of the rituals of business make sense. Now somebody comes in, we check their credit rating, we find out where they've lived the last five years. I was very rebellious and still am, but I was much more so then. I felt that big business was full of shit. Madison Avenue was just doing these soldierlike manipulations to put you in your place. No, it was to prevent the kind of things that happened to us, which was being embezzled, being robbed, having junkies nodding out in our office.

And being *Screw,* we would attract employees who were looking for a way of life instead of a job. And so in seven years I've learned to be ruthless. If somebody's fucking up, I don't care if he's got three kids and has to pay for an operation. He's going to get fired. I try to be a benevolent boss, but I've learned by now that it's me or them. But in terms of making the business grow, we knew almost nothing, and we'd occasionally have to turn to friends for advice. I remember negotiating with my distributors on how much *Screw* would get, and I was so weak at it I had to go out and get some help. I remember the first art director I fired. He wouldn't leave. I had to bring someone in to make him go. I said, "You're fired." He said, "No I'm not." I didn't know how to fire somebody. Now I'm great at it.

I didn't start *Screw* to make money. It was more pressing than that. If *Screw* were a failure it meant that I was really sick. It meant I was one of a kind and a freak. And if *Screw* were successful, it meant I wasn't alone. I mean, it was really a very strong drive, beyond money. One part of me said, gee, *Screw* can't be successful because if it's such a good idea other people would have done it. That was the big negative thing because I couldn't believe I was capable of a creative idea. Of course, what I didn't realize was that I was functioning in a very murky area of what was legal and not legal, and there was a very rapid and viable change taking place in our morality and what the publishing world would accept. So I kept asking myself why some established publisher wasn't doing it. Well, it was simply because if somebody is successful, he doesn't go into an area that's going to be a heartache. And since Buckley and I had nothing, where else could we go? We could only function in this kind of very marginal business. The first six months we didn't even have an office. But the key thing was that the paper sold. That's the thing. Because the paper was real it became successful. We printed seven thousand copies of the first issue and sold four thousand, which gave us four hundred dollars. We made a dime a copy. We gave the news dealer fifteen cents. We appealed to his greed. I knew that much. I knew he wasn't going to take me because he was a civil libertarian, but because he made fifteen cents. He only made three cents on the *New York Post.*

And so there was enough money with issue one to do issue two. And the scary thing is that if *Screw* needed more money in that early time, say another one hundred dollars, I probably wouldn't have given it and *Screw* would have folded. I told Jim I was only committing one hundred fifty dollars, that's it. And it's miraculous in publishing that we were able to make enough to keep it going. But that's because we did everything ourselves. There were no middlemen. If we had had a distributor, we wouldn't have seen the money for four or five issues, but since we dealt directly with the news dealer we got it right away. That was lucky. We didn't know.

I keep telling myself how easily it could have been different. There was nothing very cerebral or well thought out about it. It was a gut thing. *Screw* was a gut kind of publication. I didn't go to committees. We didn't say, "Well, we have to do this and balance it with that." It was almost a product of my own sickness and my own neurosis. And so cabdrivers and sanitation workers will honk their horns when they see me because they realize that if I could break out maybe so could they. Some of them resent me. Some of them will say, "Well, I have the same ideas," and I'm sure they do. There are many potential Al Goldsteins. But there were my own sexual drives, my own family conditioning, my chutzpa, my willingness to pay the price.

I mean, going to jail meant nothing to me because I had nothing. After selling insurance, my first marriage ended and I just went into a downspin. I went on welfare. I drove a cab. I worked in a carnival. And I had nothing. So going to jail—I was like a black on 125th Street. So what? It didn't mean a thing. When you're behind the eight ball you take chances. I never felt I was going to be successful with *Screw,* but I felt I had to take the chance.

GEROLD FRANK

When I was very small I wanted to be a magician. Obviously there was a need or desire to mystify or at least be in a position to make people react. Then I wanted to be an alchemist, to turn dross into gold and do miraculous things. It was the Walter Mitty story. And then I began writing.

I received BA and MA degrees: I was thinking about teaching and writing, but I became a newspaper man and a contributor to such magazines as *The New Yorker, The Nation* and *Harper's.* I began my first book about 1943 when I was still working as a reporter on the *Cleveland News.* The first wounded soldiers had come back from Guadalcanal, and I was the man who wrote their stories. There was a Private Williams who'd had a tonsillectomy by a Japanese bullet and the doctor said, "Perfect, we don't have to touch it." There was another man who had been buried in an explosion and they found him three days later still alive. These were first-person stories and would appear in the *Cleveland News* by Private So-and-so as told to Gerold Frank. That's how I started my work as a collaborator. The pieces were collected and published by Putnam's under the title *Out in the Boondocks.* And when I was writing their stories I became each of these soldiers. Maybe going back to the days of the Walter Mitty fantasy, I found that I could put myself in other people's shoes and become just as excited as they were about what they were doing. The second book was the story of the sound man on a submarine that took gold from Corregidor. He sat there all day at the bottom of the sea listening to pings and bleeps and calibrating where he was, and that fascinated me too.

Later when I was working in New York as senior editor for *Coronet,* I was asked to work on a book with Lillian Roth. I remember saying, "What do I know about Hollywood?" but when Lillian Roth came into town I went up to meet her for the first time. She was talking about her mother and started crying and left the room. I was deeply touched by her story. I wanted to listen, and to understand. My son is a psychiatrist, my daughter a psychotherapist, my son-in-law a neuropathologist, my daughter-in-law is a psychotherapist. So in some way I may be a psychiatrist manqué. I was going to study medicine in school but writing won out. I was always fascinated to listen to other people's stories because in a way I thought my own life was so mundane. I lived these stories. I wanted the fact.

You see, I have a belief that nonfiction writers and fiction writers differ. The nonfiction writer is an obedient son. If he's kept after school by the teacher and comes home late, he says, "Mom, the teacher kept me after school." He tells the truth so he won't be punished. The fiction writer-to-be will be playing ball until six o'clock and come home and say, "The teacher kept me after school." He doesn't fear the lie. To me the fact is like a life raft which is thrown me and I cling to it. It exists, it *happened.* It may be that when I was growing up reality was something I felt very alienated from. Other people seemed to be speaking a language I didn't understand, laughing at jokes I didn't quite get. All these things were going on in the world about me and I wasn't quite hep, so I wanted to experience other people's experiences, perhaps without their suffering. I don't know what it was.

So I wrote *I'll Cry Tomorrow* with Lillian Roth and when it became a best seller I was approached by various people to do other books along the same line. One day an agent asked me to do a book with Diana Barrymore, but I wasn't particularly interested. I said, "Lillian Roth was a terrific story. She was an alcoholic for eighteen years and then came back from a land no one usually returns from and made a name for herself. Diana Barrymore also has that kind of reputation—she drinks, she's outrageous—so why should I do the same kind of thing again?" He said, "Well, go meet her," and I did. She was living in a hotel next to the old Madison Square Garden which was filled with cowboys appearing at the rodeo. Even the obscenities in the men's room were misspelled. I went up and the door opened and there stood a creature slender like a broomstick with a wild

mat of hair and eyes gleaming and sort of staggering, and I
thought to myself, "Good Lord, this is the daughter of John
Barrymore, the greatest actor of his time, and Michael Strange,
the poetess." And here she is in this hotel with a husband who
is also drunk, she reeling about the room saying "dahling" and
her husband saying, "Come on, Diana, you know Tallulah does-
n't like you to imitate her." To say that my heart went out to her
sounds like the corniest of corn, but I just had to know why.
What brought this about? And then I discovered that this was
not simply the story of a girl who drank too much. It was the
story of somebody who could not live up to a heritage. As an
actress she couldn't live up to the Barrymore name. Everybody
expected that Diana, the moment she walked on stage, would be
a Barrymore, and she couldn't be. She wasn't that good. All her
life she had the arrogance of the Barrymores. She had the social
position of the Barrymores. She had everything. She went to
finishing schools and was voted the best-liked debutant of the
Stork Club set, but she was just not able to live up to her heritage. And so I decided to write the book and I threw myself into
it as I had with Lillian Roth. I went into each book as though it
fulfilled something in myself, as if I were telling my own story
in some way. There was one scene where her father dies and the
burial takes place and Diana and her uncle Lionel and her half
brother are the only ones there. And as they lower the body into
the grave, Diana is standing there thinking, "God damn Aunt
Ethel for being so arrogant and la-di-da that she can't even come
to her brother's funeral. And God damn Uncle Lionel for being
so silent and never saying a word to me. And God damn me for
being a spoiled Newport brat. God damn us all." And I remember sitting at my typewriter that night grinding the words out
under my breath. I *was* Diana Barrymore at that moment. I mean
I lived it.

After *Too Much Too Soon* came *Beloved Infidel* with Sheilah Graham. Her life was another kind of story, the little match girl, if
you want to put it in those very sentimental terms. She was an
orphan who was never adopted when the families came to the
orphanage to pick the children. She was the tallest and the
thinnest and always had a cold and once they shaved her head
—the whole thing. Then she was a skivvy, a housemaid in London who used to scrub the pavement in front of the house where

she worked. She had the most depressing kind of childhood, and then out of sheer will and energy she came to this country and worked her way up. She became a correspondent in Hollywood and met Scott Fitzgerald and fell in love with him. She had the chance to marry a titled suitor in London and turned it down to stay with Scott even though she knew she could never marry him because he would never leave his wife Zelda, who was in an institution in the South. But she stayed with him and kept him alive the last four years of his life and enabled him to begin what might have been his greatest book, *The Last Tycoon.* I was fascinated by her story and went to every length to search out the fact. I must have asked her four thousand questions, down to the slightest little thing. Sheilah would tell me one part of the story, as much as she knew, and then I'd go to other people to get the other parts of it. Then I'd go back to Sheilah and probe and probe and probe some more and ask and ask and ask.

That's how I worked with all these books. The women were my principal sources but then I'd do research by going to other people too. David Dempsey once did a piece in the *Times* in which he said that I had invented a new form, the bioautobiography. I guess I still had to be the obedient boy, the good son saying the fact just as it was. Since I seemed to have been born guilty, if you want to go into my own thing, I was always avoiding the punishment from somebody who might say it isn't so. The fact was there. It *is* so. It *did* happen. She *told* it to me. I *checked it out.* As I say, I think that's the difference between writing nonfiction and fiction.

After *Beloved Infidel* became a best seller and then a film, all sorts of people were approaching me because it seemed that for whatever reason these things worked out. And one day somebody told me that Zsa Zsa Gabor wanted to do her story and "I vill only do it wiz Ger-old Frank." Here I was, you know, somebody from Ohio and Zsa Zsa at the time was the most glamorous of the glamorous. Jack Paar once called her the most beautiful woman in the world, and she wanted to reveal her secrets to me. But I remember saying to myself, "I have to stop doing this sort of thing." Not that it wasn't interesting, but friends would come up to me and say, "Good Lord, when are you going to do *your* book?" I said to myself, "I must be sitting here thinking that these people who have suffered or who have climbed Himalayan heights and then dropped to the bottom and yet came back, that maybe there will fall from their lips the Open Sesame line, the truth about I don't know what. They will tell me something out of their experience that I don't know. I will learn the reality about people." Apparently I was still seeking reality, and now it was with Zsa Zsa, the glamour girl. And I wanted to know what lay behind that. Was there a real, thinking, calculating woman who played all these roles? Was there a great sadness somewhere? What was the secret? It sounds stupid, but again I was trying to find out what makes people tick. Again I was saying my own life is mundane but these lives are exciting and maybe I'll learn something from them.

After *Zsa Zsa* I decided that I was not going to write any more of these books, these bioautobiographies, and I went into analysis. It was a little late, but I thought that perhaps by learning more about myself I might learn why it was I had written four such books, why I was so turned on by other people's lives that I wanted to live them. I sometimes thought of myself as a hermit crab. A hermit crab has no shell of its own. It's always living in somebody else's. And I'd say to myself, "Why the deuce am I doing this?" If I were a psychiatrist I could have understood it, but I was not a psychiatrist. And even then, your training gives you a space between yourself and the patient so you don't get so involved. I don't know what I learned save that, I suppose, my mother had been unhappy and that I therefore had a tremendous sympathy for unhappy women, and that maybe as a boy I'd spent my life trying to put a smile on my mother's face and now as a man I was spending my life trying to comfort and assuage other women. But who is to know? This may be completely off the point. But there's no question that I listened. When they talked to me I listened. I participated in their lives.

After analysis I stopped writing bioautobiographies, and devoted myself to biography and history: *The Deed, The Boston Strangler, An American Death, Judy.*

ELIZABETH ASHLEY

Some idea of success is made to seem important to everyone who grows up in America. It's the most active, most evident manifestation of the Calvinist Christian Puritan Warriors of the

Lord ethic that we've got here. I mean, it's win/lose, succeed/
fail, and success is synonymous with win. They are words that
in the culture mean the same thing. Any sort of playing around
with the difference in definitions is basically bullshit. That's what
it means. And it's the American Dream, right? It justifies one's
existence. It earns one respect. And it is like the Devil. I mean,
fear is the Devil and success is the flip side. Success is the soldier
of fortune who makes love to your fear. And it is not synonymous with achievement, ever. Our culture has largely done that
separating, I think. Achievement is not respected. Labor is not
respected. Character, values, standards—there's not even a ges-
ture made in our culture towards those things. Nobody ever
refers to the nobility or honor of achievement and labor anymore. That's considered sort of an outmoded, wimping, rather
romantic point of view. They are, however, the things that give
a civilization its fiber, and I think that's one of the reasons that
civilization hasn't worked out awfully well.

Success is a ticket to ride. You've gotta have a ticket to get on
the bus. Now you only need a dollar-fifty ticket if you're getting
on Trailways and where you want to go is Poughkeepsie. If, on
the other hand, you want to go to Los Angeles, you're going to
have to come up with about thirty-five dollars, right? So there
are all kinds of tickets that will take you all kinds of distances,
but essentially they're gonna throw you off the bus if you ain't
got the ticket to ride. So if you want to travel, particularly if you
want to go any distance, you have to have some of it. And just
as it is the enemy of character, it's the enemy of art and very
much the enemy of honesty and decency. It's the Devil specter
in civilization, I think, particularly in modern civilization. And
America, the United States, my republic here, has kissed the
asshole of success for so long that it can't ever get up off its
knees. I got successful a few times and figured it out.

An enormous amount of pressure was put on me to achieve
when I was young, but I was lucky—or unlucky, however you
look at it. I grew up in the deep South and my mother was
perhaps the last of a breed in that she valued character more
than money. I was never brought up to respect money. I was not
brought up to respect power. It was perhaps in its own way a
kind of elitism or snobbery, but it's certainly the only kind I
respect. My mother was a woman who had values she lived by

every day of her life. She was a woman of character. I was brought up to respect that. I was also poor, and when you are very young you think that is kind of a drag. I mean my attitude was, oh come on, gee. My mother nailed into my spine almost from the moment I crawled out of the womb into a pink parlor spot, to the point where I almost couldn't stand it, the ethic that teaches you that the only right you have that nobody can ever take away from you, the only thing you've got that is deeply your own, is your values and what you believe in. And that believing means something. You don't believe in anything unless you stand up for it. And you should always try to keep your mind free because you might not have a lot of money and you might not have a lot of success and life can get really hard, but essentially how you live is who you are. And I believe that too.

But I caught the disease. You know, the things your parents teach you really hard are the first things you get bored with because they're the first demands that are made on you and, for the most part, you just want to get away from home and go play and have a good time and do anything you want to do and not have to worry about that kind of shit. And I was always kind of a failure. I mean I could never do anything. I mean I was a slug. I mean I was real dumb. Or so they told me. And I believed them. I was never a leader, man, and I just wanted to join. I just wanted attention. I wanted love. I wanted affection. I wanted acceptance. I wanted approval, any way I could get it. I was in for the cheap thrills and the easy shots. All the way. It's not unusual. It's pretty commonplace, I think. I just wanted to be a success. I wanted to be prom queen. I wanted to win once. I'd never won anything. Every game I played I lost. I couldn't do anything. I could never get it together. I couldn't even show up for school. I couldn't even do the showing-up part. And you see, I so desperately wanted to. I didn't want to be on the outside. I didn't want to be different. I didn't want to be stupid. I didn't want to be funny-looking. I didn't want to be a beggar. I wanted to be a winner. I would have done anything, anything, anything. And just about did. And in my mother's eyes, needless to say, I was a big disappointment, I was so frivolous and stupid. I was out there dancing and dancing and smiling and smiling and begging and groveling and doing anything to please. And those people are creeps, man. You know? I think I was kind of a creep.

I went to college for one semester, but I never even went to class. I was just sort of this lost jerk. And I was kind of wild. I could never stay in the rules. I never could stay inside the borders of situations. I wanted to be inside so desperately, but I couldn't balance there. I always fell over the edge. I didn't know what it was. It's easy to glorify it and romanticize it. Maybe I was just a creep. I don't know. I mean nine years of analysis gives you lots of snappy reasons that are perfectly acceptable anywhere on this earth. But I ran away from home. It was perfectly obvious that I was going to flunk out of college, and that was like the end of the line.

I would have liked to have been able to get married to Carroll Robert Rhinehart Reagan and moved to Magnolia, Mississippi, but I couldn't do that. I couldn't do anything. So I ran away. I'm a runner. That's my answer when it gets really tight and bad. I'll split. I'll take off. Here today, gone tomorrow. I don't like to stay around to pick up the pieces of myself. I'll just sort of leave the debris, take what's left and leave town. It's the only way I know to run my action in this life. You gotta always stay one step ahead of the cops. And there's always a cop on your butt, always.

I finally just said, "Fuck it." By that point the change that happens to people had happened to me. It's like you beat your fist bloody your whole life trying to get into their joint and finally you believe them that they don't want you in their joint. They're not going to let you in their joint. They don't like you. They don't like the way you look, the way you talk, the way you smell. Man, it's scent, it's animal scent. They don't want you in their joint. So finally if you survive all that, you say, "All right, motherfucker, I don't want to get into your joint, I'm never gonna try and cross your rope again." But there's a vengeance in that, let us not for one second kid ourselves. Because the thing that is unsaid is, "All right, cocksucker, I'll be back. And when I come back I'm gonna blow up your fucking joint." Right? "You'll see me next time with a grenade of some kind." It's a pattern, I think, a very commonplace reaction. A lot of that is what makes outlaws and desperadoettes and kids who run off and join the circus. And I'm just an old cooch dancer. I ran off and joined the circus. I mean I never had any ambition. I didn't want to do anything. I just wanted somebody to let me in their joint, to let me into a place where I could stay and be okay.

When you leave Baton Rouge, Louisiana, to go off into the world, to be an adventuress, you do not go to Cleveland or Grand Rapids. You go to New York City. There is only one Big Apple. And I came to New York City and it was terrific. It was like finding God. It was like Mohammed and the mountain. I mean I had never been north of Georgia. I'd never been anywhere. I was so green that when I got on that plane at midnight in New Orleans and the stewardess said this thing about going to Newark I thought, oh my God, I got a ticket to the wrong place. And I said, "I'm terribly sorry, but I meant New *York.*" I mean I didn't know. I had three hundred dollars that I made teaching dancing and I stayed at the YWCA. It was February ninth, 1958. I didn't know anybody here. So I looked in the paper for a job. I could type, but I thought maybe I could be a model. I didn't really care what I had to do. I was just out, man. I'd gotten out. I was anonymous. Nobody knew me. I'd lost the cop. I'd shaken the tail for a while.

My third day in New York I got a job on Seventh Avenue. I had gone to an employment agency and they looked at me and suggested that perhaps I should go to a modeling agency 'cause I was tall and weighed ninety-eight pounds and was eighteen years old and was much more peculiar-looking than I am now even. So they sent me to this model agency that handled the real *schlock,* the Seventh Avenue models, and they sent me up to this place called Jonathan Logan and I got a job as a designer's model. It's a nine to five job and you stand there while a lot of people yell and throw potato salad at each other which they're eating with their hands and they cut dresses on you. It has nothing to do with how you look or anything. It's simply that you are a very long-waisted, extremely skinny, tall size five, right? So I got the job, and there were a couple of other girls who worked there and they were hip, man. I'd never seen people like that before. One of them was Swedish. One of them was from the Bronx. And they lived in Greenwich Village.

After a couple of months I left that job and became the Chiffon Jell-O Pie Filling Girl on *The Price Is Right* 'cause I was a ballet dancer. So I jumped around with a bunch of Jell-O in my tutu, and then I found out that you make a lot more money in television commercials and I went to a commercial agency that some model told me about. And they said, "Well, you have to be able to talk, so why don't you go to acting school?" You've got to understand that I could never even get a part in the senior play. Acting school? And everybody wants to be a movie star, do you know what I mean? And meanwhile I was taking dope and living in the Village. I was just on the trash, man. All I wanted to do was break every rule I ever heard of and find out every new rule I could and break *it*. I wanted to find out everything wicked, low, evil, bad and depraved to do and *do it*. I had to find out what they were first, but I wanted to do it all, whatever it was. I mean it was the rage dance. And it's powerful music.

But it's all a double-edged sword. It's not simple. I guess I still deeply wanted to make my mother proud of me because she had worked so hard to support me. She was a child of the Depression, and that changed those people, it formed them forever. That's why many of them are so strong, I suppose. And I knew that my mother, more than anything else, would respect my going to school. But there wasn't anything I wanted to learn, because I didn't think I *could* learn anything. I mean I felt like one-eighth of a human being that had to shuck and jive my way through, you know, because I didn't have any tickets or credentials and never would have. The only thing that came easy to me was being a criminal. I could sort of steal and run action and that kind of stuff, but the only thing that came natural to me was breaking the rules. It's the only thing I ever had any instinct for. It's almost like a rule is a barrier and I wanted the barrier to open and let me inside and it never did, so consequently what I had to do was break it. And when that happens people become outlaws, I guess, which is essentially, I suppose, what I am. But I owed my mother something, and my mother was the kind of woman who never extracted payment. She was the most fiercely independent human being I have ever known and the most deeply honest and honorable human being. I have never known a person with more character. And that makes it a very hard row to hoe, having someone like that for a parent. But that's immaterial once you're an adult and you've been one long enough to file away your childhood. Then you have to deal with those very important, central people as who they are, right? Well, she was remarkable and I never figured that I would be like her, but I wanted to make her not ashamed of me. It was painful that she was ashamed of me. And rightly so, you know. I was a do-nothing, washout slug, and the only thing my mother ever wanted me to do was get a college education and be smart and strong and free and have a profession. And I couldn't do that. I didn't have what it took to do that.

I checked around and found that the Neighborhood Playhouse was sort of the best drama school in New York that was college accredited, and I went over there and tried to get in. And I got in. They took me for some peculiar reason. Well, I was a real good liar and had some real good shucking jive, you know. I'd learned to run some action. I was a pretty good hustler and a pretty good con artist. And I was good because I did not exist. There was no me, so consequently I got real good and fast at sussing out when I walked into a room—who do they need me to be, who do they want me to be, how do I score? You know? What's the rap that it will take to score here? And I would deliver it. So I went to the Neighborhood Playhouse and they accepted me, and you've got to understand that that's the first place that ever accepted me in my life. And they have thousands of applications from all over the world and they only accept seventy-five people into the first year and ask twenty-five back for the second year and all that. And it was the first time I was ever around people who seemed to be like me. It was the first time I didn't feel like a freak.

I mean I was high, man. That is like a natural-born junkie getting pure smack. You know, they tie off his arm, they cook it up, they shoot it, and he knows, he knows that there is a need he's had his whole life that is satisfied for that minute. Well, I mean you're *on* them. That's what you call tied on. And there were people there talking openly, wallowing in their emotions. . . . It's like you're a leper and you're running around loose in the world and everybody sort of goes *yah-ha!,* right? And then you are in a place where everybody looks like you do or it seems like everybody does. It was great. It was like putting into a safe harbor for me.

I wasn't very good, you understand. I was too self-conscious, too afraid. Because there wasn't a me. I just wanted to do it right so they'd let me stay. I just didn't want to get thrown out. I know that sounds silly but it's the truth. My only ambition—and it was almost the first ambition I ever had—was for them to just let me stay. Please don't throw me out. I loved it. I just loved it. And

I went to school all day and worked all night. I got about two
or three hours of sleep a night and lived in the Village in a six
floor walkup with a john down the hall and the bathtub in the
kitchen. I paid about twelve dollars a month—we split the rent
in four—and all we had in it was four army cots, some bongo
drums and a lot of drugs. And I waited on tables in the Village
and played the guitar, not really very well. I was one of those
really awful folkies, you know. But I looked right. I had a lot of
long dark hair, a lot of white rice powder and enough eye
makeup to float the Titanic, and I was dirty enough and hostile
enough to get the odd gig every now and then. And it was great.
It was one of the happiest times in my life, because I was *crazy*
about my life. All of a sudden there was a place that I could be.
There was something to do. I was waiting on tables all night to
pay my way through school all day, and my mother was very
proud of me.

I was asked back to the second year of the Neighborhood
Playhouse and given a scholarship. And at the end of the first
year, when we were doing these student plays, this young agent
at MCA named Stark Hesseltine came and left a note asking me
to come see him. I did. He said he'd like to represent me. I said,
"Terrific." I went up for summer stock jobs and *got* one. I mean
it was fantastic. And then I did a Sartre play Off Broadway in a
workshop and went back to the Playhouse in the fall with a
scholarship. And then the Theatre Guild remembered me from
a play they had tried out in summer stock, and they had to
replace a girl in the play while it was still in Philadelphia. It was
a dreadful thing that Dore Schary wrote, *The Highest Tree,* about
strontium-90. I didn't even know what strontium-90 was, but I
didn't want to ask. I didn't want them to know I was stupid. So
I left the Neighborhood Playhouse in the middle of my second
year to go do a small part in a Broadway play that closed in six
weeks. And then I was on unemployment and back on the street
again. But then I had ambition.

I had ambition. I knew there was a direction. I knew there was
something I could do. I've always been afraid of competition,
but I could go on interviews and there were people that would
listen to me. The rope wasn't up. And I worked. I got jobs. And
then when I was about twenty, I wasn't even twenty-one yet, I
scored a part in a play called *Take Her She's Mine* that Art Carney

was the star of. The play was really dreadful, essentially sort of like *Corliss Archer,* you know, but *George Abbott* directed it, right? He cast me because I was about as far away from the All American Girl as you were gonna get. And I didn't even realize it, but while we were out of town they were rewriting it all the time, changing it from a play about a man and his wife to a play about a man and his daughter. I thought it was a real piece of shit, you know? I figured it was a gig and it would close, but then I'd be able to get unemployment again. But it came into town and it was a *hit.* And I got all these terrific reviews. And there you are, you're just the hottest little piece of ass in show business. New York City has a new one every six months. It's like being prom queen. And success, well, it's always the same. The only difference is that the amounts of money get bigger and the size of the billing gets bigger, but that's really irrelevant 'cause it's always the same thing. And that's when I began to really unglue. That's when I began to go totally crazy.

You see, the point of all this is that we are conditioned to believe, we are processed, we are taught, everything in our world teaches us that success is the answer. If you are a success you are good. You have the blessings of God. He's on your side. You're at one with Jesus. You have won. Nobody fucks with a winner. Anything a winner does is okay. I mean a winner stole my country and sold it down the sewer. He got to do that because he won. And they didn't even shoot him. They're still paying his fucking way. You want to talk about winners? Okay. So you are processed to believe that it will heal all your wounds and it will solve all your problems. That's what it is. That's why it is. That's the drug the American people have OD'd on. They're junkies for it. And the reason it drives you crazy is because as long as you don't get it, as long as you're just going for it, you have a direction. You have purpose. You have a mission, one that is condoned. And then you get it. And it feels great. It's like the first time you come. You never knew anything could feel that good. It's like every itch gets scratched. Every stroke comes down. And you say, "Wow, it's all over. It's over. The devils and the demons have been defeated. I have won. It is over." And then one day you look at yourself and you notice that there's still some open sores. They're still running. There's still pain. There's still fear. Because the flip side of success is fear. And fear is the fucking Devil. And success is the Devil's dope. And you start to go crazy.

What do you do then? You're hooked. That's why people always say, "Well, So-and-so became a star and it just destroyed her, I mean they're just destructive, I mean that person had everything. Well, that's ego." You see, it's just never enough. And people get out of control. And that's when you really get ugly.

It was real interesting because I won a Tony award. I was the youngest person who'd ever won it, I think, and my agent called the producer, Hal Prince, the next morning and asked for a raise. I was getting paid about two hundred twenty-five dollars a week, but Hal Prince didn't want to give me a raise. He wanted to give me star billing instead. I've been real lucky in that there-'ve been a few people in my life who have been really fine, who it's really been a privilege to know, and one of them is Stark Hesseltine, my agent who found me when I was in the Neighborhood Playhouse. And he said, "Absolutely not, no star billing, because once you go above the title you can't go backdown. What we'll take is a raise, please." I think they gave me another fifty dollars. So then you start to get a little vision and you see how the game works. And it's no longer a matter of desperation and survival and dreams and needs. It's just a shill game then. You start to see the carnival barkers and the con men and how the game goes, and that will really just trash you. It was just slowly downhill then for me. I went and did a movie called *Carpetbaggers* and I'm gonna be a movie star. And then Neil Simon wrote a play for me called *Barefoot in the Park*. And I was on the cover of *Life* magazine the same week they shot John Kennedy, November the twenty-third. And that's success, man.

See, immediately what happens is that it is made very clear to you that, "Okay, kid, you scored. Now if you want to hang onto it, this is what you do." You know, the wolf is at the door. And I also knew that I wasn't very good. I wasn't a good actress. I didn't really know what I was doing. And you see, it's all excess. The praise is excess. The attention is excessive. You become a commodity. You become merchandisable. You see, our culture has to have successes because that's what you sell, that's what people buy. The sellers have to have some goods or else nobody's gonna buy, so you become the goods. They always let you know there's another bolt of cloth where you came from, so you better watch your Ps and Qs. So what you have is an eight-car crackup on the freeway ready to happen. I mean you have a grenade that you've pulled the plug on. Got it?

I wasn't very good, and I wanted so deeply to be good. I had no sense of achievement. I had no sense of accomplishment. I had a sense of scoring, of having gotten lucky, of having pulled a fast one. And then you get real paranoid. You feel that everybody that looks at you sees that all you are is a hustler that got lucky and scored, and the next time you pick up the dice, man, they're gonna come up low. And that makes you crazy. So it just went from bad to worse. I did *Barefoot in the Park*, which I really wasn't good in at all, and it was just an agony of despair for me. It was all my own head space, you understand, because, you see, it didn't matter to anyone else whether I was good or not. That was never discussed. It was taken for granted that I was as good as I needed to be because I had scored. And this sounds corny and pretentious and pompous and it's a cliché, but I wanted to try and be an artist. Somewhere that was the only noble thing I knew. And the more successful I got, the more of a joke that became. And I was totally dependent on the outside world for my existence: I am who they say I am, I am who they think I am, I am only as they see me, that's who I am. Because in a room by myself with the door closed there wasn't anybody there. There was just hunger and fear, that's all.

I guess there are people who simple success satisfies, but to me that's like somebody who can get off fucking a cretin. I guess that's terrific, it sure makes your life easier, but it just didn't work for me. You've got to understand I wasn't very good. I had a lot of energy and a lot of flash, you know, but I wasn't any good. And I didn't seem to get any better.

And I had gotten married when I was real young, about twenty, that's another thing. Girls grow up and are conditioned to get married, right? You're supposed to go out there and trap one: Track him, shoot him down, drag him back and loot him. Well, my mother was always very opposed to that. She didn't see that as a viable way to live. She'd say, "Any stupid little thing that works in the ten cent store can get married. It doesn't take any brains to get married. It takes brains to stay single. My God, get yourself an education, be independent so you can have some

choices in your life." I didn't want choices. I wanted to get laid.
I was twenty years old; what else do you want when you're
twenty? So I got married, but that was absurd, and we each went
our own way after a few months.

I was still living in the Village. They didn't know. The media
hadn't found a word for it yet, but I think we were like hippies,
hippy doper freaks. And I started getting real interested in politics and ideas, and in 1960 I went to Mississippi very surrepti-
tiously. I went home to Louisiana that summer to visit my family,
and New York friends of mine in SNCC asked me to rent some
cars with Louisiana plates so they could move around. That's
when they were teaching people in Mississippi to read and write
well enough to pass the literacy test so they could vote. And I
did that, and that's the first time I began to understand that in
this country they'll kill you if you break the rules and that all
these things we sort of take for granted are lies. I was really
seeing a lot of that, and that's a big thing, I think. That tidal-
waves almost anybody's head who sees it for the first time, when
it really comes clear.

But when I went into *Carpetbaggers* I had met this actor, this
very conservative man, and he was like a father figure to me. I
had never had a father. My mother divorced my father when I
was an infant and he was never around, so I never grew up
around any men. And this actor was like thirteen years older
than me and he was successful and powerful and rich and force-
ful and authoritarian. He was everything I'd always wanted a
father to be or I guess thought a father should be. And what we
want and what we need are not often the same, you know, and
what we need we tell ourselves is what we want to make it
palatable to ourselves. I needed a father so I convinced myself
I wanted the man, and I found a severe father who would punish
me for being essentially a bad girl. That's a very commonplace
neurotic pattern. So the deal was that I would stop being an
actress, which I was perfectly ready to do anyway. The rationale
that was presented to me went: "Well, of course you're unhappy
and tormented and crazy because you're living against Nature.
Because you are a woman and what you need to do is get married and stay home and cook and sew and have babies, not like
your mother. Your mother is a remarkable woman, but that's not
the way a woman's supposed to live." Blah blah blah. So I went

for it. I mean he was somebody who had an answer. At that point I was going to go with anybody who had an answer. And he was somebody who wanted me, who was gonna take me in, solve my problems, make me a happy person. So I got married again and became imprisoned in Beverly Hills. I turned in my SAG card, my eyelashes, my tap shoes and became a Beverly Hills house-wife, and that was a real interesting trip.

I had made a couple of movies before that. I did *Ship of Fools* in which I was really dreadful, and then a really low gig, after which I ran away to Europe where I did nothing but bum around. I started to turn down a lot of stuff, and everybody was always telling me that I was blowing my career, blowing my career, but I didn't care. Then I came back and did this movie called *The Third Day,* a really low fucking gig—one of the lowest I ever did—and that was really unpalatable to me, man. They say it's important to know how low you'll go for money, and I know. Pretty low. But I was a real movie star. Man, I didn't have to do anything except walk around and say, "Darling, how do you feel?" and wear a lot of clothes and hair and eye makeup, and it was ludicrous, I mean it was ludicrous. After that I got married and quit. And then I saw a lot of success. I saw the real big time, the heavyweights, and I saw it from the vantage point that you do if you're married to somebody who's in that game. I mean I saw the real believers. And I saw the casualties. And I saw the winners and the losers and the carnage. And the desolation of the soul. And the shrinkage of the mind. And the lockjaw of the heart. It was real colorful.

It was real good, too, though, because I read a lot of books and I went to school and traveled around the world and hung out with some real interesting folks on the sly. I had this whole other undercover life that I'd sneak off to. You know, people I knew who were not allowed in the house or anything. But finally I had to get out of there or die. I was living a life where my addictions and my values were at war with each other, and there comes a point where in order to survive you have to kick one of them or the other. And it's never an act of will. You cannot do it arbitrarily or because you decide to. It's almost like somehow it's your karmic destiny and if you just hang on and wait it'll happen. And so for me the only thing left was that I knew that if I couldn't live with some sense of values, I'd die. And so I left.

And I had a child. And I had to go to work again. And I'd been retired for like six years.

You've got to understand that I'd blown it in a big way. And they'd never much liked me. I mean I'd always been a loud-mouthed, smart-ass, difficult, temperamental crazylady, and I hadn't even been that good. I'd gotten real hot, but I was never that good. And when you're hot you're hot, when you're not you're not. The only difference really is that when you're hot everybody tells you how good you are, and when you're not hot anymore they let you know you never were worth a shit. That's the way it goes. And I was thirty years old, when—God knows —women, particularly actorettes, are over the hill. So I called my big-time movie agent and I told him that I was getting divorced and that I had to go to work because I wouldn't take any alimony and I had a child to support and that I didn't know what I was going to do but I had to work at something. I mean I would live in motels in Hollywood if I had to and go be somebody's wife on a television series or something. And he said to me, "Sweetheart, I think you better reconsider that divorce 'cause I can't even get you a guest shot on *Bonanza* and I don't think I ever will. You're smelly fish in this town."

Well, the first thing I figured out is that I should get myself another agent and there was a young agent at IFA who for some reason wanted to represent me. You've got to understand that I was full tilt boogie washed up, old, wasted and over with. I mean I was lower than a joke. But I started working again. I went to the Actors Studio in California and I had a couple of real good friends. My friends have saved my life, and that's why I know that the only thing I've ever done well in my life, I mean really well, the only golden instinct that I have, is for people. I know my fucking people. That's a little piece of grace that God gave me with which to save my life and my soul. And there was a man named Lou Antonio who's a marvelous actor who was moderating at the Studio then, teaching the exercise classes, and let's forget about walking, I was having a hard time with the crawling part, you know what I mean? So I went to the Actors Studio and began to get my chops up, and I went and I did every low gig. I mean I did guest shots on *Ironside* and *The Six Million Dollar Man* and *Mission Impossible* and *Marcus Welby,* and for actors those are some of the lowest gigs there are. Commercials are low gigs, but that's a whole other area. Commercials are probably as low as a performer goes for money, and it's the only thing I've never done, interestingly enough.

But I did those shows and I began to get pretty good. Because I had changed. Of course, I had to go up and read for people who are ex-used-car salesmen from Van Nuys who didn't know who I was, and there was a part of me, let us not forget, that had starred on Broadway, had a Tony award, Drama Critic's award, a Laurel award, all that shit. And it was hard, man. It makes you humble. If you never learned humility before, you learn it then. Because in the carnival there's very little grace when you're low. A bareback rider has grace when she's on the horse. When she's trying to get up on it there is no grace. And there's no forgiveness. And there's no compassion. And there's no understanding. Because failures stink. Nobody wants to be around ya. Nobody wants to know ya. And nobody'll tell you the truth. 'Cause if they told you the truth, they would have to tell you something about themselves that they don't want to know. We're all really in it together, that's the part that sticks up everybody's ass. And so I just did the gigs, and whatever sense of dignity I'll ever have was born then, I guess.

And I didn't want their success. I'd been there. Maybe I did want it, but it was a desire I knew was the Devil. I didn't respect it. I knew what it was. I'd seen the face of the Devil. I'd fucked the Devil. I'd been fucked by the Devil. We'd given each other head. That's when you know the Devil. I'd been there. It's not something you have to remind yourself about. It's with you every day of your life. You've seen it and you know, right? All I wanted to do was to survive on the outside, that's all. That's the turf I'm content to work because it's my natural turf, it's where I'm supposed to be. It's like God keeps telling you things and finally you listen. They say that you'll keep coming back in this life until you get it right, I mean that's what reincarnation is all about. Well, I obviously was a slow learner. But I began to learn, when I was about thirty I began to learn how to live. And then I started getting leads in movies for television. They were dogs, I've never been in a good movie, but I started getting real good.

I started really getting good because I knew that in terms of my work all I wanted was to be able to act, to be able to perform and play myself the way Jimi Hendrix played the guitar, the way B. B. King plays the blues. That's art. I understand that. Now art isn't something you do or that you are. It's what you shoot at. It's a target. It's where you aim. And I knew that in a world where there was very little that I could respect or even accept it was the highest thing that I could recognize. It's the highest thing, the noblest thing I know. I guess that's what the pope's supposed to feel about God, you know? And if that's a specter, it's an acceptable one for me. Do you know what I mean?

And then they offered me this television series. Not even a pilot, right? It was twenty-three to air, firm. And they were going to pay me twenty thousand dollars an episode, and that was firm even if the thing was a bomb, you know? I mean it's like you get twenty thousand dollars twenty-three times, and that's more money than I had ever made. I'd been real rich because I made a lot of money before I quit. I made one hundred fifty thousand dollars a movie. It's not the big time, but on the other hand, where I come from that's a fucking-A lot of money, and I spent it all on airplane tickets, dope, and friends. I don't regret that. And then I was married to a man who was real rich. I had Rolls-Royces and houses in Beverly Hills and Mercedes Benzes and all that stuff. I had sable jackets and suits from Chanel, I had all that shit. It was absurd, it was just absurd. But here I was thirty-five years old and I had a child and wasn't gettin' any younger, and you think, fuck it, make one smart move. You see, I've never made a smart move in my life. I don't have that kind of wisdom. Every time I've tried, I've blown it. The only things that have ever turned up right for me is when you just say fuck it and you pick up the old dice and throw them as hard as you can on a dream. They're the only ones that have ever come up for me. Somebody's telling me something, right? That's the only natural proclivity I have, I suppose. Just lucky, I guess.

Anyway, you know how with television series they'll negotiate them for months, and we were making all kinds of demands. It's all a game they play. It keeps them off the streets. And I got this telephone call from my friend Gary Lockwood, who is one of the finest human beings who's ever walked the face of the earth and a man who's been around, he's put in all the mileage. So Locks came over and he said, "You know, Bessie, you'd make a lot of money. Do you know what currency you pay for it?" And I said yeah. And he said, "The only thing I want you to think about is, you've paid hard dues but I think you ought to bet on yourself a couple more times around the track before you throw in the towel." Because when you do a television series in my space, for what I like, for what gets me off, you throw in the towel pretty much forever. It's like if Jimi Hendrix had played jingles for five years, he wouldn't have been able to play the way he played the sixth year. Do you know what I mean? He also might not have died. But on the other hand, he might have died quicker. Who knows? Those are the kind of ambiguities I like.

So I really thought about what Lockwood said, but I felt tired and I wasn't sure I had that kind of courage. I'd gotten safe. And I wanted to come in from the cold. You get tired of tap dancing. Even if it's the place you get off, you get tired, and I wanted to come in from the cold. So I was going to make a smart move. And then I got this phone call from Stark Hesseltine, my theater agent who found me back in the Neighborhood Playhouse days, and he told me that Michael Kahn called him from Stratford, the American Shakespeare Festival, and wanted to know if I'd come for the summer to do rep and do Maggie in *Cat on a Hot Tin Roof* for about five hundred dollars a week and all I could eat. I said, "Well, Stark, y'see, I'm gonna do this television series and y'know . . ." And he said, "Are you set?" and I said, "No, but they've been negotiating." He said, "Well, I understand that," and I said, "Just tell Michael Kahn no, I can't do it." And Stark called me back a couple of days later and said, "Michael Kahn says that if you're not set, he doesn't have to set the part for about another three weeks and he'll wait. If there's any chance you might consider it, he'll wait." I didn't want him to wait. I wanted it to go away. And it wouldn't go away, because call it ego, call it arrogance, vanity, anything you want, I owed myself one. And so I called up my movie agent and said, "John, guess what? There's something I want to tell you. Um, I don't think I want to do the television series." Now that's a hard one, right? That's a dude who went on the line for me, who scraped me up when he couldn't sell a slice of my ass to a horny man. And he put me on the fucking map. And it was a big score, you know? And he said, "Bessie, do what you have to do. I love ya. And we'll pay the rent somehow."

So we turned down the series, and there's a real perverse joy in that, you know, when you say, "Um, I don't think so." Because, you see, the world runs on the assumption that everybody has a price and all they have to do is find it. Now I also live my life on the assumption everybody has a price, but sometimes the currency is not quite so commonplace. And that is my big conceit. I can be bought. You can buy my tap dance cheap. I need to pay the rent, right? My tap dance doesn't cost too much. But there are parts in me that those motherfuckers don't have the currency for. And the only power I ever want is the power to not get bought with their currency. That's my perversion, perhaps. That's my rage. And so I went off to Stratford, Connecticut, with my tribe and my kid and we lived in a barn and I went to work in a work of art.

Let me tell you something, it's a privilege to be in a work of art. Do you surf? Well, it's a really high, mystical thing because the surfer, of course, has to know the board and he has to know the water and he has to have the balance and he has to have guts and balls and he has to be crazed. A lot of things. But mainly he has to have the wave. Surfers will sit around and tell you about the perfect wave, which is what they wait for. And when I was a very young actress somebody told me that if I really got lucky, maybe once in my life I would do something that was the reason that you became an actress in the first place, on the high side. Mainly, it's on the low side. Mainly it's the low cheap ones that get you up there, know what I mean? But then you become aware that there's also a high side. Most of us never touch it. We never know. So you start to disbelieve it. You know, it's like before you got fucked right, you think it's a myth. You think, "I don't know what they're talkin' . . . they're makin' it up." And so I was in a work of art. The part had my name on it. There are some things that have your name on them. That one had my name on it. It was played well before. It will be played well again. But it had my name on it. And it was a privilege to be in a work of art because it's like surfing: Now you have to be able to ride the board, man. There are dues you've had to pay, there are chops you have to have and licks you have to know. But if you've got those and you hit the wave, it's like God makes a magic bicycle and says, "Okay, kid, you get a *free ride*. Get off! That's what it's for!"

That's the highest gig I ever did in my life. It gave me something of myself that I hadn't been able to claim before, and I began to really love myself and my life and my work. And I came to know that it's not all nickle, dime, pigs and swine, con men, shill games and flat store stands. It mostly is. They own the world. But there's still stuff they can't buy. It's dreams. It's magic. It's love. It's art. It's honesty. It's compassion. And I think its days are numbered, that place, that space, whatever it is, because I think the success pushers are gonna win, you know. I also think the minute they win, they die. But all I want is to be able to live outside their world. And it's only a narrow little space. I mean, they own everything. You know, they've got all the real estate. But there are still edges that they don't own and all I want is to be able to live there. Do you know what I mean? To live there.

Now that's all a very high kind of grand and noble verbiage. I mean on a fundamental line, it's all the carnival. When you're hot you're hot, when you're not you're not. When you're in a high gig and it's a hit, they'll give you the fucking Nobel Peace Prize. A couple of turkeys, and you can't get a guest shot on *Bonanza.* That's the way it goes. But, you see, I've been counted down, out, over with, washed up and dead a number of times. The only really, I suppose, interesting thing about me from the outside looking in is that somebody keeps scraping her up and she gets out. She always seems to have a tap dance left.

Part Two

HOW THEY
FEEL ABOUT IT

Luck, Work and Challenge

QUINCY JONES

I don't know, man, sometimes you feel like it's all out of your hands. When you stop and look back and think of the difference thirty seconds one way or the other could have made in your life it's absolutely frightening. There are hundreds of instances where if you had taken the left turn instead of the right your whole life would have changed, be it with your musical career, or your wife, or whatever. It's fate and destiny and luck and everything else.

WILLIAM GAINES

My father was killed in an accident in 1947, and I was expected to take over his business. He was a comic-book publisher. I knew perfectly well that I couldn't, that I would not be able to. But I did it, I took it over because there was no one else to do it, and I just slowly got interested in it and suddenly found that I could do certain things with it. I still never expected to achieve the success that I have, and of course most of my success has been achieved through *Mad*. Before *Mad*, I had a very good-selling string of comic magazines—horror, science fiction, suspense— and they're classics in the field today, but they didn't begin to make the kind of money that *Mad* makes. *Mad* started out as just another one of those ten cent comics, but as luck would have it, it took off and the other comics were more or less killed by the Senate Subcommittee on Juvenile Delinquency.

I always felt that I kind of stumbled into success. Almost every terrible thing that happened to me turned out to be good, in an insane way, such as my first wife leaving me in effect ending up with my father's death. I'm certainly not suggesting any fault, but if she hadn't left me, my father probably would not have been killed because he wouldn't have been where he was at the time. Then my father getting killed was a further tragedy, but if that hadn't happened, I probably would have ended up a chemistry teacher. And then if the horror comics hadn't been knocked out of business, I wouldn't have devoted my attention to *Mad.* And if my distributor, who was very weak, hadn't gone bankrupt, I never would have gotten away from him and ended up with a strong distributor, which was very helpful. And of course I was extremely lucky that the right editors and creative people walked in at the right times. So what success I've achieved has been mostly accidental. And I'm not knockin' it, I'm delighted with it, but that's the truth of it, I guess.

So many, many people would be successful if they'd had the breaks, I'm sure, just as many successful people wouldn't be if they hadn't. Boy, the breaks. I'm not a big believer in fate or anything like that, it's just the way the chips fall. But if you're lucky—and I was—you make it. As I say, most of my major disappointments have turned out to be blessings in disguise. So whenever anything bad does happen to me, I kind of sit back and feel, well, if I give this enough time, it'll turn out that this was good, so I shan't worry about it too much. So far it's worked out that way.

GEOFFREY HOLDER

I am a lucky man, a lucky man. I have never asked for a job, never in my life. It just came. It all fell in place. The way I got into show business in New York is a lovely story. I was dancing in St. Thomas and Agnes Demille saw me and wanted me to audition for Hurok with my company. So after battling with immigration, the company came and Hurok came and didn't like it or couldn't use it, I don't know the story but it's unimportant. But while I was here Martha Graham was playing at the Alvin Theatre, and I went to see her all dressed up. Man, I was skinny as a brick. *Gorgeous!* Black tuxedo and rhinestones and a homberg and an umbrella because the rain was falling. So I walked into the theater and because I'm shy, literally shy, I walked to my seat in the auditorium very, very straight and sat down right in front of the producer Saint Subber, who thought, "Well, my God, look at that guy! He would be marvelous on stage but I'm sure he is a basketball player." Fate is a funny thing. My manager had set up an appointment with Saint Subber not knowing this, and I didn't even know who Saint Subber was then. Saint Subber didn't know who he was coming to see, and here was this basketball player at Carnegie Recital Hall auditioning for him, almost naked in a loincloth when nudity was out. Oiled from head to toe and bald, honey, and I was dancing off my ass! Saint freaked out! "Oh my God! You're *marvelous!* You're *wonderful! Marvelous!* You are going to be in my next production! I don't know what the show is going to be, but you have to be in my next show. I'm going to Haiti to see Truman Capote. When I return, I will call you."

He returned and called me and told me the show was called *House of Flowers* and the part was that of Baron Samadi, the king of darkness. It happened to be a part out of my concert repertoire. He didn't know this. And everything just fell in place. So I got on Broadway with *House of Flowers* with Juanita Hall, Diahann Carroll, Pearl Bailey, the whole gang. That's where I met my wife, Carmen De Lavallade. Everybody was in it—Donald McKayle, Alvin Ailey, all the gypsies. And I wound up doing my own choreography with great dancers like Arthur Mitchell and Louis Johnson, all these people who have studied dance all their lives. And I who have never taken a lesson in my life am principal dancer. It was *strange.* But fear threw me against the wall and I carried on. Then everyone began talking about it and next thing you know I'm premier dancer at the Metropolitan Opera in *Aida.*

It kept moving and kept moving and kept moving. And between performing I'm painting every day and I'm in another world, the art world, and having exhibits at the Barone Gallery, at the FAR Gallery. So my life has gone that way all the way through. And along the way I began cooking, out of necessity. To go to a restaurant in New York you have to pay a lot of money and you wind up cooking the food yourself, putting in the salt and the pepper and everything because it has no taste. Next thing you know I'm doing a cookbook. So my whole life has been like that.

EDGAR D. MITCHELL

I used to say that luck was being in the right place at the right time, even though I never really was. I now no longer believe in luck. All the work I've been doing in the consciousness areas, the futures areas and parapsychology has led me to the conclusion that the thing called coincidence does not exist. Everything is a product of someone's thought process, that's what made it happen. Just because we can't see the chain of causality all at once, there probably still is one. And so these days I talk more about how everyone really determines their own lives. They may not want to accept responsibility for it, but they do cause it, nevertheless. And when a particular event happens, you can look around and see the external causes, but generally you need to look inside your own head to find out what you did to make it happen, especially if it's something on the negative side. If you can't figure out why your world is continuously topsy-turvey and not going smoothly, ninety-nine percent of the time you'll find the answer inside your own actions and thought processes.

JERRY DELLA FEMINA

I think luck is a very bad word because that's the word those people who fail use when they decide to give it up completely and not try to succeed. I'm hardnosed about luck. I think it sucks. Yeah, if you spend seven years looking for a job as a copywriter, and then one day somebody gives you a job, you can say, "Gee, I was lucky I happened to go up to there today." But dammit, I was going to go up there sooner or later in the next seventy years. So luck, maybe it's a shortcut, but I don't think it has much to do with it. If you're persistent in trying and doing and working, you almost make your own fortune. They'll say about someone, "Gee, he's a lucky gambler." But he's not a lucky gambler. He's very confident that he's a *good* gambler. Therefore he wins a lot. Therefore those people who lose say, "God, he must be lucky," as if there's something mystical about it. I don't think there's anything mystical about success *or* failure. Luck makes it sound too much like there's a God, and I'm an atheist.

ROCKY AOKI

Sure, you've got to have luck. In business or life, you should be lucky. But do you play backgammon? A lot of people say it's just luck: "Oh, you're so lucky, the dice are lucky." But the best player tries to make moves so that even with bad dice he can still make a point. Luck, you've got to make it. Like playing backgammon. It's not the gambling. Business is not a gamble. You have to have luck, but you also have to have know-how and a lot of other things. But people say, "Rocky, you're so lucky." Of course I'm lucky. I was lucky to be here. Fourteen years ago, as a Japanese I couldn't come to the United States as a student, as a businessman, as anything. The American government wouldn't let me in. But I was lucky I wrestled. I was lucky I was a very strong wrestler. I was lucky that at that time I had the opportunity to come to the United States with the Japanese wrestling team. I was lucky I knew the coach. You know, a lot of luck. If I wasn't lucky, if I didn't get to come here with the wrestling team, I wouldn't be here now. It's the same thing with anybody. You name the guy and I can tell you how lucky he is. But there are so many people with all kinds of lucky things happening to them and they don't know how to use it.

REX REED

I think that in most cases luck has a great deal to do with it, but I don't think it had much to do with my particular case. Of course this will be misinterpreted by people as being a very snotty thing to say and I don't mean it that way, but I really do think that from the very beginning I was accepted and given the chances I was given as a writer because I had something to sell. And it was through my own ability. I didn't learn to write after I got a job. I knew how already. I wrote things and turned them in to people who hadn't even asked for them and they were impressed by the writing and asked me to do something else. I didn't wait for the job. I didn't sit around waiting for the phone to ring. And therefore I feel especially smug and comfortable in the knowledge that I don't owe anybody anything for my career. I don't know how many people can make that statement honestly, but I really can. Nobody gave me anything. Liz Smith, who gave me my first writing break at *Cosmopolitan,* has said that on many occasions. One time she was on some panel with John Simon and he said, *"You!* You're the one who is responsible for this monster Rex Reed!" And she said, "Rex Reed would have happened whether I had anything to do with it or not. I'm just lucky that I was there and able to give him his first opportunity to be in print. But even if I had refused, he would have been in something else a week later. I had nothing to do with it." And that's true. Really, I don't owe anybody anything for my career.

MARIO ANDRETTI

I can be thankful about a lot of things that happened at the right time, I must say. And luckily, because of intensive dedication and a lot of hard work, I think I was about ready to take advantage of them. In the early days I ran as many as 107 midget races a year. Three, four nights a week all over, through the winter—Hempstead, Long Island, Teaneck, New Jersey. I didn't have to run all those races, but you just want to get exposed and start winning, and from there I had my next step planned. And then my next step arrived. From three-quarter midgets I went to full-sized midgets with Mataka Brothers. Hell, I couldn't have planned it better. It worked out. We got in there, and luckily everything was pretty much right, and we started winning. They'd been around a long time and hadn't had a winner, so they were very excited. From there, I got into sprint cars and went into the Midwest. And then I made the decision that it was

going to be just full-time racing, which is a hell of a responsibility when you've just been nitpicking here and there.

I got my next upgrade when Chuck Hulse, the driver, was hurt
quite badly. You know, it was a sad situation, but I was able to
take advantage of it. It sounds almost cruel, but that's life. Somebody had to fill in the slot. My name was kind of going around
a little bit, and the men who were responsible for this team at
Indianapolis became interested. They asked me whether I'd like
to talk about it, and I casually said, "Well, I might," and meanwhile inside I was on Cloud Nine. That was probably the biggest
break I really had. It moved me a definite step up into the big
time. In fact, with this same basic team I won Indianapolis many
years later.

So I was ready for that move, but I was also really lucky.
Because it could have been a lesser team asking me to join, and
obviously with my enthusiasm at the time I would have, but the
capability of the team wouldn't have been there. This was one
of the top three teams in the United States, you see. And since
they felt that because they lost their top driver their season was
going to be somewhat uneventful anyway, they thought, what
the hell, why not try to train a young guy who's going to go
along. And Christ, that worked fantastic for me because they had
the patience, the understanding, everything that I really needed
at the time. The only pressure I had to do well was from within
myself. It was amazing, you know, because it's not always like
that. The competitive world is very cruel and cold, believe me.
I've seen drivers pushed and pressured and reprimanded for
every mistake.

These guys were just the opposite. But it was really working
for me. They used the same psychology I'd always use with any
driver with any talent, because the way I feel, if a driver needs
to be pushed and primed every time he sits in that race car, he's
not worth a damn anyway. The best thing you can do for any
competitive man is put his mind at ease and say, "Look, whatever you do is good enough for me." You know damn well that
that guy's going to go out there and bust his butt, and he'll
perform well because he doesn't have that direct outside pressure. You know damn well that he wants you to smile. To me,
that's the most sane psychology. You can't tell a guy who pole-
vaults, "This time you've got to break the world's record." All

you'd be doing is shattering the guy. Then he's just worried. If you set him at ease, you know damn well every time he jumps that's what he wants to do, so you just let him do it his own way. And that's how they were with me.

ALBERT ELLIS

Had I started my sex researches fifty years ago and done exactly the same thing, I never would have gotten as far as I have. Some people did try then. For example, Havelock Ellis partially did it fifty years ago, and he got by and became very well known, but he almost went to jail once. He had to renege rather than go to jail for his book on homosexuality, which was published in the 1890s originally, and he had to tone down his effort. He did a great deal of good and was a great pioneer, but he certainly didn't accomplish some of the things I've accomplished. His historical influence was great, but his personal influence probably wasn't. So part of that is the changing mores.

A year before I started my researches in sex, Kinsey, about whom I knew nothing at the time, started his. I began my studies in 1939. He started in 1938. His first book came out in 1948 and it made an enormous hit, even though it was dully written and most people who bought it probably didn't read much of it. But the publicity he got was enormous. The publicity on his second book, published in 1953, was even more widespread. By 1948 I had already written some articles and was the American editor of the *International Journal of Psychology,* so I was noted in the field. But without help from Kinsey and later Masters and Johnson, who partly built on my work, and from other developments in the culture, my books wouldn't have sold as well and my talks wouldn't have pulled as well. So there is both my contribution to the sex revolution and its contribution to me. Popularity in a field like sex is always partly luck.

ALICE COOPER

There's a better word than luck: timing. People say, boy, the Beatles sure were lucky to come out when they did, and the Rolling Stones. But every single person who has come out a superstar made it because he came out at the right time. Elton hit at a time when there needed to be an Elton. The Beatles hit at a time when there needed to be the Beatles. People were getting tired of the Four Seasons and the Beach Boys. And when the Beatles came out it wasn't lucky, it was good timing. Somebody was thinking. And then when the Rolling Stones counteracted the Beatles that was good timing too. I think Alice came out right at the time when people were just getting tired of the whole love and peace thing. Alice was saying, "Hey, you guys, let's just have fun, and lookit, I'm still macho but I'm going to wear eye makeup, my mom's eye makeup." It was sort of a classic play on opposites, but people liked it. Alice is like a household word now. Even on your quiz shows, you know, there are references to Alice Cooper.

JOE EULA

I think the late 1960s and the early Seventies were absolutely the open gate of all time. Anybody with a free spirit who couldn't find where they were during that time (if they were between the ages of twelve and seventy-five) might just as well hung the fucking thing up and gone on relief then and there. I'm talking literally about the five-year period between '68 and '73. That's when the thing started coming down. Everyone was doing something that made them feel good. There was no age factor. There were no criteria of beauty. There were no rules that these are the dos and these are the don'ts. All rules went and you could go with them. I had been going toward that all my life, but I think it was that marvelous open door that just clicked it off.

MILTON GLASER

I find the part played by luck or timing very hard to evaluate. I suppose in my case they had a good deal to do with it. But part of it also has to do with my own perception of the moment, my sense of fashion, time and vernacular. I have always had a good sense of context, which is really a designer's greatest skill: to understand how you appear in the context of a thousand other elements and to be conscious of what position you take in relation to what's happening. I suppose in almost a commercial way I always understood what was permissible in terms of the sensibility of an audience that existed out there. I knew how far to go, where you could take something without turning them off, how much you had to refer to the existing language. I've always had that understanding. I'm in the business of communicating information. That's what I do. My whole life is involved with in some way taking a piece of information from here to there, whether it's a book jacket or a magazine or anything else. You have to understand *exactly* what is already understood. And you have to know how to add something to it that changes it sufficiently to attract people's interest and move it incrementally towards some other objective. That's always been my issue in life, that distance between what is known and what is new. It's something I feel in a deeply intuitive way. I also try to apply whatever intelligence I can to the issue, but I think it's more of an intuitive thing, really understanding the form of address.

MIKE WALLACE

I am persuaded that luck and timing have, in my case, been very important. I think first, probably, comes motivation. And in a strange way, motivation triggers luck, triggers timing. You fill your vessel in a strange way as you grow. You don't know, really, with what you're filling it. It's a question of a variety of experiences. In the course of growing and learning and working, I've covered the theater and I've covered fires. I've been overseas and I've covered national politics. I've covered civil rights and sports. And among those have been my own interests at various times of my life, my own genuine, personal interests. Suddenly there comes a time when all those various experiences—what you've read, where you've been, whom you've seen, what you know, the questions you've asked—come into focus for some job you undertake to do. And I know that that's how it's worked in my own case, particularly with *60 Minutes.* We are generalists on *60 Minutes.* We cover everything from politics to theater, from foreign affairs to human interest, and, strangely, all of the varied experiences—indeed, the traumas within one's own life—somehow have been given a chance to come into play in preparing the stories we have done here.

HOWARD COSELL

Obviously, any person has to have the beginning luck of opportunity. After that, you still need a measure of luck, but above all you need brains and talent and industry—the willingness to work ceaselessly. Those are the qualities you need to translate the luck of opportunity into success. Even there, luck comes into it because if you're working for people who won't back you up, you're in trouble if you stand for anything. If you're working for people who don't like you personally, you're in trouble. So factors like those enter into your success. But Mr. Branch Rickey, one of the people whom I most admired in my lifetime in sports, once made a statement that I believe has truth to it. He said, "Luck is the residue of design." And if you have those qualities—industry and brains and talent—and you're in journalism, you're a reporter, it seems somehow that that becomes true, that there are reasons why you get the stories. It's almost by design that new stories keep cropping up that you and you alone can get. "Luck is the residue of design," he said. You establish relationships and connections, as any reporter must, and if you do it with people who are exceptional people, you find that they turn to you when something's going to happen. An example: The big sports story of 1974 was when three great players on the Miami Dolphins jumped to the World Football League, enabling that league to start business. Csonka, Kiick and Warfield. On the very day they did it, Larry Csonka called me at home on a Sunday morning to tell me they were going to do it, and I broke the story nationally that afternoon on my network television magazine show with the three of them sitting in a studio in Toronto. That's what Mr. Rickey meant by luck is the residue of design. Because I had spent years with Larry Csonka and he respected and trusted me.

DON KING

I feel that you have to work towards your luck, and then sometimes things will happen for you. Fate, I believe, rewards those who are really sincerely dedicated in working towards their goals. The Lord said, "If you have but the faith of a mustard seed, nothing will be impossible unto you. You can tell yonder mountain to be removed and hence in the twinkling of an eye the mountain will be removed." I take this type of faith with me, and the things just happen. You have to define what you want, make a concentrated effort to bring this conceptualization to visualization in the mind, and then you have to transform it into energy to bring it into reality.

And as you keep going it's like a person trying to climb a mountain. Every time he gets near the top he slides down, slides down, and maybe on the hundredth time because he was just so dogged and pertinacious, he gets there. Then they say, "Wow, man, ain't he lucky?" He ain't lucky. He earned that, Jack. He lay in there and lay in there and maybe on the hundredth time he put his foot down the sun just happened to shine on that rock to give him a better footing and when he stuck his foot there it didn't slide like it did the other ninety-nine times. That one time it caught and he was able to pull himself up to get to the top, to be standing at the pinnacle, the apex. So now you say, "God, how lucky that guy is, man." Sumbitch worked, man. He stuck with it, you know.

BRUNO SANMARTINO

Before I became a wrestler, I was a construction worker, and I worked darn hard in my construction job, eight or ten hours a day. But every day after I finished I used to go to the gym, still in my construction boots and overalls, and put in another four hours. I was working out seven days a week. Three days a week was with the weights and four days it was working out on a mat, wrestling. I was using the weights to develop my strength and I was wrestling to gain the experience and know-how. I was completely self-disciplined about it. I'm not bragging, but I was so darn self-disciplined that my buddies sometimes made fun of me. Someone would say, "Jeeze, go lift your stupid weights while I go out with this beautiful chick." Well, I was human, I would have liked to have gone out with a beautiful girl too, but I was determined that I was going to be something. Not that I wanted to be a big shot, a big man, but I wanted something out of life other than what I'd known up to then, and I thought wrestling would make that possible.

JACK HALEY JR.

Because I was single for so long and, you know, I certainly didn't keep a low profile in Hollywood, a lot of people always assume that it was easy for me and I was really the playboy producer-director. But there was many a night I worked straight through the clock. Poured hours into it. If you want success, I don't think you can avoid it. As lucky as I consider myself—and I'm really thrice blessed—I don't think I could ever have achieved it without truly working hard. But as I say, a great many friends can't accept that. Younger people I know say, "I wish I could do it the way you did it. All that fun." I say, "Sure." How do you tell someone? Facing air dates and things, we work sometimes twenty-four, forty-eight hours straight. And weekends you forget about when the crunch is on. You've gotta do it right, and to really do it right takes a lot of hard work, I don't care what aspect of show business you're in.

If I have a television presentation to write or a script to do, I have to really talk to myself a lot. I tend to procrastinate. A friend of mine who's a writer talks about "Sunday writers," which means you get all the way down to Sunday afternoon and you're supposed to have the first draft in on Monday, and you get the coffee pot out and just go to work. And of course you never get it done in time or done right. I have a tendency to be that way. I try to control it all the time, but that tendency is there. And writing, I guess, is the toughest discipline of all. When you're directing, you just *have* to do it. There's just no question about it. You throw yourself into the picture and that's it. You're virtually the first one on the set in the morning, and after everybody has left, you're still looking at dailies and then you go to look at yesterday's cut, what the editor has put together. The last six months of *That's Entertainment* were totally consuming. I hardly got out of the editing room. The only time I got out was to chase after one of the stars to shoot an intro.

ALBERT ELLIS

The way you really get successful is by concentration and persistence. You pick a particular field. I guess it was Emerson's famous phrase—or was it Thoreau's?—about building a better mousetrap. But then you really focus, you specialize on one thing, not on fifty other kinds of things. You don't try a mousetrap and forty-nine other things. You focus on that goddam mousetrap—promoting it, pushing it, staying with it. One of the biggest parts of getting ahead consists of persistence.

The thing that's wrong with humans is not only that they down themselves when they do poorly and don't win approval, but they also refuse to work for future gain. If you want future gain, you almost always have to discipline yourself and do some very hard work today. Horseplay is fine. But if you want future enjoyment including success, you give up certain pleasures. And I've always been that way.

When I first started in this field, for example, I didn't have any degrees. I wasn't a psychologist yet. But to do research I went through ten thousand books on sex, love, marriage and related fields. I knew that to master the field that was what you better do. So if you want to master any area—no horseshit, you don't fool around.

There are certain things I don't like to do but to get the results I want I just do them. If I'm writing a book I normally compile a fairly complete bibliography. It's just a pain in the ass, but there's really nobody else who can do it. And the same with my manuscripts. The fastest and best way I find is sitting down and typing each page on my electric typewriter—which I don't like doing. The sitting up I certainly don't like. The typing is a mechanical bore. But I simply do it. When I read those ten thousand books, I enjoyed that—enjoyed learning more. You see, that's an intrinsic kind of pleasure. I also enjoy the scores of clients I see in individual therapy every week and another hundred in group therapy. I like that kind of thing, so I don't have to say, "I had better do this rather than go out and screw," or something like that. I enjoy the screwing too, but I don't do half as much of that as I could. Because, believe it or not, I enjoy working more. And where the screwing mainly brings immediate satisfaction, some of the working brings me present *and* future gains.

WILLIAM GAINES

I have to admit that I'm very lazy and work as little as possible. I've never been one of those sixteen-hour-a day people. I work about six hours a day. I take a lot of time off. I take a good six weeks a year for vacations because I love to travel. I do not work hard and I never did. Maybe one of the reasons is that I had a successful father. I'm sure this is not a rule, there are many exceptions, but it seems like the children of wealthy people don't have the drive that the children of nonwealthy people do. I mean, my father had the drive 'cause he came out of the Lower East Side, a typical slum kid with the classic Irving Berlin–type beginnings. He was determined to make a success of himself and he pulled himself up by his bootstraps. Well, I never felt that need because I already had it. He was providing it for me. There's no drive for success like having a poor childhood.

EILEEN FORD

Success came easy, but I'm sure that the fact that I'm willing to work very hard had a lot to do with it. I'll work eighteen hours a day. I'll work twenty-four hours a day if it means that I'm going to get done what I want to get done. I'm totally capable of concentrating as long and as hard as I need to. I don't care if I eat or drink or anything. When I'm working I don't even know what's going on outside me. What I hate above all in life is when employees of mine come in and talk about the weather for the first ten minutes. If they were busy they wouldn't know whether it was hot or cold.

I believe in hard work. I know there are people who say if you can't do it in four days a week you're not successful, but I'm in a business that requires my full-time attention. Being an agent is possibly unique in that your clients don't understand that you may want a day off here and there. They really get upset if you take time off. Also I find that I can't delegate authority. The nature of my business makes it so that I can't. It's a personal service. I can tell people what to do, but I have to know what's happening all the time.

Whatever I do, I really just want to do it well. I'm obsessive about it. When I write, I rewrite every book eight times, maybe nine times. If I rewrite my latest book again it will never be published. I'm just obsessive about doing things well. Therefore I don't mind how long it takes. I don't care if it's making a pommes soufflé or a booking or writing the page of a book. Whatever it is I do, I want to do it better than I did it before or better than anyone else. Yet I'm not competitive in the sense that I don't worry about my makeup and that other women look better than I, although I do care how I dress. I don't care about playing tennis or being a good swimmer or competing on a ski slope. They couldn't matter to me less. But if they did, I would be the best tennis player or the best card player or the best whatever player.

GEROLD FRANK

I work obsessively. I know friends who write from eight to nine and stop. They play golf, they go out on a boat, they go swimming, they do things. I can't. There is nothing except the book. I wake up in the middle of the night thinking of it and I'll go to the typewriter and start typing. And the paragraph is never finished for me. It's an endless, endless improvement—I think. I mean I probably louse it up after a while. But I want it to be the best. I can only tell you that I always want it to be of the absolute highest quality, and nothing is sufficiently good, so I will work on it and work on it and work on it and worry it and worry it and worry it. It's just a natural thing for me. I'm constantly seeking to make it better.

JOAN GANZ COONEY

No one is successful who doesn't work hard. You really have to make up your mind. No, I don't really think you make up your mind. I think there are workhorses and nonworkhorses, and you are one or the other. There are certain artists and writers who are very brilliant and very lazy and they make it, but they are the exception. Most successful artists and writers work very hard, and most of those who are lazy become lazy after success and have some kind of a touch. But there's no such thing as someone not working hard in corporate America and making it. Our brightest creative people here just do nothing but work. If they're not working here, they are inventing a toy or something at home. I think—and there are psychologists who believe this is true—that creativity, inventiveness and IQ points all have an energy component that is extraordinary, and that when you see someone creative or with a high IQ you are usually going to see a high amount of energy.

I enjoy my work very much, though there are days that are absolutely hell where you are just dealing with one difficult thing after another. There are two kinds of problems I despise. One is really tough negotiations with backers, some of whom are governmental, where you really have to fight to retain your copyrights and things like that. Your very existence depends on winning those fights, so they are very unpleasant. You're never sure that you're going to come out whole. I don't often engage in them personally, but I'm kept posted while meetings are going on and sit around biting my nails. The other thing I hate is personnel problems that are really tough, where you have to either fire somebody or order the firing of somebody or put someone on probation. It's even worse when two top employees don't get along with one another and neither of them is going to get fired, so you've got to begin to separate them for the good of the organization. That sort of thing takes a lot out of me, but I've talked to other executives who say it doesn't take a lot out of them.

Everyone has his own favorite killers, where you really say to yourself, today was a carcinogenic. But there are days when I have a good time, and it's often when we are conceptualizing new projects or moving something forward, doing something creative. I don't mind getting into big messes around here when some unit has gone awry, where you are either going to take something that's dying and get it back on its feet or creating something new. And I do quite a lot outside. I'm on the board of Channel 13 and work with them on their problems, which are closely related to ours, and I'm on several other boards. It's like going to the movies. I know the problems and can be helpful, but they're not *my* problems so I can be very relaxed and very creative quite often because I'm not up so tight. So I enjoy a lot of the peripheral things that being here has brought me, and I love my work here when it is moving something. I hate it when it is just putting out some fire.

I work as long on any matter as it takes. It never crosses my mind to quit in the middle of something or not see it through to conclusion. I do try to be disciplined about walking away in the short run, though. I mean, if I find that I'm beginning to blow up or I'm not coming up with anything, I'll try to get out of here. I'll go to the movies or have dinner with a friend and come back to it the next day. The hardest thing is to know when it's counterproductive to go on with it and get away. And quite often it works. It's just amazing how counterproductive after 6 PM is on a problem. I often use 6 to 10 PM at home on the phone or reading reports, but you've only got so many good hours in you a day for a creative answer. Maybe four, maybe five. After that you're just wheelspinning. It's really an indulgence of your own neurosis not to be able to walk away.

I think compulsive-obsessive traits are the marks of almost everybody that you would call successful. Even if I walk away it's very hard for me to put the problem out of my mind. Yet it is often a productive act to get out. And I try to get other people to do the same. When you can't do it is when you are in heavy negotiations with talent. Sometimes those do go till one or two in the morning. I don't stick with them. I feel very bad about letting the lawyers do it, but sometimes it's like electing a pope. I lock them in a room and say that no one's coming out until there's white smoke. And that works. But I think if anyone's putting in long hours, chronically, in an office it's to meet some other need than the work that's required.

ROCKY AOKI

I work here maybe fourteen or fifteen hours a day, but that's my business, that's my hobby, that's my way of life. So I never call it hard work. I want to make Benihana of Tokyo a household name, so I have the Benihana Grand Prix for speedboats, Miss Benihana contests, lunches, press parties, things like that. But that's not hard work. That's pleasure. I like to talk with people. Meanwhile I'm building up the name of the restaurant. It's a lot of fun. I'm not working so hard. I love it here.

JOHN DIEBOLD

I enjoy work. There are always parts of work that I don't enjoy: the kind of housekeeping aspects, the administrative work that's necessary just to keep something moving. I like those things the least because they always seem to involve the minimum amount of creativity, but I think we all take for granted that that's what a large amount of one's time goes into. I think the problem in work is getting the right balance between the immediate and the important. I have to discipline myself very much on that. It's so easy to fill up one's time with the sort of comfortable routine, and I tend to do that. You know, on a vacation you can end up making the better part of the day the reading of the *New York Times.*

I think that Parkinson's right, that work does expand to fill the time. Often the things that I'm best at, having new ideas and seeing new patterns, are precisely the things that get the least amount of time. In one's life as well as in one's work, the immediate always tends to take precedence over the important even though you know intellectually that you should do the important things first. I'm not sure I have the answer to that. On a typical day I come in about seven and work by myself until nine or so and then with my immediate staff until about one. I can get a great deal accomplished by the discipline of just not seeing people until lunch or till evening, but sometimes you can't always control that.

I'm not obsessive about working. I love to have time to do other things that interest me, and I often push work away. I guess the main problem is that there tend to be a lot of things I want to do. I try very hard to keep windows open on a lot of different worlds, and I try to be active enough in different fields to have a feeling for what's going on. This whole business is very much formed around what I like to do, and I want very much to be part of the interesting things that are happening in the times. That leads one into being active in a group of scholars on China, in various scientific organizations, foreign affairs activities, etc. I find these kinds of things fascinating, but as you begin to spend time with them you begin to play a more important role in the various organizations and then that becomes its own kind of work. And when you have a lot of those things happening simultaneously there's a hell of a lot you have to do just to keep actively involved. But I do these things because I like to do them. I don't do them because I feel any obligation. I'm excited by and interested in a whole lot of different fields. I'm very interested in graphic design. I'm very interested in stage design. I like music. It's a rare week when I don't go to a concert, and sometimes I go to three or four. There are a lot of things I like to do, and I try to do as many of them as I can. My life is very much formed around the things I like doing, and in that sense work and play are all mixed up together. It's ideal. I live an extremely full life.

JOE EULA

Hard work is all it is, man. And you've got to enjoy it. That makes it so easy. Everybody says to me, you know, "You're killin' yourself." Oh, shit. Everyone has their own level, their own pace that they drive themselves at. Mine happens to be *boom boom boom boom!* And I adore drugs to go along with it. It's just a pity that they haven't been bright enough to legalize them. I mean, I've spelt the words on the telephone so many different ways that it's ridiculous. I don't seem to be very self-disciplined but I am. When it comes to masochistically beating myself, trying to wreck my health, I do that also. That's another discipline I've gotten myself into. And I've failed miserably because here I am fifty years old and still alive. It's just incredible. I work with total involvement, and sometimes I just can't say no. I'll take on twenty jobs at a time, keeping myself crazy and killing myself. But enjoying it. If I didn't enjoy it, I wouldn't do it.

I've never considered myself just a fashion person. Fashion is just a word that is used today. To begin with, I'm much more of a cartoonist. When I do a fashion drawing it's really a cartoon. I put down what I see in the quickest line, the quickest way possible. And if it isn't amusing it's not any good. Therefore success has a lot to do with amusement. With amusing myself. Fashion is probably the last rung on my ladder. I do films of a certain type. Big shows, like Sly Stone's wedding at Madison Square Garden. I produce. I'm consultant to Halston and to *Vogue*. I design sets and costumes for ballet and theater. I paint. I used to do a great many ads but not anymore. They're all shit. I won't let some art director tell me what to do, no way. My world's not a specialized world at all. If you put yourself in that one little cage, you're just another IBM slot. All those things in the arts, they're all related, they all work together.

GEORGE PLIMPTON

I find work extremely difficult to do. I hate it and struggle with it, so when it's over and done and the editor calls up and says he or she likes what I've done, why then there's a tremendous sense of contentment . . . the feeling that one has achieved a relative success with something, increased by the knowledge that one has truly wrestled with it.

QUINCY JONES

I tried not so much to look at it as hard work but as strong curiosity. That was almost the prevailing element. I always wanted to know why in everything. Ray Charles was like that too when he was a kid, whether it was repairing a radio or a record player or whatever it was. I guess that as an arranger that's part of your tools. You have to know why. Why can't I hear that bass flute playing with the brass section? Because the brass is too goddam loud, that's why. Put it on a piccolo, it's high enough to cut through. So you listen to *Daphnis and Chloe* and you listen to Charlie Parker and you keep asking the questions. That's how you learn to do it. I think it's really an equal balance between soul and science. The cerebral, intellectual approach to it will never make it, but you still have to balance the emotions through that. I guess the same thing applies to the writer or painter or photographer or cinematographer or whatever, because we're all basically dealing with structure.

Yeah, I enjoy work very much. Sometimes on the more important things it gets painful because your standards get to such crazy heights. You're constantly trying to put a watermelon in a coke bottle. I've talked to a lot of people about that and read a lot about it, and I guess the only consolation is that everybody has the same problem. There's that blank page, man. That blank page is a bitch. You start out with a blur of an idea and there's not a goddam thing there but air and blank paper, man, and you have to put a structure to it, you've got to put emotion, form, drama, everything. I start off sometimes with a whole lot of well-intentioned discipline in mind, but then the emotional side gets involved and sometimes takes me off the track. I guess that's a lot of what pushes me many times into the deadline trip. But down at the crunch it does get done, and I think I understand why. When the crunch comes down and it's time to deliver and you've just been mulling it over and saying, "Well, I've got it all in my head, I just haven't put it on paper yet," and all that bullshit, that's when your discipline, your craft, your emotions, your imagination and everything else all come together as one unit and you just go ahead and do it.

To me it's almost as though you break through a barrier and you're in the twilight zone and somebody else is pushing all of it through your arm. And I know what that animal is. It's the subconscious mind. When you sit down there with that goddam conscious mind in charge, man, you start worrying about what will this one say about it and, oh, that one will probably put it down and all that other very inhibiting stuff. Your fears and your confidence almost collide and contradict each other with that cerebral attitude because the conscious mind is like that. What you have to do it get to the point where you let the conscious mind be that cerebral moderator that programs the problem to the subconscious and just trust the subconscious's answer, because he doesn't go for any bullshit. He's a totally emotional animal that draws intuitively on craft and memory and everything else.

I guess that's why many times I go on those long work stretches of two or three days because I sit there, man, and try to wait until my conscious mind dozes off so I can get something done and sure enough, man, here he comes. There's the dude, man, and he says, "Let me get this fool out of the way with all his bullshit so I can get the thing done." And he's never failed, you know. Yeah, I think the worst thing you could do to me is say, "Here's three million dollars, man, for a piece of music. You have all the time you want to finish it." You wouldn't get shit. You wouldn't get a note, believe me.

REVEREND IKE

I don't like the term "hard work." I've taken out the word "hard" and substituted "diligent." I'm definitely a diligent worker, and I love my work very much. I cannot do anything I don't love doing. And I've learned how to work from a point of relaxation, which is a great discovery. Some of my best ideas have come to me when I was supposed to be on vacation. I remember when I went down to Mexico, for example, and found myself hot on the phone to operations headquarters back here giving them orders for a new series of telecasts I had just thought of. I spend a great deal of my time in what I call meditation—contemplation. I always begin my day this way, and I've also learned how to program my mind before going to sleep. If you learn how to do that and just relax, it is surprising what your mind will do for you. Doing it in the morning is good too, but the most effective time is before you go to sleep because your conscious mind is in abeyance for a longer period and all of that subconscious and superconscious mind power works best without the restraints of reason.

JERRY DELLA FEMINA

Hard work is good, but there are people who work their asses off in a bank. . . . I think it's what you're working towards more than what you're working at. I've got friends of mine who are longshoremen. That's what work is, that's hard work. Physical labor is work. I happen to think that copywriting is fun. It's tough sometimes when it doesn't come easy and it's tough sometimes when you block and it's tough when you haven't got anything going for you one day, but those are all temporary conditions. My friend who is picking up sixty pounds and trying to put it into the hold of a ship, *he's* working hard, he's working very hard. I don't think what I do is hard work. Or the bank clerk —I used to work for a bank—who knows he's never gonna make more than $150 a week and he's always gonna be there. That's not even hard work—I think that's death. I think if you're in a job where you know exactly what you're going to make, you know exactly what's going to happen to you and you don't see any great future, that's death. That's not even hard work.

DON KING

I enjoy work. I enjoy accomplishment. I enjoy being involved with people. It's an excitement that's hard to describe, but when you can see something really happen it's very fulfilling. There's only frustration when it doesn't happen, so I learned long ago that you must perform. It doesn't matter how much time and effort you put in it, how much enthusiasm and desire, if you don't perform, it's totally irrelevant and immaterial. By whatever means necessary, you got to perform within the confines of whatever rules you're dealing with.

There are so many things that I really want to do, but I recognize that in order to accomplish you must work by calculation and design rather than passion and emotion. You know, you must be able to map out a plan to deal with what you want to deal with, and even with the most scrutinized plans that you can design you're gonna have unforeseeable contingencies and you're gonna have to deal with them too. They're unknown, but I dare to challenge the unknown. I feel that I can snatch the possible out of the impossible, snatch victory out of the jaws of defeat, you dig? So I will never succumb to any situation of a negative nature. I will try to take that negative and turn it into something positive. You know: Take a lemon and make lemonade out of it.

So it's really a strong degree of positive thinking, but with that positive thinking you must put positive action. Apostle Peter said, "Prayer without good works is a dead thing," so I know you must work as well as pray. And you must watch as well as pray, you dig? You can't pray to God to give you the vision and then not use it. If your eyesight is good, look around you and don't feel that someone has done you wrong because they do you wrong. Some wrongs you do to yourself by allowing the looseness of your operation to be done wrong. So you don't get mad at the other fellow, you get mad at yourself. And you don't get mad, you get smart.

I deal with people and I feel that people are my most important assets. If I can get them involved, then whatever they have at their disposal is involved also. If you have strength and I can get you involved, then that gives me a vast resource of strength to draw from. And I deal with people one-on-one. No person's too high for me to go to. The Good Book says, "Seek and ye shall find, knock and the door shall be open, ask and you shall be given." And I believe this, you dig? So I go over there and ask, whoever it is. I seek, I knock. And if the door is open to me, then I'm gonna give it my spill and we're gonna sit down and try to work out what would be mutually beneficial to the both of us. Whoever it is, if it's Charlie Bludhorn of Gulf and Western or the Shah of Iran, if you can get him involved, then he don't want it to fail either. We're all in agreement about that. Everybody I go to has a certain apprehension about failure, so therefore I'm dealing with the odds on my side because I abhor it myself. If we can come together, then we have one unified thought, a vested interest that we can combine our energies on, which is to remove failure from existence. And that gives me an extra shot in the arm because sometimes I may slip, you know, but whoever I'm dealing with will give me the necessary help to put me back on my feet again because their reputation is involved also.

So I just deal with the people, and I think this is where the power of the situation is. All power to the people, that's what all of our declarations and constitutions say, and once you can motivate and inspire people and bring them together and snatch that type of spirit from them, it's like capturing the atom, it's like snatching nuclear energy. People are the most powerful force on earth, you know, 'cause God said He made them in His image and they are all Godlike. He gave them dominion over the fowl of the air, the fish in the sea and all the earthly abounds, so if you believe in the Godlike principle and the Superior Being, as I do, then you believe that all things are here for you. You just have to go on and take them and do what you must do with them. But you must deal with people.

When I go into any type of proposition, I want to know who I'm dealing with. When you're dealing with a corporate structure, you're dealing with a cold and calculating situation, but if you can get to the president or the chairman of the board, then you're dealing with a human being and you got the corporate structure also. So it's always people, you've always got to deal with that, and it's fundamental to my success or what semblance of success I enjoy.

MIKE WALLACE

Yes, I am a worker, and I make no excuses for it. I rather enjoy it. My wife is a painter. She is also a worker. Working hard has never really been a chore for me, a distasteful chore. I rather enjoy it, I've not had to discipline myself particularly. I'm not as good a solitary worker as I would like to be. I am a better collaborator. I like to work, for instance, here on *60 Minutes* with Don Hewitt. I used to work with Av Westin when he was here at CBS. Prior to that, with Ted Yates. I've been blessed with the opportunity to work with three of the most capable producers in television journalism, over a period of the last twenty years. Their enthusiasm and imagination spark my own. And I work better that way. I'm not sure that I would be capable of setting out by myself on a lonely chore and making a success of it. At least I never have and I'm no youngster anymore, so there must be some reason behind that pattern.

MURRAY KEMPTON

If I have anything to say about success it's that I think it's collective. Or it ought to be. Like the Basie band. And that's a problem for me because my life as a book writer is one of extraordinary isolation. I loved doing a daily column. You got around. You saw people. And I love community. I have always been sort of a Stalinist. I mean, I've never understood individualism in essence. Maybe it's a basic lack of confidence in myself. Outside of experiences with my own family, I think the best experiences of my life have been working in crowd journalism. I absolutely adored it.

I can't say that I enjoy my work all that much these days. I'm bored with this book I'm writing. I don't know, I don't find that sense of joy that you get, for example, when you hear a big band really moving. And basically I'm a very incoherent writer. I lay that to a lot of things including a certain lack of discipline. When I write I usually start without any particular notion of where I'm going to finish. You sort of pick that up when you're doing a daily column. You almost have to. I don't know if I like this kind of work.

When I was writing every day for the *New York Post* I felt that if you worked eight hours a day and got your pay for it, that was sufficient. Then I went to the *New Republic* and I was getting the same salary—which was not, let me tell you, that astronomical —for doing one piece a week and I immediately began to feel that one piece a week should be just out of this world. Now when I do a book I always have to feel that, well this chapter on such-and-such has to be different from anybody else's chapter. And also be true. And of course the problem is you don't have that many ideas. The only writer on broad general subjects I know who seems to me to have every resource in ideas is Norman Mailer. Norman can put four or five original ideas in one goddam piece. Now I'm very arrogant about myself. I think that I have developed in the course of my life maybe seven or eight pretty original ideas. But I don't have that kind of prodigality.

My problem is that I am so insecure and have so little sense of my own ideas that I actually work hard at things I don't even much want to do. When I say I work hard, I mean I put in a lot of time. Whether I work hard is another question. But I research ad nauseam, even though I notice that good books on my subjects have comparatively little research in them. Dick Rovere's book on Joe McCarthy is a marvelous book and no research shows in it at all. The only book on McCarthy that was well researched was William Buckley's and Brent Bozell's, but of course it seems to me all wrong in its estimate of McCarthy and what he was. I always think that when you are researching like hell you're really looking for something that's probably not there, and you're also avoiding work. God knows, when a man spends three weeks trying to find out from the official records how many times G. David Schine was on KP, he is either in some way avoiding work, which is more than possible, or just a nut.

And then you fall back on irony. Piss on irony. I've been making my living at it for years. I think irony is a waste of time.

There is such a thing as right and wrong, there is such a thing as evil and virtue, and irony is really the most centrist of all stances. I think the low point of my career was when I was doing sports for *Esquire* and discovered that Willie Mays hated baseball, Joe Namath was a dedicated monastic athlete, Muhammad Ali was a middle-aged man. . . . You know, I suddenly realized that I'm taking the big cliché and just substituting for it the directly opposite cliché.

REX REED

It's just a very hard life. Writing is a hard profession. You may talk to writers who say, "Oh, it's wonderful and I couldn't do anything else and I love it." Well, I don't love it. To me it's very, very hard. But it would be just as hard if I were nobody, so the fact that all this work, which doesn't come easily for me, has paid off, that is a nice feeling. But there are no intrinsic pleasures about the writing itself. The pleasures come from the success of the writing.

I work too hard now, so I don't enjoy it as much as I used to. When I didn't have any money and wasn't having to support a certain kind of life-style and I lived in a small walkup with a little fireplace that only cost $130 a month, then I could afford to do fewer things and write better. Now I have to do more things more often and I feel that the writing is not as good sometimes as it could be, but the only way you can make any money at writing is by working yourself into a position that has a lot of demands. I could still be a freelance writer, but I wouldn't be living in the Dakota. Most writers believe that the most enviable position to be in is to be syndicated and your own boss, and that's what I do now. I have a critical column on Friday and a general column on Sunday, and I have to turn those out every week. In addition, I'm the monthly film critic for *Vogue,* and I do a lot of in-depth magazine assignments. That means I have to meet a lot of deadlines, and of course you never really get used to that kind of pressure. I hate being forced to write something simply because somebody is waiting to fill some space. I hate the discipline of writing, and I hate the discipline of deadlines. I hate the logistics that are involved. I mean, I'm filling space, that's what I'm doing. I'm not writing great, brilliant things every week just because I have something to say. Now some weeks I do, and I'm proud of those columns. Other weeks I'm searching for things on Sunday night to turn in on Monday morning simply because there's a hole in the paper that has to be filled. This is the nightmare of newspaper work. But in return for that I have absolute autonomy. Nobody tells me what to do. I have no boss. I make a hell of a lot of money. And I'm famous. So, you know, what can you do? I'd rather be famous and rich and live in Vermont and raise apples, but how are you going to do that?

GEOFFREY HOLDER

All my nervous energy and all my insanity go out in creating. It's become second nature to me. That's all I know. I gave up my childhood for the arts. When other boys were out playing ball or tickling girls, I was in there with a paintbrush. My childhood was all in the arts. My older brother paints, dances, he's a musician, he choreographs. And I was there with him and the other adults, dancing and painting, and not being like the average child who has to go to school and then goes out to play cricket. My father, who was very beautiful, encouraged me. He couldn't care less as long as I was obedient at school and courteous to people. There was no loss, only gain. I am very, very fortunate because I had the parents that I did and that environment.

When I get inside myself and I raise the lid of my Pandora's Box, that's where it's at, and I have to do that very often to keep my head straight, to keep my sanity. My parents are still alive, you know, and my son, I have to be an example to him. I worry about my health. During *The Wiz* I never slept. I would stay up till four in the morning with the actors, consoling them and bitching with them and getting to know them and letting them get to know me so when we'd work the next day they'd know where my head was at and we could work in shorthand. I had to suppress all my real anger, and you have anger, you know, whenever you are trying to make a creative statement because there are always so many outside forces working against it. You have that in every business. I had a rhythm all set up and I didn't want anything to stop it, because I move very fast. It was a very lonely job.

I hate confusion. I hate too many people together and forced conversation. I love eye to eye, one to one. A third person is all right, but a fourth becomes a party. And when it becomes a party, I go into the kitchen and cook something because I know everybody in the room and they know me, so I let them get to know each other.

I sound like sugar, don't I? But it's the only way I can live. I have found a way of living and it works for me. It's a very lonely world, very lonely. It's like staring at a blank canvas and trying to see lines where there are no lines. But if you look long enough, your lines are formed. I know that if I'm alone at a certain hour of the night and I really concentrate, it all falls into place. When I get rid of the confusion in my head, it all falls together perfectly. I have to worry about my heart. I don't have a bad heart but I could, because I go, I go, I go, and I'm ruled by my heart. I'm impulsive and I want to do everything and never stop. And that I have to worry about.

ELIZABETH ASHLEY

I'm a laborer. When I go to work, I sweat. I work a six-day week, and when I finish my job I'm sweating. I believe that's a privilege. I also think it is essential. We live in a world where that is a dying thing. Not many people work a six-day week and sweat when they're doing their labor. I do. That's what I respect—tell the truth, work hard and sweat.

Work is the only thing I know or understand. I've never met anybody who works harder than I do. That's the thing I respect most about myself. When I go to work, I'm a motherfucker and I expect everybody there to work seventy-five percent as hard as I do. I don't expect them to work as hard as I do, that's too much to ask, because I'm a fanatic. If I'm gonna ask the man to pay ten dollars to sit in that chair, I have fucking-A got to deliver. He doesn't pay ten dollars to have his ass ache.

ALICE COOPER

The only time I ever get down is when I'm working with people who aren't really into it. If I go into a project, I want to go into it on the level of, damn, this is going to be great and we're all going to work at it until it gets done. So if somebody's a cry baby or something that really does bother me. I mean, if you have to work till four in the morning, you have to work till four in the morning. The idea is to get the product out the best you can. That's the only thing that really matters.

When I'm on the road, just to get all that energy up I never leave the hotel room. It doesn't make any difference if I'm in Paris or London or Toledo, I just stay there all day and rest. After eleven years in the business you really learn that discipline. I used to go out and run around, and then when I got up on stage I'd lose my energy and I had to say, "Wait a minute, that's not what you're supposed to be doing." So I got to the point where I only drink so much before a show and so much afterwards, and I know I can't eat at least six hours before a show because it makes me feel too heavy. Things like that. If you're serious about what you're doing, you really have to learn how your metabolism works.

When you are on the road you maintain a road mentality where you sit back there and are supposed to start hating all the Holiday Inns, but I got to the point where I was liking them, really liking them. Those three turquoise horses on the wall that you see in every single Holiday Inn in the world. And, you know, you do about two months on the road and you start saying, "God, I can't wait to get back home, I'm never going to tour again." But then you get back home, and about two weeks later you find your fingers tapping and you start saying, "Well, when's the next ship?"

HALSTON

You have to have the right talent. You have to have the stick-to-itiveness. And you have to have, certainly, the interest. I think that's probably the most important ingredient, more than anything else. The older I get, the more I realize that the business-man who always complains about working on the weekends and working at night is really doing it because he likes it. He might complain to the outside world, but it's something you have total control over if you are your own chief executive officer. And it becomes fun. It's more fun than social life. It's more fun than almost anything else. So therefore one spends most of one's life doing that.

With the creative aspects of it, sometimes it's a little difficult to get the adrenaline up to the point where, you know, you can just sock them out like that. But if the climate is right, I would prefer to work than almost anything. We just had this very hot weekend, it was ninety-eight degrees, and the air conditioning was blown out at my house so I thought I'd come to work. Well, the air conditioning here was blown out too, except on the third floor, which is a sort of showroom. So I worked the entire week-end, down on the floor and most of the time alone. I enjoyed it.

I've never had to discipline myself to work. What I have to discipline myself to is to take time off. I mean, one needs that. It's not a matter of recharging one's batteries, because the more I do, the better off I am as far as my creative experiment is concerned. It's just removing yourself from it and then coming back with fresh eyes.

I'm very selfish. My work certainly comes first. And I think that's the rule of thumb with most professional people. If a friend or an emotional thing gets in the way of it, I'm very selfish. I must have my work first. It's of utmost interest to me. I take it seriously and I have an enormous lot of people who depend on me for their livelihood and I just like it. It's a big responsibil-ity. But I wouldn't say that it's the only thing in my life. I cer-tainly have friends and social life like everyone else.

MARTIN SCORSESE

I've been termed a workaholic, but I have to discipline myself to work all the time. I'm terrible. Disciplining is very, very im-portant. But I usually work with other people who say, "Three o'clock tomorrow, right?" I'll say, "Three o'clock, uh, yeah. I may be a few minutes late." "Be there on time." "If I'm a few minutes late start without me." "Well, we can't." "Okay. I'll be there on time." It goes back and forth like that. I come in usually very harried and I'll take a few phone calls at the beginning of the meeting, anything to push off the work. But then we get down to it and it gets done.

When I'm shooting I usually work pretty much the way I talk. Very fast. I'll say, "Do this, do that," and then I'll sit down and wait and read something while they do it. That's the big difference between low-budget and big-budget filmmaking at this point, low-budget being five thousand dollars and big-budget being about two million right now, which is considered low-budget in Hollywood. In the five-thousand-dollar days you had to do everything. You couldn't sit down and wait. But with the two-million-dollar thing you can explain to your cameraman exactly what you want and then you can wait a little while. You can do some work, you can read, that sort of thing. It takes some of the pressure off. That's really the only difference I can see. And sometimes that works against you because it makes you lazy.

My favorite period is the editing process. You give the work to the editor to do and the next morning you can do your own things—go to your doctor, go shopping, or come to the office and make phone calls or look at a film—and then in the afternoon when the work is done you see the results of the work you did the day before. So you have a little more leeway. And also, editing for me is where you really create the picture. I can't understand directors who turn it over and walk away from it. I worked on *Taxi Driver* with three editors, two Kems, four Moviolas, everything. It was real craziness, the worst situation since the editing of *Woodstock.* It was even harder than the shooting but I enjoy it better because you can actually see the thing come alive.

But I have my ways of relaxing. If I'm doing preproduction, I like to look at a lot of films, old films. They usually relate to the picture I'm doing, but it's my way of relaxing too, even though I'm still working. Sometimes you're doing something that's a period piece and you want to make sure certain things look just right. Or sometimes it's a cleansing-out process. Sometimes it's a recharging. You look at the old films and you see what those directors did and you're inspired again.

MILTON GLASER

I love to work. I work all the time. Yes, I have to be very self-disciplined. I don't think of myself necessarily as a disciplined person, but I have a method for always getting the work done. I never miss deadlines. The work always goes out when it has to. I never thought I was self-disciplined. In fact, the reason I always wanted to have a studio situation with other people was to make sure I'd have someplace to go in the morning, that I'd have to report in and do the job. Early on, I had a horror that if I stayed at home, when I woke up and went to the drawing board, I'd say, "Aw, fuck, I'll watch a little television," that if I were left to my own devices, the fear of moving toward pleasure, I guess, would overcome my need to accomplish. So I always had the feeling I wasn't really terribly disciplined. I'm not terribly disciplined, but the work always goes out.

I would say that to a large extent the focus of my life has always been on the work. That's always been the methodology for my own perception of myself, my own sense of justification, my own position in the world. I cannot say that I have given up pleasure for that, though I certainly have changed the focus of what people think might be pleasurable. It gives me more pleasure than anything else I can think of.

F. LEE BAILEY

I did a film for a company in Chicago that trains executives and executive salesmen in motivation, in the ability to get out there and be effective. It was in three parts with myself, Bill Lear and Michael De Bakey, and it was broken into confidence, determination, and discipline. Lear was determination because he started projects that people said just can't hack it and he usually won out. De Bakey was discipline. Every day he reads over the book on how to do this heart transplant even though he did three of them the day before. And the section I did was the one on self-confidence. I know I can do it. Sometimes I'm wrong, but I usually turn right around the next day and say I still know I can do it, which simply makes life tolerable if you take on substantial projects. That was probably a pretty good synopsis of what you'll find in successful people. In the top corporate executives in this society, for example, you rarely find a guy without some measure of self-confidence, discipline—that is, doing that which is unpleasant to get the damn thing done—and determination, which is a no-quit attitude.

Self-discipline is probably my weakest suit. I'm inclined to put off until tomorrow what doesn't have to be done today in some areas. But that really is an attribute of a trial lawyer. Most trial lawyers were crammers in law school. They attended classes spasmodically if at all—I think the third year of law school I went to four—but they acquire the ability to sit down and memorize at a very high rate and retain for forty-eight hours and just go in and regurgitate what they've memorized, in addition to having working principles. If you've got enough factual data, and you know the ballpark that you're in, you can put together a pretty satisfactory answer to any hairline question, and law school examinations are nothing but hairline questions where you're balancing on the razor's edge. And trial lawyers have to have the same ability. You may have to sit down the day before a trial—and it's a mistake to do it two weeks before—and learn enough about engineering, say, to demolish an engineer. You've got to know his language, and when he's going off the track, or where he's weak.

This is enough to give some lawyers heart attacks unless they enjoy that sort of life. I can remember when I was still in law school how other students would just be terribly resentful. They'd say, "Damn, I studied and went to the bar review and everything else, and you march in and do that." Well, the intensity of the effort in those forty-eight hours was enough to compensate for what they thought was all their agonizing work, which nonetheless still left them time to go to the late show.

I think most successful people do better under pressure. It motivates them. I suppose that they are all very well equipped to defend themselves, and the urge to defend yourself is greatest when you are under the gun. That's probably when you function at your own highest level. But if their self-confidence begins to wobble you see tremendous changes and you will find them with heart attacks because they worry too much. You can't live in a world of anxiety if you're going to undertake to do more than logic would seem to indicate as reasonable.

EDGAR D. MITCHELL

I use my own body and my own thinking as a laboratory all the time. I'm a continual tester and tryer. To use the test pilot lingo, I'm always "testing the envelope" to find out just what will happen. Unfortunately, my wife thinks I do it with the family too. I'm always pushing them to the limit. Not so much in terms of their attainment but in reaching their own capability. I'm a much better psychologist than to insist on fixed goals. I don't demand the impossible of them, but I do believe in testing people through stress to see what they can do. I know that you grow under stress. What I've had to learn is the recognition that you grow best in alternating stress and relaxation, not continual stress. But I do stress people, everybody I work with. I expect the best of them. I want them to attain what they can attain. From my experience in the military, I guess I'm a pretty good leader, but the military programing of command contains an element of driving people instead of leading them and I have to fight that continually. Not to be too short, not to be too demanding, not to be too authoritative. But if I can cope with that, I can get people to work for me very nicely.

Many people think I'm a workaholic. I'm sure I used to be, but I've been doing my damnedest these days to break that habit. I've found that people are more successful when they learn how to turn it off. Regardless of what it is, you've got to have a break from it. Working all the time is an addiction, and any addiction is, I think, detrimental to you, whether it's drinking too much milk or playing tennis twenty-four hours a day or thinking your job is the only thing in the world that matters. Those sorts of addictions are not healthy emotionally or mentally, and I think it becomes particularly deleterious when you exclude everything else in your life for your job. I think an individual needs to be broader than that. In the past, I could always give intellectual acknowledgment to that idea, but I found myself working eighteen hours a day anyhow. As a result, I wasn't enjoying my family as much as I might have and they weren't getting very much enjoyment out of me. But I suddenly realized that I was putting all of my energy into my job and excluding everything else around me, and I decided that I didn't like that, that I wanted to experience a broader spectrum of life than just my work activities. I think the change mostly took place after I left the space program. My life took quite a turnabout after I came back from the moon.

AL GOLDSTEIN

I'm hardworking but more chaotic than the usual. I can work twenty hours in a row. That's the best way. I was in the hospital, and I'm really behind. That big pile on my desk is all pressing stuff. I'm still healing from my operation, and when I left the hospital I came back to the office too soon and the doctor said, "You better get the hell out of New York because it's not good for you, you've had major surgery." So I went up to my house in the country where I was on the phone ten times a day, but at least I couldn't get lost in heavy conferences. And I've learned with *Screw* to delegate. When I delegate, it never comes out the way I want it to, but it frees me to enjoy life and also to have other enterprises.

I probably work about sixty hours a week. I used to work about ninety. I'm learning to enjoy myself. I tell my wife that for somebody in my financial bracket who's running a publishing operation, I'm one of the few people who takes off his weekends. Saturdays and Sundays we go to the country. I feel that because of my age, I really want to know my wife. I really want to know my son. So going upstate for me is a forced kind of relaxation. My big decisions there are when will I go to the general store four miles away for the *New York Times.* I really slow down tremendously and it's great 'cause I can come here Monday and function again.

I used to be in the office from eight-thirty in the morning till around ten at night. Now it's generally from ten until around seven, five days a week. And of course I'm constantly clipping articles, etc. The mind's always working. This is where I think hours get to be difficult. If you can actualize something from idea to reality, that's a tremendous incentive to keep at it, very positive reinforcement. And I can make things happen. I can make three phone calls and things will happen, so I'm always on the phone. I have a phone in my car. I have a radio-controlled phone away from the house. I have a phone in my attaché case. I have beepers. Being in touch is so important to me. I want to know everything that's happening if it's a problem. If it's good, I don't want to know, but if it's a problem, I have to tend to it.

I would say I probably don't work as hard as I think I should, but that's maybe because of analysis. I'm trying to be good to the other parts of myself that are not entwined with dollars and cents. And also I feel that after seven years at *Screw* and nine arrests and this federal indictment coming down on me, I want to get some immediate nonmonetary pleasure out of life. Maybe analysis is changing the drive. Maybe I feel I'm nice enough as a person that I can start enjoying some of the fruits of my success. I'm not sure.

MILTON H. GREENE

Work for me is a habit, it's conditioning. It's not a matter of discipline. If you want to do something you just do it, and if you don't want to do it you find a thousand and one reasons why you shouldn't. There are certain pictures in the back of my head that I want very much to do whether I sell them or not. Certain commercial jobs I'll do because they're interesting and exciting. Other jobs I won't take because I feel they're not for me. I'm trying to earn a living, that's all.

And believe me, when I do a bad job it hurts. I'm my own worst critic, which is also not the best thing. So I feel the need to keep working at what I'm doing to improve more. I've forgotten so much that I knew when I was younger and just starting out. I didn't actually forget it 'cause when I need it I can pull it out of the back of my brain, but I'm not working with it all the time. I was brought up in an old-fashioned photographer's way: an eight-by-ten camera, making your own color prints, going into all the changes. Today, if you have an eye for photography you could get a camera, hire a technician and shoot. It's not exactly the same. It may even be better that way, though I think it's good to know what you know technically so you can apply it and get the right result.

I originally majored in art and when I went into photography

I went into it as an art, not as a commercial venture, but I found myself into it so deeply that before I knew it I was in business. When I was assistant to Louise Dahl Wolfe, who was one of the top fashion photographers at *Harper's Bazaar* in the 1940s, we used to discuss it. She'd say, "It's a business," and I'd say, "No, that's not the way I look at it. For you it's a business, for me it isn't." Well, I got so involved in business that everyone started saying, "Milton has a business head, he's a good businessman." But I'm not a businessman, I'm serious. The only business sense I may have, which is not that good, is from the experience of making mistakes, that's all. Or from allowing the people that represent me to make the mistakes for me. They can't be blamed. You blame yourself. You blame yourself for all the faults and you take very little credit for your success because other people allowed you to become successful.

I used to have an accountant and leave everything to him, but you can't do that. You've got to take time out. If you have a business you're responsible for everybody who works for you, you're responsible for the lease, you're responsible for everything you do. Everything has to be looked into or else you'll get a bad reputation. So after I get through work I have to sit down and check through the books and everything else. My head doesn't want to, but I have to do it. When things were swingin' you could overlook a lot because so many things were coming in. I'm not talking about waste 'cause I'm not cut out that way. If I get a job for X dollars, I always try to bring it in on budget. But you could spend another couple of hundred here and there and try a little this or that. But now there are times when you don't get jobs, or jobs are canceled on you and you're stuck.

Photography has changed. It's not as big as it used to be for photographers like myself because magazines have closed, agencies don't advertise that much, it's gone into television, all sorts of different things. But at the same time, more than ever we live in a visual world, and circumstances and conditions push you towards another area, which is photography as an art form. People are buying photographs now and putting them on their walls. So the cycle has come back to what I originally started to do and maybe it will end up that way. At least I'll have enjoyed it.

MARIO ANDRETTI

There's always a down side to everything, but then you look at the bright part of it, and I feel, how many people today can say that they really enjoy their work? Very few. People ask me, they say, "Hey, what are your hobbies, what else do you like to do?" My hobby is my work. There's nothing wrong with hobbies, but airline pilots and people like that have all got these really strong hobbies only because they're bored to death with their jobs. Their work is not exciting enough. So they get that out of the way, those eighty hours a month, and then the rest has to be a hobby of some sort to occupy their minds and satisfy themselves. But I satisfy myself in my work, and the rest is just free play.

In the things that I want, you're damn right I'm self-disciplined. I'm that way in business too. Auto racing at the moment is my main line, but I also have other things going, and it's all the same discipline. If you're going to excel, there's no easy way. If things are going to be easy, you have to *make* them become easy. At least that's the way it's always been with me. I've just never been handed things. Yeah, I enjoy it. There's a certain incentive that goes with it. I enjoy the challenge of it all. There's nothing like that wholesome feeling of accomplishment somewhere inside. Nobody has to pat you on the back. You just *know*. And you walk proud and you have a certain amount of confidence. You say, "I know what I'm doing even if they may not think so." Just to know what's going on, to know what makes things tick . . .

On the other hand, I feel I'm my own worst critic, like most people feel about themselves. And many times you feel, dammit, I know I can do better than that, so why am I dropping the ball? And you start worrying about it. But then you look around and you see how many people are really screwing up and how very few you'd like to associate with because they're really on the ball. And you feel, well, I'm not so bad off. You know what I mean? All you have to do is look around. Like you can watch people work, just the way they go about a certain plan or the kind of methods they use, you can usually evaluate whether they're really heads-up or just don't know what the hell they're doing. Driving or anything else—whatever it is.

I feel that this world is very competitive in every sense. You've got the same competition I do because you've got a lot of damn good people who can do the job that you're doing quite well. Now for you to excel, you've got to be just a little bit better. So that's your competition right there. Sure, I'm doing something different, but basically, you know, it's the same thing. We all have the same basic wars. That's the way I see it, anyway.

I think competition is the only thing that really motivates you. I think that's all of it, right there. Accepting the challenge, that's where the real satisfaction comes in, in my opinion. Meeting it. Overcoming it. And then if you have conquered that part, let's go on to the next. That means that you're progressing. You look back every year at your life and you ask, what the hell have I done this year? Am I better off than I was last year? Did I make a step forward, step backwards or what? And as long as you can feel that you've inched ahead, you know, even just a little bit, well, then you've got to feel good.

ALICE COOPER

I'm real competitive in everything. I always was. When I was a kid I was a miler, you know, a cross-country runner and a track runner. I swear, I used to train by running eight miles every night. I loved competing. I couldn't stand the idea of anybody being in front of me. I still hold the state record in Arizona for the twenty-four-mile marathon. I broke my nose when I came across the finish line and passed out, but I refused to let anybody beat me in that.

I never doubted that Alice Cooper was going to make it, just because of the fact that I had a drive that said nobody's going to stop this. I was very confident. I think the only people who can ever succeed are those who have confidence in what they're doing. It's like hitting a golf ball. You step up to a golf ball and if you don't have confidence so you can hit your five iron, you're never going to hit it. You're not going to hit it by accident. It's the same way in business. A lot of the Alice character evolved out of pure frustration. Alice is kind of a brat, you know. He really doesn't answer to anybody. And that attitude developed out of people saying to me, "Hey, you haven't got a shot at making it. *You're* going to draw as many people as Crosby, Stills and Nash?" And I kept saying, "Yeah. Wait." Because I really believed that you give an audience something to watch and they're going to watch it.

I really believe in the Barnum and Bailey, Ziegfeld attitude. That's why my show is like this. I poured four hundred thousand dollars into the show because I refuse to go up there and just do something average. I want the audience to go back to school the next day and say, *"Jeeze!* You can't *believe* what I saw last night!" Yeah, I just love the idea of entertaining the audience. I'm getting paid, say, sixty thousand dollars a night, and if I were in the audience I'd like to see something for sixty thousand dollars.

F. LEE BAILEY

I'm usually motivated by somebody saying, "You can't do that." When anyone says, "You can't do that," if it's at all interesting, I suppose it's worth doing just to say I told you so. The Sam Sheppard case is a good example of that. It was the judgment of the legal profession, number one, that he was innocent and, number two, that there was nothing that could be done about it. He'd lost eleven appeals, and when I took the case a bunch of the older lawyers kept saying, "I hope you're being well paid because you can't possibly win." But I just stayed with it for five years when I was not being well paid at all until it was finally brought to a conclusion. The same with my helicopter company. When I bought it it was shut down and the scions of the industry said, "It can't be saved. You'll never get it back on its feet." So I spent an inordinate amount of time collecting good management and getting the product back together and now it's thriving. If they hadn't said that, I probably just would have let it lope along. Yeah, I suppose challenge interests me generically.

JOAN GANZ COONEY

I don't think I would want the challenge of trying to rescue a shoe factory that's in trouble, which someone else, who really thought he could, might love. But I love the challenge of starting a new project. There's nothing I'd rather do. I'm a born obstetrician, not a pediatrician. I really like delivering the baby. But I have a strong sense of what this organization ought to do, and many potential projects are brought to us that I don't think would fit into it, so I don't immediately rise to them just because they represent a challenge. I say, "That's not for us," even though I might see it as a real possibility for other people and might even help get it started elsewhere.

I try never to take up a challenge that I don't see a real possibility of succeeding at. If I think it's an idea whose time has not come, I'm not interested. I'm in the business of popular television. Even though we're experimental we're still using something that exists and is finite. A new project is so expensive that unless it has a real shot at attracting a large audience we have no right to be playing around in it, in my view. I would love to have an experimental studio where you could really fool around at low risk and low cost on half-inch tape just to try different experiments and then test them out on test audiences. But I don't believe in high risk once you know you're going over the air. That's why we do so much formative research here, where our researchers feed back information while we're still in production. No, I'm very success oriented, whatever that means. I want to see the achievement done right and well received, and I want to know I've got a shot at it before I undertake it. I guess it comes from wanting approval. It probably goes back to the childhood thing of wanting to succeed on that test.

BUDDY RICH

Challenge is the whole thing. That's the only reason it's worth doing what I do. The challenge is there every night. The challenge is there musically. The challenge is there to the audience. The challenge is there with the band. And the biggest challenge is against me. I meet that challenge every night and I love it. I love it because I can say, "Aha, I beat you, you son of a bitch!"

When I lose, that's a night when I don't want anybody in here in this dressing room. I don't want to talk to anybody because I'm in here calling myself every kind of dumb motherfucker you can think of. When I drop a stick or I hit the rims or I do something that's really childish, I come in here and I start talking to myself and I'm really mad and I don't want to see anybody. I don't want anybody else to tell me because I *know it.*

GEOFFREY HOLDER

I cried opening night at *The Wiz* when the Lion and Dorothy sang "Be a Lion" only because I identified with the Lion. I'm a Leo astrologically, and we always have to keep proving, proving that we are lions. We are basically cowards. When I get on stage I'm terrified, but through fear I make fear work for me. If I'm cornered, *look out,* I'm gonna either sink or swim. But I won't sink. I will swim. That's how I learned to swim in Barbados, somebody pushed me off a boat. It's the challenge, you know. The challenge. Challenge me, ask me to write a book, and I say, "Yes, I can." I'll never say, "Maybe, I don't know, I am not sure whether I can." I say yes, and then worry about it after.

I do worry, but, you see, we really do have all the answers in our subconscious minds. You've heard it all before but it's in that storage room, and you just have to clear that garbage out of the way and then you have it. Or you might meet a friend, that's why I love friends, and unconsciously they might answer or confirm something you already know. I love the risk of challenge. I get my kicks out of that, you know.

MILTON GLASER

I feel the need to stay interested in what I'm doing and to move towards resistances. It's always been an issue in my life. A lot of it is just overcoming the father, you know. But I had a kind of ideal context for accomplishment, which was a supportive mother—I really could do anything—and a resistant father to whom I'd have to prove it: "I want you to work in the tailor shop, so don't fool around with those stupid drawings." That's really an ideal situation in terms of psychic conditioning. I used the support of my mother to overcome my father, and my father became transformed into the establishment, the judgment of the world, the client, everything that resisted my own movement. But I always felt because of my mother that I could do it. I always felt strong enough to do it. So that metaphor is always part of me. As a consequence, I've always moved toward resistance in some way. I find nourishment in situations where I'm resisted because I just keep leaning on something until I finally get through it. I have a good friend who's absolutely the opposite, and it's very interesting spending time with him. He moves toward pleasure when something's tough for him. A West Coast guy. I say, "Oh, that's tough? We'll just stay here and keep pushing."

I find it energizing to meet something, be resisted and be forced to press harder. For instance, if I do something and present it and somebody says, "Naw, I don't like it, you're fulla shit, get outta here," instead of feeling that that represents a position of compromise or a stepping-down, one just has to be tougher and stronger. I have to make it better to overcome the standards. So my tendency is to try to use the energy in resistance to overcome resistance. And I've had a high degree of success with it. It's been paid out. I mean, there's little frustration around that. I've been encouraged by my own success in that so I have no apprehension about the notion to begin with.

The other thing is really understanding the no-win game, which I understand very well. There are some situations that have nothing to do with the quality of the job and there isn't any way to overcome by increasing the quality, and in those I disengage. I mean, I will not beat my head against a situation that is not possible. I think that is perhaps one of the attributes very common to success, just knowing when you can't succeed. Not that you ever know entirely, but there are some indications in every situation that there ain't no way, and you really have to understand that. And I have a good smell for that. But I must say that's a very subtle and beautiful perception because of its complexity, because you don't want to create risk-free situations. You don't want to anticipate what can and cannot be accomplished. So you don't really want to eliminate things out of hand so far as that struggle goes. I guess it's just a balance between understanding what can be and what cannot be, and how sensitive you are to that.

I may be more involved with resistance than I am with pleasure in some cases. I mean, maybe part of it is not taking what's in effect easily available and going towards a path that would be rewarding in another way. It may, in fact, exclude alternatives which also would be very rich.

DON KING

It's very difficult for a black man because he's not counted in the game, you understand? I recognize the things I would have done had I been white. That doesn't mean I'm supposed to feel sorry for myself. I don't deal with crutches and excuses, I only deal with results. So since I recognize that it's gonna be much more difficult for me to go through the door than it is for you, that means I must muster that much more energy and dedication than you. When you look at it dispassionately and realistically, this is what it is. I would never allow anyone to use me as the criterion to other blacks to say, "Lookit here, he made it, he did it." Bullshit, you understand? Circumstances and events really laid out a situation for me that isn't there for others. Systematically they're excluded.

They used to have us thinking that if we got a degree that your education would be a panacea, if you got some money you would be acceptable. But you find out that if you got the education and the money and the position that you're still just a nigger. You ain't gonna change, you dig, so you might just as well recognize from the beginning that I'm a nigger and I'm gonna deal with being a nigger. You understand? Now whatever comes, you know you're getting it as you're supposed to get it and you deal with it as such. And then the people that you're dealing with, you have relieved them greatly because now they don't have to play that foolish game with you. They can be honest with you. And it's a hell of a relief when someone knows he can look at you and say, "Goddammit, I don't like you and you understand my position and I understand yours, but let us mutually make some money together and I will dislike you all the way to my bank and you will dislike me all the way to your bank, but we both go to the bank." That's honest, man.

Nothing in the world gives me more gratification than turning a bigot around, just to get into a conversation with him and for me and him to do actions together to change some of that limited view. His view is so limited because it's a shade of ignorance. He's accepting clichés that are nonexistent in reality, but he's making them exist, you dig? What I want to do is add a little dubiousness, a little doubt to his assumption that a black man can't perform with proficiency and effectiveness. This is what I wanted to do and this is what I'm doing.

EILEEN FORD

I talk to women all day long, and they're easier to talk to than men because you're both sort of equal. When you are talking to men in business, they all think you're tough and mean if you disagree with them, and they wouldn't think that if it were another man. An art director said to me, "You have no heart!" and I burst right out laughing. I wouldn't do what he wanted, and he said, "You have *no heart!*" I couldn't help it but I broke out laughing, and he hung up on me. It wasn't a love affair. It was business. It had nothing to do with my heart one way or the other.

I'll tell you another thing: I have a friend who doesn't speak to me anymore and I just found out why yesterday. It's because he asked me for the phone number of his ex–girl friend, a client of mine, and I wouldn't give it to him. For me it was business, but he considered it friendship. Well, that's just too bad. I'm perfectly capable of dividing business and friendship. I wouldn't do it, that's all, and so the head of one of the major corporations in America doesn't speak to me.

I never worry whether people think I'm a good lady or a bad lady because I always know I'm doing the right thing. That's how single-minded I am. I work for my models, I don't work for anybody else, and if I have to do something for them that somebody else doesn't like, that doesn't concern me at all.

MARIO ANDRETTI

If you haven't really pushed yourself to the limit, even though guys say, "Hey, nice job," *bullshit,* you know damn well you haven't done your job. You can't be honest with yourself and feel good, you see. So that's the thing: You've just got to be able to satisfy yourself. There's a certain pride involved. It's the same thing when a driver reaches a certain age. I've seen some great champions retire in style. Others linger along and almost kill everything they accomplished only because they didn't know when to quit. A man should know inside when he's doing a job, and he should know when he's no longer really sparkling. And when he can no longer do that, then you might as well be honest with yourself because otherwise all you're going to do is live in misery, you see. When the time comes, I just hope the hell I'm man enough to say to myself, "Hey, it's not the way you used to be. Better hang it up." It all goes back to really being honest with yourself and knowing whether you're doing the job or not.

MILTON GLASER

I've always understood the difference between external and internal perceptions of success, and I've never felt that people's judgment about me is what I cared about. I never care what people say about my work. I never believe anybody's judgment about what I do or use it as a criterion for my own self-perception. I mean, I like the fact that my work is acceptable, but I've never felt that people have the capacity to tell meaningful from nonmeaningful parts of it. So if somebody says, "That's a marvelous thing," it doesn't really mean anything to me unless I internally understand where it succeeds and where it fails. I've always had my own judgment about the nature of my success. I suppose a very important part of the success issue is how it's

internalized. For a part of my work I feel I deserve to be successful. For other parts I don't. And I really can separate them, I
think, clearly.

Is it Rilke who said that fame is the sum total of all the misunderstandings that surround a person's work? There's a tremendous amount of misunderstanding of everybody's work in the
world, and part of it has to do with its usefulness and its nonuse-
fulness. I have, I think, a very objective sense of the value of my
own work. I don't elevate it beyond its true value to the world
or to myself. It very easily could have happened that I produced
exactly the same work and remained totally invisible. The fame
itself is an accident of circumstance. The peculiar visibility that
I have right now comes from being at the right existential position at the right moment. You know how that happens. But that
visibility neither enhances nor reduces the quality of the work
itself. It's essentially an irrelevance. I would say that it's always
been more important to me to feel that I'm getting through to
the people who are my peers, those who have some more objective sense of the criteria for my work, than to have a broad
acceptance or a high visibility.

I was at a commencement recently at the Philadelphia College
of Art. They gave me an honorary doctorate, and I said, "You
know, I'm deeply honored to get this, but I have to admit something to you. At the same time, internally, I really resent the idea
that anybody, including you people, have the right to judge the
quality of my work." Because suppose they decided not to like
it? It would have meant that I was putting myself in their hands
basically. I was saying, "Fuck you, I don't want to be in your
hands," right? I don't want to relinquish my own autonomy to
someone else and say, "Approve me."

REX REED

When I think I've done a really first-rate piece of work it's
usually reflected in the opinion of others. I usually get a lot of
compliments on the pieces I think are very good. But sometimes
I'll do a newspaper piece and I'll think it's better than most
newspaper pieces and you don't hear a word from anyone. And

then you'll do something that it took you an hour to write and people will say, "Oh, what a terrific piece. I really enjoyed that piece on Sunday." And you think, "Oh, I'm not even going to say anything. Don't complain, don't explain." But it wasn't very good and I know it. I really don't rely too much on the opinions of other people. I know when I'm good, and I know when I'm bad.

BUDDY RICH

I'm hardly ever satisfied with what I play. I've had nights when I just thought I was seven different kinds of motherfucker, man, I thought I was so good. And those nights when I think I'm really that good, they are not the nights necessarily when the audience agrees. But I've had other nights when I thought I played bull-shit and I've had standing ovations, and I come into the dressing room and I say to whoever may be around, "Can you *believe* that?" When somebody says to me, "Gee, you really sounded great tonight, Buddy," if I don't think I sounded great I'll say it: "No, man, that wasn't great, it wasn't even fair." But there are other nights when I'll beat you to it. I'll say, "Man, I played *my ass* off tonight." Because I listen to what I play, you see.

I don't think I've really met my highest standards yet. I still shoot for something. I'm never satisfied. I want to keep making it better. That's the whole challenge of playing, the idea that what you did last night was really good but tonight it should be a hell of a lot better. But then there are the nights when you had difficulties at home or with the cabdriver or some drunk and you come in and that blows the whole thing for you. But I can't really count that as being a bad night. That's just circumstances that make you play bad. Once you've accomplished a certain standard for yourself, I don't think you ever play bad, you never do anything really bad. Just because Ali got knocked down one time does not mean he's lost his ability to fight. He had a bad night, that's all. If you have a succession of bad nights, you're in trouble. But, you know, if you only get knocked down once, that's pretty cool.

HALSTON

I never like anything that's finished. I like it until it's finished, and then I always think it can be done better. I think there are certain things that one likes maybe more than others. But generally speaking, once the exercise is completed, I would have done it ten other ways if I had the time. It's really funny. You sort of want to change it, make it grow more.

GEROLD FRANK

Nothing I've written is good enough. And everything I've written is better than I thought it would be. And everything I've written is very good. All three statements are true—I think. But I am full of doubts. I would still like to be a man who could paint in fiction, invent a complete world, give something to people that they could experience with absolute vividness. I read my own books marveling that I wrote them, at the same time realizing that there are such big leagues I aspire to be in but that I haven't written the fiction that goes there. I think I've done pretty well so far as it is possible within this straitjacket I've put myself into. Is there any more limiting straitjacket than that which makes you tell what you wish and feel in terms of somebody else's life because you fear that if you attribute it to yourself, if you take full responsibility for it, you may be punished? So what is it? I don't know the answer.

JOHN DIEBOLD

I'm never satisfied with anything I do. I think it's very bad to be satisfied. It's my job not to be satisfied. My own impression is that to a greater extent than one might realize the striving process is really the important part of life, much more, I think, than the actual achievement. One keeps changing one's sights. When you achieve something you want, you constantly set new sights, new objectives.

Risk, Failure and Security

F. LEE BAILEY

I suppose you can't separate risk from challenge because they usually go hand in hand. As an airman I'm a very conservative guy, having gone through the hot pilot stage and flown under a few bridges and come close a few times. I think I've done that as a practitioner too. But to the extent that risk is diminished very sharply by confidence, I don't perceive a lot of risk where other people do, so I'm apt to be in what others would view as a high-risk business.

EDGAR D. MITCHELL

I find that if other people have done it and it's well under control and well understood, I'm not particularly interested in it anymore. So yes, I'm very definitely responsive to challenge. But I'm not a daredevil. I won't do something just because somebody comes along and says, "I bet you can't do it." I'm only interested in challenges that make sense in my framework, that seem to fit into my goals, the direction I'm going, my way of thinking. The risk element to me is the by-product. Like with anybody else who's been out front in certain things, the risk does become part of your way of life and you do get a certain exhilaration out of it, but I don't go looking for it. I accept risk as part of the consequences of the fact that I like to be plowing new ground. I accept it as part of exploring the unknown. If you're out there and the answers are unknown, then you are going to make mistakes, and I accept that but I don't go looking for it. As a matter of fact, I will always do my very damnedest to eliminate as many risks as I possibly can. I'm not foolhardy. I like to assure myself of success, and risk simply means that you might not be successful, so I try to do everything in my power to make the risk minimal.

MARIO ANDRETTI

The risk is what makes it special. Naturally, I don't want to hurt a finger any more than you do, and I want to enjoy life today, tomorrow and the next day, but what makes it special is the calculated risk. To be able to take a risk and get away with it. You know, to do something that's daring and do it well, to feel that you've got things under control. The guy who claims to be a hotrodder just can't do it. That's what makes it worthwhile. But I'm not shooting into the unknown. I'm not jumping the canyon like Evel Knievel. You know, the one-shot deal. That's a type of risk that I myself couldn't appreciate. That's a different type of risk entirely because it's not calculated. Maybe it'll work, maybe it won't. Well, in my case, this can work. It's up to me. You see what I mean? It's up to me to set the limits, to say, "This is the edge right here. How close and for how long can you be right on that ragged edge without falling over?" That's the thing. That's the difference between winning and losing, first or second. How close can you stay to that edge for how long without messing up? That's the whole works.

GEORGE PLIMPTON

I admire artistic people who take risks. I have a friend, the author Peter Matthiesson, who takes risks in his writing. He says about writing about nature, which he does enormously well, "I can do it so easily. It's just like a carpenter building wood cabinets, I know how it's done." So he's just finished this novel called *Far Tortuga,* about turtle fishing in the South Atlantic. The story is straightforward, and one wonders why he doesn't use a wooden cabinet to house it, really. But he doesn't. He utilizes all sorts of devices, calligraphic spacings, the elimination of common fictional usages . . . taking risks to try something new. Which is absolutely admirable. Taking risks of that sort is to make absolutely no compromise with public taste. In my own case, it's not especially an issue. In the work that I do there's not much to be gained—either for the reader or my own esthetic consideration—by taking that course. As an editor I value and exult in it; as a writer I know better.

ALBERT ELLIS

I was one of the very first who got up in public and said very direct things in favor of premarital sex relations. And a little later I started to say four-letter words in public. I was a professional by the time I started to give those talks, a psychologist with a Ph.D., so I knew damn well that I was risking professional censure. Academic psychologists often criticize popular writings —and in those days if anyone popularized psychology without any four-letter words and without any sex, they'd still resent it. So I was taking a chance by doing popular writing in newspapers and magazines and by making public presentations over radio and TV. And in favor of premarital sex, no less! So I knew it was risky.

I was chief psychologist of the state of New Jersey in 1951 when my first book, *The Folklore of Sex,* was published. It was a liberal sex book, one of the most liberal up to that time. It examined all the mores and folkways of sex as outlined in the mass media, newspapers, magazines, novels, movies, songs, etc. It got a lot of opposition, and largely because of that I was asked to resign from my post. The head of the Department of Institutions and Agencies in New Jersey clearly thought that I was too liberal sexually. So they found excuses to try to get me out. Not wanting to work under such bigoted conditions, I resigned.

Well, I persevered in what I was doing because my goal, my own ideal, is to have liberation, not just sexually but in love and family relations, and in general. That's why I gave up my early radical political alliances, because I found out that most of the socialist and communist groups were dictatorial rather than democratic. So I went for liberation. And I will fight for a cause.

Being a sexual or general libertarian is not as nutty as it may at first seem. People who speak out against custom and tradition can do so sanely because they recognize that there are advantages as well as disadvantages to revolting and rebelling. Because you always get a minority, usually an enlightened minority, on your side. The same articles and speeches that aroused opposition also brought clients and referrals. Because there always exists a minority of psychologists—and psychologists are more liberal than average—who will go along with iconoclasm. So I hardly got one hundred percent disapproval.

We'll never know, but I suspect if all the personal advantages and disadvantages were ever weighed up, I garnered more disadvantages than advantages from my rebelliousness. Because if I had gone along like certain conservatives in my field, as a result of the large amount of research and writing I did, I would have been probably even better known and certainly much more "respectable." I have colleagues who are less creative and powerful contributors than I, but they are more respected. So I probably could have been a better and bigger leader in the field had I been willing to junk some of my liberal views. I would have lost something valuable, but I probably would have gained more accolades.

But it worked out. I did much better in private practice than I ever would have done if I had stayed with the state of New Jersey; so that was a success. And it wasn't that hard to be considered "controversial" or to be bad-mouthed by "respectable" psychologists, because my attitude is, "Fuck it! If I get opposition, I get opposition!" I never took the calumny personally. I never felt "hurt," but only disappointed, when my colleagues didn't support me. I just said, "Well, shit, this is the way they behave. Tough!" Most hardness or cynicism arises when you feel hurt, not when you feel opposed or frustrated. So I only got frustrated. And I never got terribly frustrated because I just kept plodding along.

After I quit the state of New Jersey I didn't know for a few months whether my private practice was going to build up; but as it happened I did very well, so that was okay. Before I knew that would happen, I applied for teaching jobs at Columbia, my own university, and other schools in New York, and I got solid refusals. My first book had already been published. I had lots of highly respectable articles in professional journals, most of them on nonsexual topics. I was already one of the best-known psychologists in the field. But I got no offers. And for a man of my established scientific reputation, I normally would have gotten them fairly easily. But I didn't feel hurt. I just felt opposed. So therefore it wasn't so hard. If you don't whine about opposition, you just go ahead with what you are determined to do.

My commitment was sufficiently strong not to worry about dissension and even at that time I fortunately didn't have much "ego." Ego, as I teach in rational-emotive therapy, is largely disturbance. Because ego means a self-rating. "I am a good person if they like me or I do well. And as soon as I don't do well and they dislike me, I fall back to shithood." At that time I just felt, "Hell, I *want* to do well, but I don't *have* to." So I didn't attach that much to my self-rating, my ego. Ironically, I had "ego strength" because, largely, I had no "ego." Most so-called successful people are screwballs of the worst sort because they do it for ego, to show how noble they are, to lord it over others, and to get into heaven. That's their real goal. They're trying to get somewhere on earth, but they're also trying to prove that they're holier than thou, better than the other humans—in fact, superhuman. So they have very strong success drives—but disturbed drives. I didn't have too much of that. I won't say that I didn't have any, but I had relatively little. I have practically none today, now that I've used so much RET on myself. But even then I had less "ego" than the average because I focused on working—on doing a problem well rather than on rating myself as noble and great for succeeding at it.

AL GOLDSTEIN

There's part of me that's still constantly testing. In terms of the libel actions against *Screw,* wherever the boundary is I will go two feet past it. No one knows what pornography is, but if someone gave me a definite, absolute definition and the district attorney said, "If you go beyond this, you're going to get busted," I probably would stick to it the first two issues. The third issue I'd be right on the boundary. The fourth issue I'd say, "Aw, what the fuck. Who are they to tell me this is wrong?" and I'd be over. I think that's self-destructive. I do not have the capability to be moderate. I overeat. I overfuck. I overwork. I will overrisk. I will take chances. It may be a death wish. I'm sure it's also a desire for failure. We've had the Mafia up here with guns. That's why we have bulletproof windows out there in the reception area. And there are times I've written some vicious things about people and actually had to walk around with a .38 strapped on my hip. I think that like a junkie the excitement makes me feel alive. There's one danger for me—that *Screw* may become so successful that I'll be so bored I'll sell it. One of the joys is the constant harangues and tensions we function under. But I think there is a part of me that would like to fail, that feels I don't deserve all this.

JOAN GANZ COONEY

I have no attraction to failure. I'm unequivocal on that point, and I'll bet you most successful people feel the same way. They have a neurotic drive to succeed. I mean, there is a neurosis there. Do I fear failure? Well, I'd say that the *Feeling Good* show the first time around was considered a failure, but it didn't bother me much nor did I fear it in advance. It never crossed my mind. My instant reaction was to try to correct it within a few shows. We did pull it off the air and I think returned it to air reasonably successfully. But I think to try something new and fail at it isn't something to fear. I mean, I recognize that I will have some successes and some failures and that's part of the game. I don't want too many failures because it would affect other things in the company. But the reason is not personal. I don't have any ego problems with it. In fact, I wish I had more freedom to fail for the sake of television itself.

WILLIAM GAINES

Every time you put out an issue and determine how many copies you're going to print, you're taking a chance. Sometimes you win and sometimes you lose. I generally am on the conservative side. What I tried to do with *Mad* was build slowly. Sometimes it raced away even faster than I would have wanted it to. I know my own limitations, and as a consequence I have built the kind of business in which I can keep track of everything. I have a very, very tiny business here. It is not in my nature to be able to take care of a large, sprawling business where I have to delegate authority to many people. I just can't work that way. I deliberately keep it very small so I know exactly what's going on down to, you know, how many envelopes we've got. This is not the proper way to run a business but it's my way and it's the only way I can, so I do it. It works for me.

As a result, I have been very cautious, and I've tried to build the business slowly but solidly so that it isn't a flash in the pan. For example, I didn't want a *Ballyhoo. Ballyhoo* magazine was the perfect example of the other way to do it. It came upon the scene and rose like a rocket. It achieved a tremendous circulation within a year. Within two more years, I think, it was dead or practically dead. And I wanted just the opposite. I wanted a slow, solid growth for *Mad* and for the things associated with it. Because just instinctively, rightly or wrongly, I feel that when you grow slowly, you can grow securely, and if you grow too quickly, you can topple. We've had about seventy imitators. At the moment there are only about three or four left.

MIKE WALLACE

The single biggest example of risk-taking in my own professional life—and I suppose to some degree in my own personal life as well—was about thirteen years ago. That was at a time when I had fallen back into the trap of doing too many various things. I had done a talk show called *PM East.* I was doing *Biography,* the television series about the lives of the famous. A piece here, a piece there. And I determined that I had about enough money saved to take a year off. I quit everything. I was forty-five years old. I quit everything, and wrote to Dick Salant over here at CBS, Bill McAndrew at NBC and Jim Hagerty at ABC and said, "I want to go back to work at a network. I want to work exclusively in news. Salary is no object. I've come to a certain time in my life when I want to do what I want to do, and if you have an opening please talk to me about it." And months went by, and I wasn't getting any calls. Finally, a local station out in California offered me a job anchoring the seven and eleven o'clock news out there. I went out and we negotiated a contract and I asked for three days to think about it before I made a final decision. I came back to New York, and Dick Salant had heard about my going out there and said, "If you're that serious and if you'll take what amounts to about a two-thirds cut from your last salary, I think we can find a job for you here at CBS." And of course I grabbed it. That was in 1963. And it was a sensible decision. It had been a wise investment to make. I had been out of work for four or five months, but it had been an investment in trying to find myself.

ROCKY AOKI

We spend close to a million dollars per unit to open up a restaurant, and I'm asked, "Why don't you spend three hundred thousand dollars like Howard Johnson?" I don't want to be Howard Johnson. I want to be Benihana. Every Benihana you go to has a different atmosphere, yet they all have the same concept, the same food, the same service. People are sometimes tired of eating the same food, but the atmosphere sells the food. So Benihana Las Vegas they go to, and Benihana Los Angeles, Benihana Boston, Benihana Miami. They all have different atmospheres, different exteriors.

For me to spend a million dollars I know I have to get back a million dollars in a couple of years. It seems risky. So I asked myself, "Rocky, why don't you spend three hundred thousand dollars? You can fake it. You can have plastic beams or fiberglass beams." But I don't like those fakes. I want the real stuff. So a lot of competition came in the last ten years, but we still use the same big beams and the customers are still interested in the atmosphere because we spend money. So we can survive longer. So it's not really risk. It's more like foresight, investment.

MARTIN SCORSESE

Everything in filmmaking is a risk. That's all we're doing. I don't like it, actually, but sometimes it's fun. People said that *Mean Streets* was directed with so much energy, but the energy was because we were so crazy from the risk of doing the picture under those financial circumstances that we didn't have time to look back. It was all "We gotta get the shot! Let's get the shot!" The same thing with *Who's That Knocking on My Door?*, which was the first part of *Mean Streets*, the same characters only eight years younger. *Taxi Driver* is probably one of the biggest risks I've undertaken. It's a question about its commerciality. The film was made to get certain things off our chests. We all did it for certain deals and for certain prices to keep the budget as low as possible, so we all knew what we were getting into, even the studio. We were quite honest about making it for our reasons, but, still, it's a big risk for me, y'know? So we deal with it, what else can we do? In this business everything is risky.

I'm gonna do a new musical with Liza Minnelli and Bobby DeNiro, and everybody thinks it's not a risk. Well, you never can tell. There's no such thing as a sure thing. Remember when they did *Star*? That was not supposed to be a risk. But I intend to keep within the budget and keep it straight, keep moving forward, be honest about it and keep moving. It's better than being stuck making pictures you don't want to make.

But you can feel miserable sometimes. The censorship laws change every minute, and I've had terrible problems with the censors on *Taxi Driver*. I've fought with them on it, but their laws have changed. Not their laws but their whims—whatever, their feelings have changed. But it's like my friend Brian Da Palma says. When he sees me really miserable, when we're hanging out with our eyes propped open watching late films on television or something and can't go to sleep because we know we're going to have to wake up and go through the same shit the next morning, he always looks at me and smiles and says, "Well, it's what we always wanted, kid. This is the rest of our lives." And I say, "You're right, Brian. Thank you very much. That's it. This is the rest of our lives. It's what we always wanted."

DON KING

An old hustler told me, "Anything that's undertaken without risk will never be undertaken." You will always be standing on dead center, and dead center means retrogression so you're going backwards. Robert Kennedy, whom I greatly admired, said that only those who dare to fail greatly can achieve greatly. Shakespeare says that some men are born great, others achieve greatness and others have greatness thrust upon them. So when you look at them all, you just have to get out there and really roll with it.

When I was incarcerated in 1970 it was a real moment of truth for me. You know, you have to make a reassessment, a reevaluation of your own life and what you've been doing with it. You have to be able to really deal with yourself. I find that the most important thing. To thine own self one must be true. You can jive some of the people some of the time but you can't jive all the people all the time, you dig? And the thing with me is I can't afford to jive myself at no time. I must recognize the stark reality of whatever the situation is and speak to the issues. So I try to be pragmatic and realistic in anything that I do. What I'm selling may be some type of pie in the sky at that particular time, but within me I know that I must deliver this. So once I get out there and it's accepted, then I have to go and make it happen. When it happens, it's no longer pie in the sky. Then it's a reality. So I believe in the transformation of my dreams. I feel that everything begins with thought. If you can think it out and work very hard on this concept, you can then visualize it, and from the visualization you can then transform it into something in reality, something tangible that you can feel.

Sometimes I get so locked in that I just have to perform. I don't have no choice, even if it means working eighteen or twenty hours a day until you just fall out from sheer exhaustion. You have so many people so correlated into your life that you must do your job. I get locked in sometimes by shooting off my mouth, so it's a price to pay. It's all right when you can say that I'm good and I can perform, and you do perform. But when you say this and don't perform, then you're in trouble. So it keeps me trying to perform at all times.

ELIZABETH ASHLEY

I can never sign my name on a piece of paper saying I'll deliver artistry. I don't know, that's an accident. That's like hitting a home run. I can sign my name on a piece of paper saying that I will deliver labor of such high quality that it will be professionalism to the highest degree that I know. I will give you my word that I'll deliver that. I'm a professional. If I can't get it up, I can fake it. The thrill you get sitting out there may not be as high as the people on Thursday night got, but you're not going to know the difference.

It's like surfing. Sometimes you get the perfect wave, but you still have to know how to ride them even when they're choppy. And fear is the Devil and my demon is in my work. If I get insecure when I go to do my job, if I get afraid, then I'll get tight and play safe, and I hate that. The man isn't paying ten dollars to have something you can mail out in a brown manila envelope that he can sit home and read. He's paying for an emotional event, and I've got to give that to him. He needs to sit in that chair and have me risk for him. That's the deal that's negotiated between him and me, karmically, when he sits down. He is the dancee, I am the dancer. I owe him. And if I do my job well, he could never afford what it would cost if you wanted to measure it out. You always give more than anybody can pay for. That's what we do. That's what we're supposed to do. That's what they pay us money to do.

When I go out on stage, if I'm working well, I have absolutely no idea what will happen. And I really don't like performers who come on stage with a plan. A plan somehow has got to be bullshit. What can I tell you? Freedom only comes from discipline. Art only comes from professionalism. It's like when Jimi Hendrix was running riffs, he didn't make a plan, he wasn't playing a chart. Do you know that I mean? I can read the music but I don't want to play the chart. But on the other hand, if I don't get the perfect wave it doesn't mean I'm gonna pack up my tap shoes and go home either. There are a lot of ways to skin a pig and performers have to know every single one of them. I've done shows when my throat was shot, when I was tired, when technically all kinds of things were going wrong. You know, the magician reaches into the hat to pull out the rabbit and he's forgotten to put it there in the first place. That's a hard trick to pull off, but you've got to find some way around it. Because performing is on the line. There's no rewrite for that night. The people are really out there. That's it.

And the audience is never wrong. There's no such thing as an audience that's wrong. You hear old-time actors who will come out and say, "How are they tonight?" What do you mean, how are *they*? How are *you*? They're as good as you are, that's just about how good they are. What you feel, they feel.

MILTON H. GREENE

There's risk every day I wake up and go to work. When I took that shot of Elizabeth Taylor at the Hermitage in Leningrad, do you think I knew what I was getting? My wife felt confident. Everyone else felt confident. Elizabeth's children said, "We all want one of those." But in the back of my head I said, "I hope I got it." I wasn't sure.

People magazine wanted to do a picture of Elizabeth Taylor while she was working in Russia doing the film of *The Blue Bird,* and they couldn't get her okay. Everyone else was turned down, so they asked me if I could get her. I asked and she agreed so I went over there, but then everything started to go wrong. First I had problems with the Russians. I wanted to shoot her sitting on the throne in the Hermitage, and the curator of the museum agreed. He couldn't have been nicer. I got a letter from him and everything. But then he left for America, and while I had Elizabeth waiting at the hotel I had to fight with his assistants for an hour and a half because they were afraid to let me do it. You know, nobody sits on that throne. So I said, "Well, can she *stand* by it? Nobody will touch it." I figured, take the risk, when she comes it'll be different. And when she came it was different. But in the meantime I started running into all kinds of technical difficulties with my equipment. I went over with three thousand dollars' worth of special lights that I had tested, but now as I was setting up they didn't work.

You know, if you play the piano, after a while you don't look at the keys anymore. I know my camera and I know my lights, but if the technical things fail me when I need them, then I have a problem. And that's what happened. I was going to have to take the shot with a single little cockamamy light, the kind you use at a wedding, and this one room in the Hermitage is the length of a whole house and it's dark. That light doesn't travel that far. There's just a little move on the strobe meter, so I had to push the film. It wasn't the film I was going to use, but I always bring high-speed color film with me in case I'm stuck. And I always bring this old little unit that is reliable. The new unit I brought was five times as powerful and would have given me the beautiful quality I wanted, but I couldn't use it with this high-speed film.

So I'm sweating and trying to set up and Elizabeth finally comes in with the hair and the makeup and the costume and everything, and she sits against the window watching me and she's saying, "Miltie, you're blowing it. Miltie, you're blowing it." Meanwhile I'm thinking the lights aren't working and I don't know if that wedding light is going to give me what I need. I'm gonna have to do an eight-second exposure and what if she moves? If I don't get it, I just blew it. It's me that's wrong no matter what happens. There are no excuses, okay? So I walk over to her and she says, "How long will you be?" She's biting her teeth and she's very upset. And her boy friend was with her and now they're getting ideas of their own from things I've been talking about. He's a used-car salesman, a nice guy but he just started photography. And I'm thinking and I turn around and I say, "Okay, let's go." She sits down. I said, "Here, hold the meter." I'm upset too, but I'm not going to blow it. So she holds the meter and I flash it off. I leave everything set up so it looks like everything's going and I just put this little wedding light under the umbrella, because if they see everything taken away the whole attitude would be different. I said to myself, "Okay, I'll push it a stop and a half, whatever. I know I'm not going to get the best color, but I'm gonna get a picture and that's what we have to get now."

At the beginning you could see the lack of rapport between us. I said, "Elizabeth, cool. Hey, it's gonna show up." I said, "You and I will straighten this out later, not now. Between you and the camera it's another story now, okay?" I'll show you pictures where she's just beautiful, and I'll show you some where she looks great. I made some copies, retouched them, sent them to her, and she said, "They're beautiful!" and that was it. One of the last of the superstars.

REVEREND IKE

There was a great risk when I left the more traditional church to start my own ministry, but I didn't calculate the cost because I'm the type of person who does what he believes in. I do what I feel is right. I do what I feel is good. And if I feel that the doctrines of the church are no longer valid, which I did at some point, I have to be honest with myself. I can't just go out there and preach to the people simply because they have been programed for centuries into this type of thing, and just go along and make good money out of the system and be comfortable and know better. And I daresay a lot of preachers are doing that. As a matter of fact, I know they are because ministers come to me privately and say, "We know you're right. But we can't say what you're saying. We wish we could." It would surprise people to know the people who say that to me, but, you know, I keep all of this in confidence so anybody can speak to me. But, as I say, I didn't analyze that change too much. I'm an evolving kind of person, and the more light I see, the more light I walk in.

MIKE WALLACE

I'm going through a bit of a struggle at this moment, trying to figure out where I want to spend the rest of my professional career. Doing what? But barring that—and I'm sure I'll get that straightened out—I cannot say there have been very many frustrations in my career. Really, it's been a process of learning, learning all the way. And still. This is not to say that it hasn't been painful and insecure and worrisome at times, but the obstacles have been useful ones and I suppose each one of them overcome forges a new understanding.

GEOFFREY HOLDER

My whole thing is that there is no such thing as defeat. There's no such thing as failure. There's no such thing as mistakes. I make them work for me. I'll use them for another job. And I don't envy anyone for getting ahead of me, because it's their turn, the moon is in the right place for them.

ALICE COOPER

You learn from all your mistakes, so you get up there and make as many as possible so you can learn faster. I'll look out at the audience and say, "I'm gonna try something tonight, I'm gonna do a number on them, maybe some sort of reaction thing just to see how they would respond to me maybe covering everybody in feathers," and then I'll ask myself, "Okay, did that work or didn't it work?" And that's the only way you learn. You have to try it. 'Cause you could sit back in rehearsal and say, I *know* this is going to make it, and you could have worked on it for months, but when you take it on stage it might just be a total bomb. You can spend thirty thousand dollars on a prop like a guillotine or that whole thing we were using with the hanging in the old show, and it's really a gamble, because you spent all that money and what if they didn't like it? On the other hand, you might accidentally do something that completely destroys the audience. And it's funny, a lot of your mistakes on stage end up being the best things that happen.

MILTON GLASER

When I started to design *New York* magazine about eight years ago I had a profound misunderstanding of the problem. It was a very complicated problem, I must say: trying to maintain the success of the old format in the *New York Herald Tribune* while making a transition to a new one, going from large format, dull paper to small format, slick paper and still hold on to a lot of the principles, the modes of presentation. But at any rate, the first two years were a disaster for me. Every week was like a visible failure. I was making a fool of myself. Everybody was telling me how terrible it was, how badly laid out, badly conceived. For two years it was a source of enormous pain because I literally didn't understand what the hell I was doing.

I couldn't get past the success of the previous form, and there was no way to invent a new one. I just couldn't put it together. Now I wasn't alone in this, in the sense that the magazine itself had the same problems editorially. It was a reflection of the same confusion that was expressing itself graphically as well. But nevertheless I was making an ass of myself in public every single week. If *New York* had gone out of business at the end of two years I would have considered my performance absolutely disastrous, humiliating and highly visible. But it didn't, and I finally began to understand what I was doing.

JERRY DELLA FEMINA

There were accounts I wanted to get that I didn't get. This business when we first started looked like it wasn't going to make it. But they weren't really major disappointments. A major disappointment is when you stop and you know you're not going on. There haven't been any of those. It's been remarkably smooth. Somebody said, a Giant baseball player in 1928 or '29, I think his name was Russ Youngs, "Gee, it's great to be young and a New York Giant." He was twenty-one years old. He had just come up to play for John McGraw. "It's great to be young and a New York Giant." Well, it's great to be young and in advertising—and going downhill.

MARIO ANDRETTI

As time goes by and the older you get, the harder it is to accept losing. Believe me. Because I used to feel, okay, something broke. I could have won this big race, but what the hell, I've got plenty of time, I'll win the next one. I just didn't think about it so much. Now all of a sudden I'm beginning to think, Christ, every one that I lose I'll never recapture again. It's lost, it's lost forever, even though I might win the one next week. And that's really got to possess you, I'll tell you. I used to be able to shrug it off a little better, which you've really got to do. I don't want to live in misery. But I must be honest and say that it's been bugging me more than it's ever done in my life. Like just this past weekend, in this 5000 Series, here I am sucking hind tit when I had led every race, set records, and could have won every race if the damn chariot would have just stayed together. I used to say to Jim McGee, my mechanic, "It'll take us to Wednesday to get over this one." Now it's taking me till Thursday, Thursday night.

ROCKY AOKI

I'm always looking for a miracle. I want to go in ten directions at the same time. I feel I'm too slow. The institution management people say we have the biggest profits in the restaurant business, so we could go all over. But somehow to me it's taking too long. Me, I want to just move . . . without making any mistakes. So I'm starting Orient Express restaurants for fast food. I started *Genesis* magazine. I thought PLAYBOY and *Penthouse* are doing fantastic business, why not somebody else? Why not me? The same with speedboat racing. I'm doing pretty good. I've won two of my first five races and came in second once.

But I've had failure too. I don't like to accumulate money, I want to invest it, so I opened up a place called Club Genesis in New York. We had a new concept: a country club in the middle of New York City with a discotheque, a restaurant, steambath, sauna, exercise rooms, health club, whirlpool treatments, tennis courts. I rented a whole building plus a garage roof for the three outdoor tennis courts. I thought I had a fantastic idea. I could have opened up so many of them in other cities. We failed. I lost a bundle of my own money. That was two years ago. The idea still makes sense. But if an idea is too advanced, it's no good. I cannot go two steps ahead. Only one step ahead, I finally realized.

JOHN DIEBOLD

My main failures have been when I've delegated too much too fast. My tendency is to delegate tremendously, and the problem is that that's very difficult in brand-new things until you get patterns and proper controls established. It's essential to delegate in large going organizations to get them to operate efficiently, but you're dealing there with fairly well-structured situations. But almost everything I've done has been in completely new areas, and I've too much underestimated their uniqueness, the time required by managers to really develop in those fields before you can delegate and walk away.

ALEXIS LICHINE

I started off Alexis Lichine & Company way in the late Forties, with twenty-eight thousand dollars. Had I had enough money at that time I would have been able to build up a much larger company, even though it did become the number-one fine wine exporter of France. I was always underfinanced. I could have bought other châteaux in Bordeaux because I saw the trend coming. Why? Because I was creating the trend. I remember that for two hundred fifty thousand dollars I could have lined up all the great domaines of Burgundy. I tried to sell this to various people. No one would budge. People would take a fling of two thousand, five thousand, ten thousand dollars maximum, but I could never raise big money.

My greatest disappointment was that what I was doing in those days was not understood and that it was only much later on, some four or five years ago, that the phone started ringing endlessly from morning to night and people came to me practically with moneybags in their hands. All of a sudden they had discovered wine and in their enthusiasm went into a wild euphoria. Speculators got into the act, and people started to form syndicates here and in California. They thought there was a shortage of wine, and all kinds of money was being offered. Two million dollars, three million dollars, four million dollars. But by then it was too late. The prices had become vastly inflated. And I had already sold my wine company and my hands were tied by certain noncompete clauses. I had sold my company in 1965 because I couldn't get French banks to finance me, I couldn't get American banks to finance me, I couldn't get anybody to finance me. It was coming my way, but my cash flow position was too static.

I guess I was also ready for a respite. I used to work days, nights, weekends. I didn't take holidays or anything else. So when I saw the possibility of being able to get a breather, I sold out.

EDGAR D. MITCHELL

My definition of success is the accomplishment of what you set out to accomplish, whatever it is. Now there are many ways in which I do not feel successful. If I look back over the things I've done I could say, "Well, there's a pretty neat track record there," but I find that in many instances my expectations were much greater than what was actually accomplished and therefore I don't feel as much of a success as I might. Yes, I'm my own worst critic. I set very high and difficult standards for myself. This is, of course, really an ego thing, an internal security system that forces you to drive to meet your own imaging of success. I guess to a certain extent it's healthy because that's what provides your motivation, but if you get too rigid about it, it can become a source of enormous internal frustration. I've had to recognize in my life that it's all right for the reach to exceed the grasp but if it's too much it becomes detrimental and you just can't cope with it.

I started this Noetics Institute out in California that is funding research in the consciousness and futures areas. By most standards it's doing very well, going great guns, but I expected it to be more successful in a shorter period of time, so I have some ambivalent feelings about its success. But it's taught me some significant lessons. I've had to become fully cognizant in the last few years of the phenomenon I call "getting the carrot too far in front of the donkey," and I've had to learn to pull my carrots way back. After twenty-five years of dealing with research and development with the government and the military, it was a shock to learn how plodding and conservative the business community really is. They're just not open to new ideas at all, so you can only give them the tiniest extensions of ideas that are already accepted as solid and proven. Instead of going for grandiose long-range plans, you only reveal the first tiny steps of it, and you only give them those one at a time.

But I cope with frustration and disappointment pretty well, and these days I am probably coping with them even better. I used to internalize them, just go through periods of despair and rejection and then get angry and determined and go charging off again. I've learned to roll with all that a lot better, to express my feelings at the time, talk it out, recognize that most of the time it's not a personal affront. I say to myself, you can't control everybody else's inputs into this thing, they are doing things for reasons of their own that are beyond your immediate control. Rationalizing it this way, I then continue to persevere and go on. I guess I consider perseverance ninety percent of the formula for success.

ALBERT ELLIS

I frequently say to my clients, "I fail more than you do because I try many more things, and I am frustrated more than you are because I keep trying hard tasks." For example, maybe twenty times people have come to me with big TV ideas which would have promulgated my work greatly, and every one of them fell through. Some stupid vice-president killed them. Sometimes for good reasons, of course—the idea just wasn't practical—but sometimes they were against my sexual liberalism or against my radical views on psychotherapy. All the big series of shows that were planned got killed. In the realm of writing, some of my books would have been enormous best sellers, but the publishers screwed them up. So there are always disappointments. For good reasons or bad, people just let you down. But I don't get upset. I just persist. I go on. I develop other ways of doing things. I just take it as a blocking: "This is a problem—now how do I overcome it? Or if I can't (and I frequently can't), how do I live with it?"

DON KING

I never use the word "failure." I've totally eradicated it from my vocabulary. "Setback," perhaps, every now and then, but "failure," never. If I'm trying to get from one point to the other and you put it on a chart of A to F, if I make it to D and something happens to me, then I will go back to B and reconnoiter and redeploy my forces and attack again to try to get to F. It's a situation where you cannot be a total failure whichever way it goes. You just fall short of the mark. You know, you had to do something right to get from A to D in the first place. So I take whatever happens and I call it an experience and then I put it in a file cabinet to be utilized at a later date.

QUINCY JONES

Oh, shit, yeah, there were tons of disappointments and failures. Are you kidding? There's a lot of shit you have to go through. But I think the thing that really throws you off the most is not understanding it beforehand. If you have the suspicion that there's that possibility, you can cushion the blow a little bit. It's like seeing yourself fall and not breaking all your arms. So you have to step back and really try to look it in the eye and say, "Okay, am I a victim of my own mistakes or of viciousness, man, or jealousy, or whatever it is?" And you have to be able to put all those things together because sometimes it's a combination of all of that. Sometimes you've made a mistake and there's also some other element involved.

It can be a racial trip, you know, which you run into all the time. That's such a thin line that you can't always permeate it because sometimes it seems almost like it's part of human nature. Being in Europe taught me that, because in America when I was young and wanted to write for strings in New York they said, "Man, niggers can't write for strings. Write for bebop horns, man, blues—that's it." And so I went to Paris and studied with Nadia Boulanger and did two hundred fifty sessions with strings for Barclay Records. I just kept doing it over and over again with Aznavour and Jacques Brel and everyone else, and finally I said, "Hey, man, it's got nothing to do with being black." It's like when they asked Stravinsky was he thinking about Greece when he wrote *Apollo* and he said, "Shit, no. I was thinking about violins."

F. LEE BAILEY

I deal with failure pretty stoically at this point. I can recall when there used to be a shudder when a jury came back with a result which I thought was inappropriate. If the result is appropriate, that isn't a loss in my view. If a guilty man gets convicted, the system has operated and we should all celebrate. But when one I think is not guilty is sent off to jail, even today it's a terribly depressing experience. When a jury is out you're usually as tight as a drumhead because you're waiting for a result over which you no longer have any control whatsoever. When it comes in, if it's an adverse result, the drumhead remains tense and you go on to pursue the remedies, even though they are greatly diminished in scope. If you win, it's like somebody undid all the straps around the edges of the drum and you feel terribly exhausted. The recovery is usually nice, but there is in the throes of an individual success, in the legal profession at least, a great letdown, simply because there has been a high expenditure of adrenaline right up to the crucial point, the crescendo.

MILTON H. GREENE

In the past five years there have been many disappointments, and a close friend who I respect very much said to me, "Look, what's the worst that can happen? You hit the bottom of the barrel and you come up." So I called him up one day and said, "Okay, it happened. I hit the bottom of the barrel." And he sounded kind of happy for me. I know he means well for me. I said, "I hit the bottom of the barrel and guess what happened?" He's waiting for the happy news. I said, "I found another hole." And that's what happened. I went through a very bad period. But that's all part of the cycle, you know? It seems everything always repeats itself, and you're either on an up side, a straight line or a down side. And when it's on the down side you suffer and you try to survive, that's all.

BRUNO SANMARTINO

After I picked up Haystack Calhoun I became a sort of somebody. Not big, you know, but I was getting up there and doing a lot of wrestling all around the country. But I had signed a contract with some people, and the more I traveled the more I realized that it was impossible for me to make it on the kind of money I was being given. I had to pay all my own expenses, and

I guess I didn't understand how much all that would cost. I never had much of an education. Nobody forced me to sign it so I can't blame anyone but myself, but the contract was really pitiful. I wasn't able to take care of my wife and kid even though I was getting some main bouts here and there, and then my wife ran into very serious health problems and had to go into the hospital for a long time, so there were some pretty good bills piling up from that. And being young and stupid, I made the mistake of buying a home. It wasn't a very expensive home, I think it was something like nineteen thousand dollars, but with everything else, it put me in a terrible mess. So I thought to myself, boy, I'm getting some main bouts and the arenas are kind of full and I can't even earn a living. I started becoming pretty bitter about it and complained to the people I signed with. They more or less said, "Well, tough, you signed the contract." I said that I was going to break it even if I had to go to court, and I quit.

Well, promoters stick together in a lot of ways, and when I quit, the people I signed with booked me into Baltimore without telling me and when I didn't show up the State Athletic Commission asked the local promoter what happened to me, and he said that he didn't know, that I was supposed to be there. So the commission sent out a suspension keeping me from wrestling in thirty-eight different states. I started moving around the country to other promoters who would take my services. I went out to California and had one match, but then the notice came from the commission and the promoter told me I couldn't work for him anymore until the suspension was cleared. I went to Omaha, Nebraska, and the same thing happened. Then to Indianapolis and, again, the same thing.

By now I'm making no money and I have no money. I was stumbling around like a blind man, not knowing which way to turn. And then a real tragedy happened. I was in Indianapolis, very depressed, very, very down, and I get a telegram that my brother's wife has died. God Almighty, I needed the money to get home and I didn't have a cent. Nothing. Whenever I got hold of five or ten dollars I'd send it home to my wife. I had to walk the streets at night because I couldn't afford to check into a hotel. So even though I was a very bashful guy, I had to hitchhike for the first time in my life to get back to Pittsburgh and barely made it home in time for the funeral. It was a very rough period for me and I became very bitter.

But I refused to let myself be beat by it. I told my wife, "There are some people out to hurt me and they're making me suffer terribly, but so help me God, they'll never stop me. I think I have the ability. I think I have the talent, and I'm going to go through this hell but then I'm gonna come back, I'm gonna make it." And my wife said, "Do what you have to do," and she suffered with me. So I went to Canada and got a decent break there. I started doing well, and finally the suspension was settled and I could come back to the United States.

I like to think I came out of it a lot wiser. I don't think that could ever happen to me again. After that I was much more careful about every move I made and I always made sure I had lawyers to look out for me. But I had to learn the hard way. Coming from the old country, I think this was the big problem. I was kind of too easy and too trusting in believing people. If somebody gave me a piece of paper and told me what it meant, I tended to believe too easily, and it was not always the way they told it, you know. It was my fault for not doing it the proper way, but, really, it was because of trusting too much that I got hurt like that.

JOE EULA

I really freak out at my mistakes because certainly by my age I should be intelligent enough to know when I'm gettin' into trouble. And that really is a bummer, when you're that masochistic. You can't say you enjoy something that you know is a big foolish mistake. But I'll tell you, I've made some marvelous fuckups, full-out flops that have been very successful for me. I hate that old adage, well-I-was-taught-a-lesson, but I *was* taught a lesson. There are certain dos and don'ts in all societies. When you're dealing with the business community, for example, you're dealing with outside influences. Before you ever say yes to anything, make sure you know what you're getting into. You better get the story straight. And when you fuck up it can be very successful because you won't ever be able to go that route again. You never forget it. You forget all the easy successful trips that you just pull out of the sky, but the ones you fail miserably at, man, what a marvelous success lesson they can teach you. Whenever I'm in meetings with people and they're askin' questions, I always say, "Okay, now what do you want? What do you want from me? What can I do for you? Let's talk about it." That's why I hate lawyers. They never talk plain like that. You can add doctors to that list.

JOHN DIEBOLD

I think the thing I've learned most is the importance of following my own instincts. My major mistakes have been when I was argued out of what I believed I ought to do by people who showed me logically why what I wanted to do was illogical. I'm surrounded by very bright people, much brighter than I am, but I have very, very good instincts and I've had to learn to trust them. I've learned to have total confidence in my own mind if I really feel strongly about something after thinking it out, even if everyone else around the table disagrees. I have one of those meetings coming up at four o'clock. I don't want to give you the idea that it's all gut reaction. There's a high amount of logic involved, but in the end on a major decision you do very often come to the point where the modes of reasoning disagree. The problem with logical decisions, of course, is people's premises. One of my major strengths is the ability to think in an analog rather than a digital way, if you can use that analogy. In a digital manner things go through a counting and sorting. In an analog manner there's an instant perception of the result. I usually see the patterns in things instantly, and that's a strength. It's also a weakness because people can go through logic to disprove them.

MARTIN SCORSESE

There's always frustration, incredible frustration. Every day's a different one, in a sense. You never really get quite what you want, or you think you never quite get what you want even though very often you do. You're never quite satisfied with your work. *Mean Streets* is a very sloppy picture. It's still my favorite, but I never thought it was going to get received like that. Sometimes you find yourself in a situation and the idea is to just get yourself out with dignity of some sort. Do the best job you can and finish it.

I always try to give myself some sort of guidelines. It's like when I did *Boxcar Bertha* with Roger Corman, you had to work within the genre and the style but within that you had a great deal of freedom. But even though you always think that your original screenplay is never gonna change, when you go into the editing room you usually end up saying, "Oh, Jesus" or "That scene will work better up front." I don't enjoy that. I really would like to get to the point where the structure is straight and you can improvise within that without ruining the picture.

There's a point when you're editing a film where you don't quite know what's happening and you need the friends that you trust to sit down with you and tell you what they think. Sometimes it'll be very drastic—"Listen, cut out the entire last scene" —but at least you know they're giving you their honest opinion and you can take it or not take it. Other times you'll be looking at your film with other people and you'll immediately know what's wrong with it. Sometimes it just reveals itself. They'll say something and you say, "Thanks, but I just decided to take that out of the picture myself"—that kind of thing.

GEORGE PLIMPTON

I was disappointed a little in the reception of my second book about football, *Mad Ducks and Bears.* I thought it was really better than *Paper Lion.* It looked very hard at two athletes, Alex Karras who was the mad duck of the title and John Gordy who was the bear, and I thought it really told much more about what it was like to play football than *Paper Lion* did. Of course, it didn't have quite the "adventure" of the first time around—the idea of the amateur walking into this strange, extraordinary world. But the best writing I've done is in there. Some critics were pretty tough on it. "You can't go home again." Of course, one of the things you very quickly discover is that with success you become an immediate target. The critics get tougher and your friends get tougher and the gossip people get more gossipy. So it's a good idea to be wary and prepared the second time around because very often you're going to get popped, and popped hard. It happened with *Mad Ducks and Bears.* I got a very vicious review in the *New York Times* by a humorless woman who wrote about how much she hated sports and how little my book had done to assuage her view. That was hardly my function.

Well, you've got to just keep on going. It would be a terrible mistake if you took to heart the criticism of people who really don't know what you're doing. Every once in a while you read someone who's perceptive and you say, "Yes, that's so." But if you spend your time worrying about what people outside are going to think, you'll have an awful hard time. So you just have to reckon yourself a bad night or two as you walk around composing imaginary letters to the *Times* and throwing the paper across the room. It's no fun. There's a sort of sinking feeling, a terrible sinking feeling because you know the criticism's being read by three or four hundred thousand other people. Perhaps they're taking a sort of perverse delight in your misfortune. You imagine your literary friends reading it and saying, "Well, there's another one out of the running." A lot of paranoia of this sort.

But the main sinking feeling comes with the loss of contentment, of peace of mind. It means that the book is not going to be read by as many people as you hoped it was going to be read by. And it makes you wonder whether you did a good job, really. It chips away at your confidence and thus indirectly at your peace of mind.

MURRAY KEMPTON

One of the problems with writing books is that you can reach a certain level of success where you're never going to get a bad review. One of the reasons for cronyism, I think, is that if you've grown up with a guy and you have lived with him and you have worked with him and you and he are on a general plane of equality, if you say his work is bad, to some extent you're also saying that your work is bad. And there's a need to feel that you are important, that your generation is better than prior generations. So it is almost impossible for me to write a book that will get bad reviews. I think it's getting less and less possible for *anyone* to write a book that will get bad reviews unless it's an extraordinarily good one. I think *The Power Broker* is the most wonderful book I've read in years, and any book of mine will get less mixed reviews than that did, because fundamentally—and it's very curious—I don't think I really write anything that is taken seriously in that sense.

During the fifties I was far to the left of anyone who wasn't a party member—and when I say "far to the left" I mean that my politics and Estes Kefauver's were roughly the same—but I ran around with communists and the extreme right wingers never got angry at me. They hated Jimmy Wechsler of the *New York Post,* and they violently hated Joe Barnes, who was my editor at Simon and Schuster, but these guys were well to the right of me. I have often wondered about this. The right wing and I have always been very good friends, and I think that's probably a failure of moral seriousness on my part. Somehow or other, I have never been a man who has been taken that seriously.

I have no enemies except people who have been close to me one time or another, and I think that is a failure. I mean, I hate to be hated. My only virtue is that I really have no desire to be feared. But I loathe being disliked, and I think really first-class people don't mind it. I don't mean disliked by people who work for them or things like that because I don't think any really first-class person yells at his employees, but the enemies people earn seem to me to be a measure of their success. Why was Bob Kennedy hated more than his brother ever was? Because he was a more serious man and you expected more from him. It was a compliment for the right wing to go after Wechsler and Barnes. They were being given the stature that's accorded people whose character is firm enough for them to do wicked things. There was also another reason for this intensity: Wechsler was a crashing success at the age of twenty and Joe Barnes was a crashing success at the age of twenty or twenty-one. I was never much of a success and when I approached being one, it was well into my thirties, safely into my thirties.

AL GOLDSTEIN

I'm frustrated that *Screw* isn't taken seriously and that I don't have the options of the average businessman. I've had the same distributor for six years. I like him very much, but why hasn't any other distributor come to me? In New York I'm on fifty percent of the newsstands, and in the rest of the country I'm probably on one percent. Why am I so much like contraband? Why haven't I gotten access to a wider marketplace? That frustrates me. I'm frustrated that the paper is so ahead of its time that our circulation is 120,000 when it should really be two or three million. I should be selling as much as the *Enquirer.* Everyone who reads it is fascinated by it and wants it. I'm frustrated that my rights are constantly violated with taps. I'm audited every year, constantly harassed by the government. I'm not outraged, but it's not a thrill. I'm upset that first-class postal subscriptions are constantly opened by the Post Office. It's a federal rap to interfere with the mail. I'm treated like a communist in the fifties, that frustrates me.

I hate to use the putdown of the racial epithet, but that's why I'm nigger rich in a way. I mean, I want to buy the shiniest watch, the flashiest car because I feel that at any time my life can be ended by a bullet or incarceration, and I want to have as much as I can while I'm still here to enjoy it. I mean, there's a loaded gun in that drawer. I've had bodyguards in some situations where I've been threatened. I'm conscious that if they can reach the Kennedys they can get to Al Goldstein with the greatest of ease. That's difficult to deal with and scary, and I'm not heroic and get frightened. The fright lasts two days and then I'm back with my arrogant fuck-you-I'm-gonna-win attitude, which is probably why I am successful. But the fear is there.

ROCKY AOKI

No, I have no fears about my restaurant business failing. I'm thirty-seven years old. I'm not afraid. I can do it again, or I can do something else. Sure, I'm even a little bit tired of what I've been doing. That's why I go into this and I go into that. I look for maybe happiness, maybe for more profit. Who knows? I don't know. I don't think I'm doing this for money. More for competition. I want to win the competition. I enjoy competition, especially boat racing. Now I want to be a world champion. I go crazy with it. I made one boat, now I'm making bigger boats. I'm making one boat here and another in Europe so I can compete in the world championship circle.

Next year, you never know, it could be something else. When I go into anything, I go in very heavy. Within a year after I started playing backgammon I beat Oswald Jacoby, who wrote books about it. I was champion of a big tournament, beating Oswald Jacoby. Everybody was surprised. A guy who came out of nowhere a couple of months before beat him in a twenty-one-point match one-two-three. Because I studied it. I hired the top people to teach me. I spent a lot of money and learned the lessons from all the top people. Now I'm one of the good back-gammon players in the United States. And now I'm getting tired of it.

I fly airplanes too. I had two airplanes, a Comanche 250 and a Cessna 310 dual engine, and I also used to rent a Lear jet for the corporation. In twelve hours I learned to solo myself. In wrestling I was a national champion in 1962, '63, '64. I don't like to talk about how great I am, but somehow I have a feeling that if I like something, I know I'll be tops right away. The restaurant business is the same way. That's been my experience. That's why I have no fear. I can go into any business. Somebody came to me and wanted to open up an advertising agency, and I invested one hundred percent of the capital. And the next year this advertising agency hit five or six big awards for radio and TV commercials. Prestigewise, they became one of the top crea-tive agencies. Within one year. So I have a feeling—only a feel-ing—that anything I want to go into heavy, I know I can do it.

JERRY DELLA FEMINA

I feel very secure in my success. I never worry about it disap-pearing because the other side of it wasn't that terrible. All it would entail would be to work very hard and try to do it again. Yeah, it would be a nightmare if I had to stop and go back to carrying checks for National City Bank, but even that would be okay if I could think to myself as I'm doing it that I'm getting something out of it and some day I'm going to be successful again. I remember carrying them. I was about seventeen or eighteen, a kid, and my job was to take these giant bags from 10 Exchange Place to their 42nd Street branch. And I said, how can I get something out of this job, what will I learn from this other than the subway system? Then I hit on the fact the bags weighed about sixty pounds each, really very heavy, and I could walk along the street and press and lift them. I may be the only person in America who can say that the National City Bank developed his arms. So I did get something out of it even then.

F. LEE BAILEY

When the government laid an indictment on me, knowing as I do that juries can come back every which way and that the appellate system is far from insurance against a bad result, I gave very realistic thought to the possibility of being thrown into the can and having all my assets gobbled up and not being able to practice law anymore. But it wasn't as frightening a proposition as I think it would have been for most people because I've spent a hell of a lot of time in prison as a guest and had been involved in prison reform. I viewed it as just a bad piece of luck that came along. You could easily say, "Well, he's had enough good luck so that this is no more than a balance."

But, no, I don't have many conscious nightmares. I think everyone has them while sleeping. You know, terrible things happen, but then you wake up. I usually have enough optimism to say, "Well, even though things look very bad right now in the law office or with the company or with the client, even though everything is just gloom hanging from every corner of the rafters, it's going to turn out all right." In order to survive without being terribly anguished, I think it is necessary to take that attitude that, you know, we're not going to fold. I think a professional has an obligation to be realistic but to stay on the bright side of realism as far as honesty will allow.

MARIO ANDRETTI

It's strange. A lot of the times you dream about some of the things that in your subconscious mind maybe bother you the most or could bother you if they actually happened, and lately I've been going through some of that. Like being late for a race. I've never done that in my life, never missed one in my life. But I don't know why, it's just gotten into my thoughts—not being ready, arriving late for the start, and things like that. I don't know, maybe that's going to happen next. Part of my nightmares, you know.

GEORGE PLIMPTON

One is always terrified that you're not going to be able to write the next morning. It's a curiously American phenomenon. I doubt the French worry about such things at all. What you hope is that the success is really going to be relative to what you yourself think of it. It's always a disappointment if someone doesn't like what you've done. I mean, occasionally they say, "Well, this isn't up to snuff," or something. But as long as you have some sense in your own mind that you've done a good job, I suppose that's enough . . . almost enough.

HALSTON

I think a lot of people worry about their talent suddenly drying up on them, but that's not my problem. I happen to be very prolific in what I do. My only problem right now is editing down the ideas. I have sketches for five hundred long dresses, and I can only have twelve for my next collection. And how do I weed through five hundred ideas and make it realistic as far as the manufacturing is concerned? I can do a collection a day. That's no problem at all for me. The hardship post is getting enough good people around to follow through so you don't have to do it all yourself. But the ideas and the drawings and all that are there. I have, I think, about six collections going right at this moment, and I have too much for each one of them. That is the only big frustration. Being able to edit the ideas down, that's your problem. It's a business problem. Time again. It's hard to simply look through five hundred sketches and say, "These and not those," because they are all ideas of validity, you know. I'd just like to do them all, but you can't. And then how do you hold back and still continue on with each individual experiment?

MARTIN SCORSESE

Security? In this business? When you see a guy like Bernard Herrmann, one of the greatest film composers ever, and the last Hollywood picture he did was *Marnie* and then after years of neglect he dies in this room in a commercial hotel overlooking the Universal lot? And then you look at Samuel Fuller, a marvelous filmmaker and he can't make pictures anymore. What a business, you know? You try to deal with it but it's very hard because once you're not hot you are not hot, that's all there is to it.

JOAN GANZ COONEY

You want to keep going and to come up with new things that are respectable. We tried health education for adults with the *Feeling Good* show, and while I think it was one of the most interesting things we've done, a lot of critics hated it because it was highly experimental. We were trying to reach the poor and less well educated and we knew we couldn't do that with straight slick documentaries. So it was an undertaking very worth doing, and I'm really sorry that the society and television are such that you either have to have a smash or you're off the air. That really is the way it works. I accept that, but I'm not content with it.

EDGAR D. MITCHELL

No, I never have the feeling that one day I'll wake up and it'll all be gone. What you're really asking about is internal fear, the fear of dying. But to me the difficulty is not in dying, the difficulty is in living, in learning to live in a fulfilled, productive, competent manner. I think my years of test pilot experience brought me into contact with the possibility of death, and I was able to confront it. And my studies of metaphysical science have always convinced me that physical death isn't the end of anything. It's simply a change of phase. So I was able to get over those anxieties.

BUDDY RICH

No, I don't feel secure in anything. You feel secure in anything? What the hell is security, man? I'm here, and that's pretty good security for now. I don't take a bet on tomorrow. I suppose I've had doubts, I've had doubts. But they only last until I hear myself play good and then I say, what the hell was I all upset about? You know, sure. I'm not Superman. I have as many weak structures in my frame as anybody else.

REX REED

I feel I get into these terrible ruts, but I think every writer feels that. Every time I sit down at the typewriter I think, Well, this is just terrible and how much better somebody else would have written it. And I think, well, I've gone dry and I'm stale and I'm tired. This happens almost every week. There's no way to combat that. Even when I have vacations, which are rare, I can't turn it off. I'll say, "Great, I'm going to go and replenish my supply of thoughts and feed my creative process again," but then I worry about work and think about what I'm going to do when I get back and what the first column will be.

You know, you can't really turn it off. I guess that's part of the creative neurosis connected to being a writer. I don't know any writers who are not neurotic. They're all neurotic. Actors are neurotic too, but writers are much more so because they're alone so much with their work and they have no idea of what anyone thinks of them. I mean, an actor can be neurotic and wonder if he's any good, but the minute they applaud he thinks, Well, everything is okay. A writer never knows.

ELIZABETH ASHLEY

I think performers are people who for whatever reason, whatever you want to call it, have some kind of spiritual, psychic hunger that does not get fed. Something starves. No matter how much is going on everywhere else, no matter how filled up other parts of you are, there is some part of you that has some hunger that isn't being fed, and it feels like a hunger for attention, love, approval, all those things. It's ego, ego hunger. Some pocket, some corner, some dark murky place in that ego is not being fed what it needs. And it's like an addiction. We don't have a choice. Anybody that can make that choice doesn't do it. I think the people that become performers are the people that really don't have a choice.

GEROLD FRANK

I will never write the book that is good enough. Every book I begin I begin in fear and trembling that I won't be able to do it, and in order to encourage myself I go back to my earlier books and read them and say, "You know, they're good." And then I'll say, "Well, isn't this stupid? If the fellow could do those, he can do this." In short, I reassure myself from books written by a man who needs reassurance. Does that make sense?

My own conviction is that nearly every artist, whatever that word means, begins from behind the eight ball. Nearly all of them have had less than happy childhoods. I mean, what makes you want to tell something to people? I've tried writing aphorisms about it. One of them is "I feel across the street from everything." Another is "I'm a guest in my own life and I don't know who the host is." A third is "Who is this all-understanding, all-forgiving, all-powerful presence whose approval I seek so badly?" I don't know who it is. Maybe every writer does that.

So, no, I don't think I'm secure. Danny Kaye once told me that when a singer wakes in the morning the first thing he does is sing some scales to find out whether the voice is still there. Perhaps the gift has been taken away as magically as it was given him. It is not impossible that out of insecurity flows the most Herculean effort. I make no outlines. I can't follow an outline. The chapter goes the way it goes and then it stops and I have to think, now, what next? I don't know how much further it will go. All I know is that I'm trying to impose a sense of order on chaos, because a life really doesn't fall into place ABCD, and if you try to write it that way it's boring as hell.

BRUNO SANMARTINO

When I first won the championship belt all I thought about was, Boy, this is great, I hope I can hang onto it for six months. Then a year went by, three years, five years, eight years, nine, ten. So the way I look at it, if it happens that it goes, I'm still in America and I can still feed my family. That's the one thing I couldn't cope with, I'll tell you the truth. If I ever saw one of my kids crying because he was hungry, that would destroy me. But as far as no longer being a champion wrestler or even a wrestler, if it goes down the drain, as long as God keeps me healthy and strong I'll find something, I'll do something else. It's not the end of the world. Hell, I'm a man. I can be a garbage man, a ditch digger, I can be anything. As long as I can take care of my family, that's it.

DON KING

I'm not in love with any of this materialistic situation that you see around here. If it's taken away from me tomorrow and the secretary leaves and the phone is cut off and the bills can't be paid, I promised Rockefeller, my landlord, that I wouldn't jump off the building. I don't ever have any apprehensions about anything like that, but it's a fact that the possibility is always there. It's only when you bury your head in the sand like an ostrich that you fail to recognize it. You understand? You must always be cognizant of how your business is going, what you're doing and what your direction is and how much you have to have in order to fulfill your obligations and stay around. See, getting here was a hell of a hard job. I'm here. Now staying here is gonna be even tougher. But I don't feel bad about it because I think I've broken all records and all odds to get here. The least I'll be able to say is that I was here. So I'm not gonna worry about whether I ain't gonna be here or not. I'm just gonna keep performing. And it should be just an exercise of business that will keep me here as long as I desire to stay here. When I change my mind, I'll do something else.

I never have any fear about being thrown out because there are so many people who are with me who understand my sincerity and my dedication and, more importantly, my performance that if I slip, like I said, somebody will give me a boost. It's only when you have eliminated yourself from your people and your power base and have tried to assimilate into another world that you can't assimilate into that you find yourself wandering in a void, what I call standing alone in the safety zone. You understand? Then if anyone went to push Don King there would be no opposition. If I left my black world and tried to assimilate to the white world, I might just find myself floating around out there in outer space. No, I want somebody to scream. I want a team, you dig? I don't want to be alone. Individualism is something that we cannot afford. I feel the luxury of divisiveness is much too high a price for us to pay. My strength comes from blackness and my commitment is to blackness, but this is not a strength or commitment of alienation, polarization, isolation. This is a commitment of togetherness, but dealing with each other from a position of strength and equality rather than one of subordination and supplication. That's all. I ain't got no hang-ups with nobody.

MILTON GLASER

I think the dark part of success is that it can be an impediment to your own development and growth and can put you in a position where its maintenance becomes the most important thing in your life. But I don't think I consciously have any anxiety about that. I'm not really at a point now where the perception of my own boundary is clear to me. I don't really know how far I can go and where my talent and interest run out. If I did, then the issue of holding on to my success might well become the most prevailing matter in my life and I really would try to do whatever I could to cling to it. I've seen this happen to a lot of people. Success really does become a limitation.

But I studied yoga for a long time, and one of the things you learn is a sense of detachment from whatever you hold most dear. I think that has helped me be able to observe my success in a detached way rather than be caught in it. Attachment really is the issue: what you're attached to and how much you need the attachment and how limiting the attachment is. So once you have the capacity to observe what those attachments are, at least you're able to maintain some kind of choice in the situation.

QUINCY JONES

I never worry about it not being there tomorrow, and I'm probably wrong too. I see a lot of very young kids in the business with that attitude of, "Man, this thing can't last forever so I'm making the wise investments. I'm not fucking up any money." That's probably a good thing. I should probably have more of that, you know, because I have fucked up a lot of money, man, made a lot of foolish moves, pissed away a lot of bread and not done some of those cautious kind of well-insulated things. But there's just something underneath that says, "Hey, man, it's the same dude that started over again twenty times." Fuck it, you know?

JOE EULA

I have no fear whatsoever. How can you have fear if you don't give a shit about material things? Have you ever just closed the door and walked out? I've done it about six times in my life. What a gas! You know that you take yourself with you all the time and there you are, that marvelous fuckin' thing called "makin' the decision of your own choice." There it is. Shit, I can always go be a gardener. I dig diggin' in the earth. I love that, putting a bulb or a seed in the ground and watchin' it come up. My God, what a successful thing, what an adventure to be able to take care of that.

The Rewards

JERRY DELLA FEMINA

I love all the trappings. All the things that people told me to watch out for. Love it, love it! I love the fact that it's gone to my head. I think that that's the best part of it, really. That's the most delicious part. There's nothing I don't like about it. What's not to like? People say they wish they could go back to the days when their lives were simple. No, my life is complicated and it should be complicated. There's a lot to do. There's a lot to enjoy. There's a lot to have. There's a lot to see. There are places to go to. It's very beautiful, it really is.

WILLIAM GAINES

I enjoy the freedom and the independence and the ability to go my own way and do my own thing. As long as I don't break the law, nobody bothers me. Money gives you such independence. I think the most wonderful thing about being successful is that you don't have to take all the shit the world hands out to the average person. Somewhere in some novel, I don't remember where it was that I read it, somebody was talking about fuck-you money. The term struck me as very appropriate. When you're successful and have it made moneywise, you've got fuck-you money. Now I don't mean fuck-you money in an aggressive sense. I mean it in a defensive sense. If somebody comes to you and tries to step on you in some way which most people have to take, you have the clout and the wherewithal to say, "Fuck you, leave me alone." I think that maybe is the most important thing I've gotten out of my success because it's given me a lot of happiness and freedom that a lot of people just don't have.

MILTON GLASER

I suppose its deepest reward now is that it's on the record. That I really can say to everybody who ever humiliated me, "See? I deserve to live. That proved it." I was thinking the other day, I have a show at the Museum of Modern Art now and the only feeling I have around the show is not one of gratitude but of revenge. I mean, that was the real center of my feeling. "See? I told ya! You never believed me." Who am I talking to? The world, my father, the kid that beat me up in the locker room when I was seven years old, the people at the museum who would never look at my work before. I mean, the whole thing.

I suppose the other thing, really, has to do with a sense of having altered to one extent or another people's perceptions of the world. To say, "I see it this way," and have it shared, that's a tremendously rich experience. I teach a lot. I find teaching very exciting. I've been teaching fifteen years. I get so much out of it.

MIKE WALLACE

I enjoy immensely the fact that I'm doing something I can take a certain pride in. That's important to me. I've been able to make a decent living at it, and that of course is also important. And the recognition, particularly the recognition of one's peers, that comes with being involved in something like *60 Minutes,* that's important too.

CLIVE DAVIS

What I like about it is that my track record enables me to deal with artists on a level of equality from the point of view of constructive criticism. Without the recognition that comes with success, executives in this business are not given to take that position. Artists like Harry Nilsson or Elton John or Paul Simon are much more ready to say to someone who is purely a business executive without a successful track record, "Here is my product, here is my album. Now just merchandise it as best you can. I want a lot of ads and a lot of promotion." But when you have shown that creatively you have made your own mark with your own contributions, whether they be in talent recognition or song finding or producing or just creative awareness, you are much more able to participate. Not because of a need to participate, but to the extent that you do have ideas about a song or a production, the artists on your label will listen to what you have to say. It helps enormously in being able to deal and be listened to, assuming that you're right. I feel that my track record has been good, and because they recognize it, it's not as difficult, I don't have to be quite as ginger as when I was on the way up. I can deal with a Barry Manilow or a Barbra Streisand.

With Barry Manilow, I urged him, "Hold up your album because you don't have a big single in it." And this is an example of where it comes off. Barry Manilow had one album out before I became associated with him, and he had not yet made it. I listened to his new album when he delivered it to me, and I said, "It's a very nice album, but it's just not going to break because you don't have a big hit single." The very fact that he was willing to hold it up was in itself a trusting of my creative judgment. Then it was a question of finding the song that could break his career. And there I was fortunate. I found the song. It had been called *Brandy*. I retitled it *Mandy*. And I ended up coproducing it. Manilow and his coproducer Ron Dante were producing it in a different manner, which was not capable of having it break out in a Top Forty sense. And when I disagreed with what they were doing—I felt they were just not capitalizing on a major song— they then asked me to help produce it myself. And I did, and it became a million-and-a-half seller and launched an enormous career which was mutually rewarding because now he's a major star.

Well, the ability to lay on an artist, to say, "Hold up," and then, "Hey, do this song. Hey, you're not doing it right. Let me go in and at least show you how I think it should be done," and then for the results to speak as they did speak, only came about because of the track record I had and their ability to trust me because of it. The normal reaction is, "Hey, leave the music to me, and you just take care of the business side." But I think that what had occurred in the past allowed them to say, "Well, maybe he's right." They're not going to cede responsibility on a silver platter. They all have their own egos, as they should. But it does enable you to have creative discussions without being impeded by constant apologies and all the other defense mechanisms.

AL GOLDSTEIN

I feel I'm successful because I think of the money I make and I'm in awe of it. Sure, then I think of somebody who's making three times as much, but I roll the figures quietly over my tongue like a good wine. I feel successful because I'm making fifteen times more than the highest-paid person here. I feel I deserve it because I'm the one who goes to jail. I'm the one who's not replaceable. They are. I'm replaceable too, but it would take them five days to replace me and in five hours I can replace anybody else.

I think I'm a success because I'm visible, I'm seen. My mother and father think I'm successful because people work for me. I'm a boss. I'm impressed that all the boring shit I don't have to do. I'm difficult at home now because I want my wife to dial my phone calls. I mean, I've become a lump. I don't do anything myself. I'm surprised I don't have anyone drinking my coffee or feeding it to me via an IV. When I hired my new secretary, who's magnificent, a really superb executive secretary, I told her, "Everything that's unpleasant and disagreeable, you will do. If it's fun, I'll do it. If you're into women's lib and fairness, you don't want to work for me 'cause there's no such thing as fair. So long as I sign your check every week, you're doing all the shit work."

I'm a success because I can be saved from some of the irritations of life. I have a house upstate and I have a Montgomery Ward garbage compacter and it leaks. Now I don't just go to Montgomery Ward and complain. My secretary writes to the president of Montgomery Ward and we get a letter from fourteen executives genuflecting to my power and prowess, and of course it will be fixed. And that's what I love. I have a card that lets me into a chain of really nice theaters here in New York any time I want to see a film. I love it. That's almost more important than not having to pay. I feel important because I guess I feel alive. When I was a cabdriver I felt so much like a failure. I was immersed in gloom and doom simply because I always took other people to places where I wanted to go. I took these guys with these beautiful model-type women to movies and to great restaurants. I really felt like the kid of nine or ten with his nose pressed up against the bakery window while his stomach was growling. I'm a success now because my stomach rarely growls.

If I'm with a friend in a restaurant and I'm paying, I don't worry what the price is. My eyes don't automatically dart to the right. I don't care what things cost. Immediate gratification. I saw someone with this silver razorblade I'm wearing around my neck and I asked him where he got it. He told me and I walked in and said, "I want it." Now it was cheap—it was thirty-two dollars—but if it was a hundred dollars I would have bought it. Money becomes unimportant. There are so many stories about Teddy Kennedy running around without money. I wish I were that way. Of course, I was too poor, so I'm still conscious of money. I remember before *Screw* started, I used to do what women did in Williamsburg, I would hide mad money, five dollars, because I was always afraid, God forbid, I would wind up in some strange town, I can't make a phone call. And also, I can't eat. I don't want to be hungry anyplace. That's why I'm so fat. Anyway, now my mad money is eight hundred dollars, eight one hundred dollar bills. And I realize how everything has changed.

I mean, the trappings of success amaze me. I moved into a duplex five years ago with my second wife. It was wonderful and I loved it, and for two months now I've been hating it—also I have a son now and a new wife—so I'm moving up to Bloomingdale's country with a doorman. I'm like a Jewish "The Jeffersons." I want all those trappings, and at last I can afford them.

I can look at the *Times* travel section, and any place advertised I can go to. I can buy a Rolls-Royce, which I think of but maybe it's too ostentatious. I don't drive that much. I had a Javelin that was stolen eight months ago. I walked into the showroom of the Ford dealer and I saw a car which I had read bad reports on, the Thunderbird, but it was big, it had a sliding roof, and it said,

"Take me, take me!" Well, I bought it, and I drive it with the sliding roof. I feel like some garment center mogul. And the car handles truly like a balloon in a strong wind. It's a bad handling car, but it's comfortable, and the windows—it's got all this gadgetry and it does everything but stroke my cock. And I love it. I should have had enough class—if I were middle-class, not lower-middle-class, I probably would have bought a Continental. I still don't have it. I still have failings. Caddy came out with a new car, the Seville—twelve, thirteen thousand dollars. I can buy it. I can buy the TV set I want, the watch I want. That is a certain kind of power. I don't fight with my wife over what she spent last week. I recently bought her an expensive watch, and it made me feel good. Because I'm good to me, I like being nice to her.

And I don't have to answer to anybody. This is one of the problems I had with my partnership with Jim Buckley. Buckley and I got along very well and hated each other but loved each other too. We were in jail together. You have no idea what a close bond develops. His ass was on the line too. But since he owned fifty percent of the paper, he could check out what I did and say, "Well, Al, you know, you're spending too much on *Screw.*" And now I don't have to answer to him. I surely don't answer to my wife. I don't answer to my staff. As long as the company is making money, I only answer to me. It's liberating, it's freeing. When I bought Jim out, to me that was the total breakthrough. Even though I was making nice money before, I hadn't realized that I was a success. Now that I own the company, it's changing. I'm not uptown on Madison Avenue, but I say, "Jesus, I really am a success." And even though it's been seven years, it's hard for me still to believe. 'Cause deep down I guess I still think I'm the guy who was driving a cab or the kid in Williamsburg who was left back. It's frightening. I'm still Fat Alvin.

JACK HALEY JR.

I'm at a certain level of achievement, and I don't look for much more out of life than what I have now. I have a wife I adore and respect, and we look forward to having children. I'm very pleased, very happy, very secure. I've always felt secure, unlike a lot of children who grew up in Hollywood. You know those old Hollywood jokes: One kid says to the other, "My father can beat your father," and the other one says, "What do you mean? He *is* my father!" Well, I never had that. My parents both gave me a lot of love and affection at home, and my father always encouraged me: "If you want show business, fine. If you don't want it, I'm not pushing you and insisting you be in it." There was also my father's wealth and my reluctance to share it with him. I always knew it was there, and in the past I would borrow money from him when I really needed it. I was always very careful to repay it, but knowing that a considerable amount of money someday is going to be mine if I outlive him gave me a certain courage to tell somebody to go jump if I didn't want to do what they were telling me to do, and I have walked away from a few things with no regrets. But that's the kind of courage that you can only get, I think, by divorcing yourself from family wealth.

Only in the most dire necessity do you fall back on someone else's productivity. You know, you're just hooking up the cord again, and I don't think either party is pleased by that. But, boy, having it there is a big cushion, a big emotional cushion. You know, "Jeez, what if I'm out of a job tomorrow?" Well, I've always known I'm not going to starve. I've known that since I was a child. So that's a big leg up, a big leg up in any kind of business you're in.

JOHN DIEBOLD

My parents had very high ideals and they always emphasized that money did not matter but that it was important to do the best you could in whatever you were doing. Success for them was always differentiated from accumulating wealth, and I think that was a very important distinction for me. It was ingrained very early and became quite basic to my nature. I always assumed that if I put my whole effort into something and did a first-class job that the money would take care of itself. I have never, to my knowledge, made any important decision on the basis of money. To whatever extent there's been financial success, it has always followed along upon the rest. I suppose I've achieved wealth, but I've never considered it important. It means nothing to me except that it does make things easier and you can do more things you want to do. One is almost embarrassed about it. It's part of success, but one never talks about it. That's the way I was brought up.

REVEREND IKE

The financial part of success overtook me without my noticing it or necessarily trying for it. In 1966 I came back to New York in mass evangelism, and we just kept getting on more and more radio stations and picking up more and more supporters all over the country. Not only all over the country but in different parts of the world. For example, when I was on international radio on one of the Mexican stations, among the followers and supporters of this ministry we had Eskimos thirty-five miles above the Arctic Circle. They would write and send contributions and so on. So it just kept happening. I was just busy conducting services, ministering, counseling, getting on more and more radio stations. The first time I was ever on television was in Madison Square Garden. I had never been to Madison Square Garden before and never been on television before and I said, "Hey, we're going to videotape this and put it on television for all the people who can't get in." I'm still amazed at how many people watch you on television. And so success from the perspective of fame and money sort of happened without me going for them as such. They were really by-products. But I find them quite agreeable.

REX REED

I think we have to abolish this whole idea that money corrupts, that money is evil. I don't particularly feel that way. I feel that it depends entirely on how you use it. But certainly having it is not a terrible thing. I grew up in a world of venetian blinds and chenille bedspreads and rented houses. I went to thirteen different schools before I ever graduated from the twelfth grade, so that means that I lived in a lot of tacky little houses that oil field people had to rent in those tiny little towns where there's no such thing as decent living accomodations. And I knew that there was something better. All you had to do was go to the movies and see Fred Astaire dancing through rooms with Louis Quinze furniture, and you think, wait a minute, there's something better out there. I didn't want to settle for that, and if you're not going to settle for that you'd better find a way to make some money.

And so, yes, money has always been important to me. It unfortunately becomes more important as you make more of it, because you owe more money and you spend more money and it costs more money to maintain your life-style. But I've never been ashamed of the fact that I've made a lot of money as a writer. There seems to be a snobbish tendency on the part of some writers to think that if you make any money at writing then you can't be any good. They distrust you immediately if you are read by more than ten people. I don't understand that. I mean, I have made a hundred thousand dollars a year and more for the last two or three years, and they want to write you out of the human race when they find this out. You can't be any good and make money. Well, you know, I could write for the *Partisan Review* for nothing too, but I'm not willing to settle for that. What else have you got, really, to show for your ability if you don't get paid for what you do? I'm told that I have a vast readership out there, seventy million readers. Well, I don't know any of them. I don't get letters from the ones who can spell. I get mostly letters from idiots who write on Big Chief tablet paper with soft lead pencils. And, you know, I'm not living for that public. I have to have something else to show for it besides the adulation of faceless people.

DON KING

I don't really put all my hopes on money per se, but I do feel it's necessary. You must have affluence to do the things you want to do in an affluent society. My race has lived through the hard-core era of segregation, the more ameliorated era of separation, and I feel that it's now time for a new era of togetherness. It's time to come together, but we must do so from a position of economic strength. I feel that many of us have been enslaved through the Bible. The Bible is one of the greatest books that was ever written, but you must understand it the right way. You must understand the reality of what is being said for your every-day life. So many of my people have been terribly misled through the Scriptures. They have been taught that they'll get their pie in the sky when they die but nothing solid on the ground while we're around, you dig? "In the sweet by and by. Swing low, sweet chariot, coming for to carry me home. The torment won't be like it is now. The pain will be gone. And when we go to our Father's house, where there are many mansions, the streets will be paved with gold."

And they have been taught that a rich man has as much chance of getting into Heaven as a camel through the eye of a needle, and in their unenlightened minds they look at that small hole in the head of a needle and they look at that gigantic camel and they figure this rich man will never get there, not recognizing that their hell is right here on earth, you dig? So what it does is orient us for death rather than for life. And when we would die, they would have big funerals with bands playing behind the procession and everybody getting sharp 'cause old Lucy or John, you know, they ain't got to suffer no more. They really send ol' John off. He's starved, you know, all through his life eking out a meager and intolerable existence, and now that he's dead you give him the best funeral and really bust everybody else so they be starving too. Yes, I got to understand this real well when I was growing up.

MARIO ANDRETTI

My father worked all his life to achieve what he wanted to achieve, and then because of the Second World War he lost everything and had to come to the United States and start over. So when I was young we could never have the things we wanted. There was always this financial barrier there. But when things started coming together for me I was able to overcome that, and I appreciate it. It kind of puts me more at ease than it might some other people, only because I've experienced the other side of it. I don't know how it has changed my life, though. I mean, I'm not an extravagant person, but I do have just about everything that I really want. I lead a pretty simple life. But comfortable. The way I want it.

QUINCY JONES

Money means one very important thing to me. It means independence, man. It means I can say that I don't want to do that piece of shit that I might have had to do ten years ago just for the bread. Now I don't even want to know about it. I'd rather do something else that I might not make anything on at all, and I've earned that because I have enough money to say no. It also means that I don't have to have a dishonest relationship with a person just for financial reasons. I don't have to smile at somebody I don't like, pretend to like them because I'm making money at it. See, I can't live with that, I cannot live with it.

MARTIN SCORSESE

Fortune, unfortunately, I don't think is part of my situation, the way I make pictures. I don't know yet, you see. Possibly they'll make back their money, but I don't know if the kind of thing I do is really ever gonna be a blockbuster, even though I love those kinds of films, the blockbuster films which bring a lot of fortune. I tend to make a much more personal sort of picture. I'm trying to figure out how to keep doing that in a way that still makes commercial sense, if that can be done. I'm sure it has been done. I think *2001* is very personal. My next one is very personal but it's a musical with Liza Minnelli and Bobby DeNiro. It deals with the relationship between a man and a woman in a way that is extremely personal to me.

I'm trying hard to erase that conflict because if you do one just for commercial reasons you can really find yourself not wanting to get up in the morning to shoot that scene. And then what the hell do you do? How do you do the scene? Just take a master and a closeup and a medium shot and that's it? There's no soul behind that. And if there's no soul behind it you can forget it. One of the last things Bernard Herrmann said to me, I was talking about another project I have and he says, "Be sure you really want to make it. You have to want to go to the gallows for the picture." And that's what you have to do.

F. LEE BAILEY

The accretion of wealth for its own sake doesn't interest me, but if you can get a very substantial fee in a case you can devote a tremendous amount of time to it and go in prepared like a razor that's just been stropped, and that's a delightful way to practice law. To have to go in less prepared than that is simply a compromise, and the only saving grace is that the other side is in the same condition or worse.

Numbers on a piece of paper, whether that be a savings account or something else, have never really motivated me. If I wanted something as a kid I would go out and work twelve, fourteen hours a day until I got it, and to that extent, since money was the tradable item, I suppose you could say it was motivating. But in my mind, money is really a value to the extent that it gives you elbow room. For instance, my life would be absolutely impossible if I couldn't highly integrate air travel in private aircraft and helicopters with my destination because it would simply cut my available useful hours in half or leave me so exhausted because I would be doing nothing but working, and I don't want to fall into that trap either.

In many senses I don't have a great deal of money, certainly not fluid money, but as a substitute I have an earning capacity which I know is extraordinary. As long as I'm healthy it's as good as a savings account or better, because no matter what the economy does I can always take more cases, give more speeches and make more helicopters. But it usually would have to be against some goal. If I wanted to buy a company I suppose I would be going hammer and tongs until I'd acquired the assets to do that.

BUDDY RICH

Money of course is important. You have to sustain, to live. You have to have nice things. That's also part of success. But that's not the main drive. The main drive is to continue to do what I do and enjoy it. I think that when I stop enjoying it, when it ceases to become play and I say I'm going to *work* tonight, that will be the beginning of the end for me. Sure, there are times when I don't particularly feel like it. I have moods like you have and anybody else, and there are some times when those moods are very depressing and I don't feel good. But a funny thing happens when I get up on the bandstand. For the time I'm up there—forty-five minutes, an hour, whatever—I forget all the pain in the ass things that go on, so that's another way of feeling success.

I've been a millionaire about three different times in my career. Probably up until this point I've made maybe seven or eight million dollars and I had the best time in my life spending it. It was lovely. But if I had ten million lying in stacks like this in the bank, I'd still be down here at nine-thirty tonight playing my drums and my music. The only thing that ten million dollars would do to me is make me eight million dollars richer.

ALICE COOPER

After going through starving all that time, when we finally started to make so much money we didn't know what to do with it, it was extremely important to flaunt it. And so I found myself directing a whole stage show towards the idea of America making it and then flaunting it. That was the whole idea behind *Billion Dollar Babies*. I treat Alice as a character, not as anything other than that, so anything Alice does on stage is about ten times more extreme than what I normally think. But I do love the idea of having a Rolls-Royce and a big house and things like that. That's great. Because I really feel I worked for it. I broke my ass for eleven years, and I say if you work for it you deserve it. I really believe in that system. In Europe they call me the All American Boy.

I've got enough money now where I don't ever have to worry about it, but that never was really the whole punch for me. The punch for me was the fact that I didn't like the idea of going through life without anybody knowing I was here. I was going to leave my mark no matter what. That was much more important to me than the money because the money was automatic. And once you've got it, you really do forget about it. I mean, you think about it while you're making it—*how much have I got?*—but if you have over a hundred, two hundred thousand dollars you can live the rest of your life easily. The rest of it is just excess.

I used to live on one egg salad sandwich a day. And now, you know, I still do. But I know I can afford a pizza if I want one. It sounds silly, but I'm so satisfied with a case of Budweiser and a television. I mean, I like all the frills—I like the idea of having a color TV in my Rolls and things, I love that—but I spend most of my day either golfing or watching TV and drinking Budweiser. As long as my color TV works I'm happy because I got to see my quiz shows, you know. *"Take the car! No, take the curtain!"* So long as all the things I really do care about are around me and as long as I'm really satisfied with my performance on stage, that's success to me.

BILL GRAHAM

Money was never the drive. If I was going to work this hard, I wanted to make it, sure, but I live considerably below my means because I have very strange habits. I don't dress very well. I don't live very lavishly. Why not? I don't know. I have nothing against people who do dress well, who have fancy cars, but that kind of stuff doesn't mean that much to me. I have a 1970 Jag and a house that is very unpretentious. I'm not saying, "Boy, I'm gonna live this way to show people how unpretentious I am," and then have a villa that nobody can see, which is how a lot of the artists in the music business are. They don't want to show what they have. Well, that's what I got. But when I come to New York I derive great pleasure sitting here in this hotel suite looking out there at Central Park, and if they told me it would cost me two thousand dollars to stay here today, I'd probably pay it. I've done things that have cost me a lot of money because at that particular moment that's what I wanted.

That doesn't mean I throw my money around. I'll fight you for an act over ten cents, but if I want something I have a right to have it if it's available and doesn't hurt anybody. You know why? Because I work and I earned what I have and I have the right to decide what my pleasures are.

ROCKY AOKI

I used to work for a dollar an hour parking cars. I enjoyed it. I know the value of money, so I don't waste it. I personally try not to waste it. I realize that the Rocky Aoki of a dollar an hour of eleven, twelve years ago is not the same Rocky Aoki as now, but I still know the value of money. That's why I can sleep anywhere. I slept in the bathroom one wintertime when it was very cold when we were operating one small restaurant and almost went bankrupt. I didn't want to go back to where I used to live. It was too far away. I didn't want to take the subway, so I had a foldup bed in the bathroom, the only place where it was hot. And I can sleep in the bathroom today. When I travel, I take care of my friends first, but I can sleep in the car without telling anybody.

EILEEN FORD

I'm a spendthrift, the worst, and I always was. I never had a cent left at the end of the week in my life. If I made a hundred cents a week, I would spend a hundred and two. If I made five hundred, I would spend five hundred and two. Money just doesn't mean a thing to me, except that my bills are paid and I can live how I live.

EDGAR D. MITCHELL

I like to live nicely, I like to live very nicely, but amassing great wealth is just not part of my makeup. If it were to happen, that would be very nice, it would be super, but generally it doesn't happen unless you really go for it, unless you make it a goal. I have never made amassing wealth a goal. I have always made being fiscally responsible a goal and providing well for my family, but once past that I'm interested in other things. I think that one's struggle for survival is really paramount, but once you are surviving in a way you're happy with, then you can become more culturally based and look at other things. My thrust for survival is very high. I like an affluent life. But once beyond that, I couldn't care less about money.

ELIZABETH ASHLEY

I'd love to have enough money so I wouldn't have to worry about it. Now my "enough" is probably different from somebody else's "enough," but I'd like to make enough money so I don't have to tap dance when I'm sixty if I don't want to. But I've never been able to make a plan and I've finally sort of stopped trying. I will always be spared the pitfalls of rarefied air because people like me don't make a lot of money. We get good salaries but we can't afford to not work for very long. Performers don't get rich in the theater, and not many of them make money in movies anymore. The only performers that make any money are those who do television series and even that's sort of rare.

I don't own anything, I don't have any investments or anything like that, so I kind of live hand-to-mouth. I would like to have enough money in the bank to buy airplane tickets and nice wine and a couple of other substances I'm fond of and cook good grub for my friends and go to Baja occasionally. That's not cheap, but then on the other hand it's not a whole lot. You see, I've lived long enough to know how I like to live. I mean I've had Rolls-Royces and drivers and sable coats and Balenciaga dresses and been totally, absolutely miserable. I really OD'd on the vulgarity of it. The kind of people that get into that are just not my kind of people. It doesn't mean I wouldn't enjoy a Rolls-Royce, but where I go I would feel silly in one.

WILLIAM GAINES

I've always had a tremendous guilt about appearing prosperous. When I was married, I wouldn't let my wife have a fur coat and that kind of thing because if all my friends' wives didn't have fur coats, I felt it wasn't nice that my wife should have one. Of course, my wife didn't see it that way, and this led to difficulties. It was a long time before I allowed myself to buy a Cadillac because I thought that was too ostentatious. And then I did get a Cadillac, and maybe for seven or eight years I drove them. Then for a variety of reasons I gave them up, and I think after I gave them up I was a little more comfortable again.

I've never believed in expanding my standard of living in proportion to my income because I am always expecting my income to plummet. I'm really a born pessimist that way. I live my whole life as though tomorrow I'm going to suddenly find myself having to make do on a lot less, and philosophically I think it'll be a lot easier for me if I never get used to too much. So I live what I think is very modestly in proportion to what I could afford. I live in a five-room rented apartment. I own no homes for the winter and no homes for the summer nor any kind of home for that matter, because I don't like houses. I like to live in my apartment, where I can hole up with my air conditioner. And I drive a Torino, so I don't care what happens to it. I don't even own it, I rent it. You can see I spend nothing on clothing. My only extravagances are travel and food and wine. I will spend anything on food and wine, and I really only travel to get to more and different food and wine. I have this one overriding, highly neurotic passion, which is to stuff my face with the very finest wine and food available. My idea of a good vacation is to go to France for a week and just jump in a car and ride around to the vineyards and drink and eat at two- and three-star restaurants. That's my extravagance, and I really have no other.

HOWARD COSELL

America has easy yardsticks for success. One is to make a very good income. That's probably primary in the average mind. But I don't consider myself a successful person because I do that. I consider myself a successful person because of my home, because of the life I've created with my wife, my two daughters, my son-in-law and my three grandchildren. That's where all my real success is. And they are two totally separate things, except for this: Without the support of my wife over the years, and for that matter my two daughters who are now adults, I don't think I could have possibly achieved that other "success."

I grew up in the Depression. My parents had a very hard time of it. It's a miracle my dad, by borrowing from the banks every three months, was able to put me through college and law school. Based upon that upbringing my drive has always been for financial security for my family. So my attitude toward money must necessarily have changed. When I began I had none. Now I've got a goodly sum. But I still need more to insure my family's security forevermore. If I didn't have to do that, quite frankly I'd quit now.

BRUNO SANMARTINO

It makes me feel good inside that I can send my boy to the school where he wanted to go. It makes me feel good that I can buy a home and put a big swimming pool in the backyard. I travel a lot, so if I can't be like the regular Joe who takes his two weeks vacation every year, at least I can provide this. Maybe it's not the same, but if they've got their pool to swim in they're happy, they're having a good time. So the fact that you can do all this is a great feeling.

But you know what a newspaper man asked me last week? He said to me, "You know, I've been looking over the records of what you've been doing as an attraction and I see that you sell out Boston, you sell out Madison Square Garden, you sell out Baltimore. Yet I've been inquiring about your earnings and I see you make between two hundred thousand dollars and two hundred fifty thousand dollars a year." Now he says, "I'm figuring out what kind of gates you're drawing and if you got the right percentage you could be making four hundred fifty thousand dollars a year." He says, "How come you don't demand it and how come you accept this and how come you accept that?" I guess he was more or less saying, "What's the matter with you, are you stupid? Don't you know that Joe Namath is making half a million?"

Well, I don't buy that kind of thinking at all. The way I see it, athletes overprice themselves. They think too darn much of themselves. I make over two hundred thousand dollars a year and here I am, an uneducated guy from Italy who was starving to death, who never knew what it was like to have a full meal in his stomach. Now I come over here. I trained my guts out. I did. I didn't just become a professional wrestler because somebody looked at me and said, "Hey, how'd you like to be a wrestler?" It didn't come that easy. I had to work hard for it. But everybody works in this life. Who works harder than the guy in the steel mill by the blast furnaces? Who's working harder than the guy who's walking on those steel beams five hundred feet in the air? You know what I mean? No matter what you do, you have to produce and produce hard.

But the way I look at it, I'm earning more money than I ever dreamed of, certainly enough money to give my family the kind of life I never knew as a kid and to provide for my future if I'm lucky enough to live to a ripe old age. And I don't want to make twice what I'm making if it's going to mean that the wrestlers who don't earn as much as I do are going to be making even less because of my greed. The man who promotes you is going to have to get that money from someplace. If they gave me more, maybe they wouldn't be making what they need to continue on as promoters. I often hear that baseball teams are owned by millionaires who love the game and if they lose money they use it as a tax write-off. Maybe it's true. I don't know about other sports. But in wrestling, promoters are always taking a chance and if they don't make a buck out of it they go out of business. I've seen promoters go out of business and I don't want that to happen to anyone because I think I should be making four hundred thousand dollars a year. I say let everybody live.

And I just can't understand how any athlete can take himself so seriously that he believes he is really worth that much. People like Jonas Salk, who discovered the vaccine that can cure people of polio, for God Almighty's sake, this is truly important. A guy like that, if I heard he makes a million dollars a year, I would say, man, let him make two million. This man is really doing something. What am I doing? I go to Madison Square Garden. Yeah, I may sell it out. So people come and cheer. They let everything out of their system, they're happy, they go home. So what can I credit myself for, perhaps giving some people some entertainment for twenty minutes, thirty minutes, an hour?

DON KING

I recognize the difference between power and money. Usually they put money before your eyes and try to mesmerize you with the glamour of money and what it can do, but they preclude you from dealing with the real entity, which is power. Power is basic and fundamental. In anything that you deal with, you must search out the real crux of the situation. When you do this you come face to face with the reality of the situation, and power is the most important. You see, money is incidental. If you have power over a nation you can print its money, you can make whatever you want to be the money, the medium of exchange. The masses of the people have been trained and oriented to this medium of exchange, and they begin to worship it because it can give them the possessions they desire. But sitting up on top of the heap is the man who prints the money, you understand? And he's got us all down on the bottom using the money as the god. I give you ten dollars and you give me the cigarette lighter. In my own life I used to be like the rest of them running around that were somewhat dead in their perspective. Money was the real thing for me too. Money is now. You know, money is a necessity. But I understand that when you can deal and perform, then it's automatic that the money must come along.

BILL GRAHAM

People always relate success to power. The owner of a building will throw out the cleaning man who's standing in the lobby rather than say, "Would you please get out of the lobby? We're ready to close the building." But then when the owner isn't there, the cleaning man will say to some kid who's thrown down a chewing gum wrapper, "Get that fucking chewing gum wrapper up!"Because of our titles we obtain this supposed power, and I act the same way sometimes. Someone will go, "Well, why can't I throw the orange peel on the floor?" and I'll say, "Because it's my fucking building, asshole! And you pick it up!" We all have this power. I suppose it's what we do with it that counts.

AL GOLDSTEIN

You never have enough power. I would like to be really important. I'd like people to cluck, "That's Al Goldstein!" In certain circles I'm hot shit and important, I'm sort of like the Vincent Canby of porn films. I can make one or break one. I like that. People are obsequious to me and nice and a lot of fake friends are interested in me. I'm aware that they're not really my friends, but I like knowing that I was instrumental in the success of *Deep Throat,* that if I zing a movie, instead of playing seven weeks in New York, it's gonna play one day. Sometimes it scares me. It mostly scares me when I meet the person who made the film because then there's a human element and it's more complicated.

Linda Lovelace, I was the first person to interview her, and when I found those shots of her having sex with a dog I ran them. And she felt betrayed because she thought we were friends, but I am a journalist, so it means I'm really a whore, more so than she is. I have no loyalty. My loyalty is to next week's newspaper.

So the power is exciting in the small areas. I have it. I want more. I wish I were important in viewing some of the big studio films. I know I'm not. I do try to be a realist. One of the things

I love about flying—I've been taking flying lessons—is that I can overcome gravity. It makes me feel important and in command. I think the larger the boundaries in which we can exercise power, the better we are. I would like to be Kissinger. That seems exciting to me, that kind of power. Of course, he's encouraging, Kissinger, because he's fatter and uglier than I am, and I always think of dashing diplomats. So he's a step forward for Everyman. But power I would like more of. It's exhausting, but it's exciting.

GEORGE PLIMPTON

I always thought the so-called influence of *The Paris Review* crowd was something of a joke. It's true that some time back the literary establishment was supposed to have been controlled by the people associated with *The Paris Review,* and a number of articles and books came out saying that you really couldn't get anywhere as a writer in New York unless you scratched a lot of backs of the people around the magazine. But that sort of influence in the literary world has just always seemed overstated to me. It might exist in the art world, where the artist's reputation depends so much on dealers and museum curators. I mean, if Henry Geldzahler of the Metropolitan Museum puts his check mark next to somebody, that person is automatically an extremely important painter. But there's no way that could be done with a writer. I don't know of any critic or editor with that power. Front page reviews in the *New York Times* don't automatically push a book onto any sort of best seller list at all. Of course, people who can't get their works published refuse to admit to themselves that their writing really isn't very good; their excuse is that they're not being published because there's a literary power complex and they're not members of it.

REX REED

I have no real proof that I have any influence, and I think you start sounding very snarky when you begin talking about all of your power and everything. I don't know about that because I've never really analyzed it. I'm told by the various polls that are conducted that I am influential as a critic. I don't know who anybody polls in these things, but the Ford Foundation went to the people on the street and asked theater managers to conduct similar polls from their patronage, and as a result I came out the second most influential film critic in America, the most influential in the printed media. Number one is Gene Shalit on the *Today Show.* I'm told these things, but I don't really know. I'm skeptical, and I think any critic should be. I think criticism is highly overrated anyway. Critics tend to believe they are in the position to make or break works of art, and I really don't think they are. I didn't like *The Sound of Music.* It's one of the highest-grossing films of all time. I thought *Jaws* was a B movie for television, and you couldn't beat them off with a stick.

But even in movie reviews I am able to get certain social points across, some of the things that are important to me. I'm always exposing things I feel are wrong in society, and I like being able to reach people who might not otherwise be exposed to them. For example, the *Daily News* was a very conservative paper for a long time, and when I came there I started getting away with murder. I started sneaking in all kinds of liberal political ideology that was diametrically opposed to their editorial page. Consequently, all the writers at the *News* were up in arms because I was being allowed to say things nobody else could say, and eventually I feel in a small way I helped to change the texture of the whole paper. The *News* is very different today from the way it used to be, and that makes me feel good. That's kind of tangible evidence that I do achieve something.

JOHN DIEBOLD

I am in a position where I can get an awful lot of things accomplished if I believe in them and want to do them. We are a tiny organization, yet we have a tremendous fulcrum, which is the multiplier effect of working with enormous organizations, the biggest organizations in the world, governments and private businesses. Part of what I've been interested in is having some effect on my times, and in the times in which we live things are largely done through enormously complex organizational relationships. So by working through these organizations we have tremendous impact on very large numbers of people and on public policies and all in a way that virtually no layman understands. The general popular understanding of it would be nil, yet the real impact is enormous.

BUDDY RICH

Yeah, I suppose I've influenced a great many young drummers. I don't suppose they really understand it because they won't admit to people who've played before them as being an influence, yet I can go see some young cats play drums and I feel as though I'm looking at a picture of myself. But they don't admit that they may be playing like somebody else. When I started out there weren't that many drummers to listen to so you had to develop your own particular thing, your own particular style. That's what made everybody so great. Each one of the cats delivered a personal message when they were playing. But the young guys today listen to one guy and then all the other drummers feed off that particular thing, so there's a whole lot of little one-style rock drummers running around. But I suppose that's their success.

MILTON GLASER

The nature of my particular business is to be effective and influential. That's what it's supposed to be, so I don't mind it when my work is adapted by other designers. I think it's sad when it's taken without understanding, when people use it for solutions it doesn't work for. There is one problem in that if a form is too frequently duplicated, you no longer can use it yourself. It just takes it away from you so that you begin to look like a cliché. That has happened to me occasionally, but it's also been useful because it's moved me off something. I mean, if something that I do becomes highly visible and widely duplicated, I tend not to repeat it myself.

ALICE COOPER

Influence is an important thing to me because I actually did become one of those people that people looked at and said, "Well, what's he going to say about this, what's he going to say about that?" But I refuse to get involved in politics because I don't think it has anything to do with the entertainment business. If a Robert Redford or a Paul Newman or any of those guys go up and do a speech for a candidate, you *know* there's going to be a housewife who's there just because she likes his movies and she'll vote for the candidate just because her movie star told her to.

I really don't think that's very fair at all. They're not voting for the guy, they're voting for what their movie stars say. So when they call me and say, "Will you do a concert here for this guy and a concert for that guy and support him?" I always say no. I don't want anything to do with that. I'm an entertainer. I'm not a politician.

QUINCY JONES

To know that the dues you've paid and the position you've gotten to can let you open the door for somebody else is to me almost a greater reward for the success than the bread is. To know that you can do that, whether it's for Black Expo or the Panthers' breakfast parties or a funding thing for sickle cell anemia, well, that's just a wonderful feeling. And it helps you too, man. It makes you sit back and evaluate yourself. You say, "Wait, am I being an asshole here politically? I don't really know anything about this. I'm not just going to say yes because it's the nice thing to do." So you have to go out and find out what you're getting involved in, and that makes you keep up your social awareness.

Political people hit on you for a lot of things, and naturally sometimes you find there's some bullshit going down. Every now and then you run across elements and personalities and motivations that are ambiguous, that you can't really put your finger on, that you can't really define, but I don't want to be cynical or withdrawn so for the most part I usually stay pretty open. That means you can get your ass kicked. You get loved a lot, but you can also get your ass kicked hard when somebody disappoints you because somebody you really like can really hurt you, you know.

But I find that your antenna gets stronger and stronger. Mine's pretty strong anyway, the way it's got to be when you come from the South Side of Chicago. And generally when you get to a certain point a lot of the things you run into are pretty goddam standard. If you let the ego get carried away you could say, "Oh, man, I'm so special. So-and-so is calling me up for this," when he's called everybody on that same frequency range simultaneously, with that same emotion in his voice. I have a tendency to lean to the overbelieving side sometimes and I have to settle back every now and then to get my sights set, but for the most part I can pretty well clock it, and I'll say, "No, man, I don't want anything to do with it," or "Solid, I'll be there."

ALEXIS LICHINE

I'd say I'm successful mainly because of the recognition. If I walk into a restaurant in the United States or Europe, my name is recognized. My name has become synonymous with wine. I've become sort of the symbol of wine in the United States. As a result, when I'm introduced to someone at a cocktail party or a dinner or if I make myself known in a restaurant or hotel, immediately I see a sort of twinkle of interest, a sign of recognition which in itself, I suppose, means success. Outside of living well —and living lavishly well—I cannot say that I'm successful in terms of what Texans or the average American businessman would call success. There are tens of thousands of people in this country who have big bank accounts and big holdings, which I don't have, who may be totally unknown, who may not be respected at all except for their wealth. And very often they brandish around their bank accounts to get themselves recognized. In their own eyes they're successful. In the eyes of the small group of people who surround them they're successful. But insofar as fame, reputation or respect for a particular expertise are concerned, I don't think they are.

It's not anyone's fault if by making a considerable amount of money in nuts and bolts he's not recognized. American industry is such that a great deal of successful people are unknown. On the other hand, a lot of successful people have both recognition and money, and although I've lived very well, I don't think that the two naturally belong together. I've been referred to as a millionaire, but I'm not. I'd be a millionaire, I suppose, if I took all my holdings together and remained without house and home. I suppose that without having a roof over my head I would be one. But when it comes to bank accounts and shares and so forth, that is not the category I fall into. But people do know who I am.

AL GOLDSTEIN

I think I'm a success because I'm visible, I'm seen. The Play-boy Interview made me feel really like I was hot shit. It made me feel important until PLAYBOY went off sale. That's the worst thing about that kind of fame, it's so fleeting. I mean, daily writers have it all the time. They have a great exclusive, a great story, but nothing ever continues. We really are a thirty-second culture. In and out so quickly. You have a new book, you do a couple of talk shows, but you're passé three weeks later. To me the imagery is of Johnny Carson interviewing people. He gives you four minutes and you slide down that bench. I always want someone at the end to say, "Hey, I'm not through yet," and fight with the person who's now right next to Carson. It never happens because there's an etiquette to that kind of hucksterism.

JOE EULA

I've never been a person of stellar quality. I shun that. I don't give a damn about my name being up there in lights. I don't even care about signing a piece of work, I really don't. It's something a little bit different from that. I'm not going to be one of those idiots and say that I don't like the limelight when it happens correctly, but on the other hand it's such a bunch of shit.

MARIO ANDRETTI

We all have a little bit of ham in us, you know, and to me, it's so wonderful, it's so important, really, to know that people appreciate what you're doing. I enjoy the recognition. I truly do. I would be less than honest to say that I didn't, because then I know that the people care. I read a lot of the mail that comes in. I know what a pain in the neck it is for me to write a letter, and for someone to take the time and write down his thoughts and maybe want an autograph or something, I think that's really damn nice. And I must say I do enjoy it.

BUDDY RICH

Recognition is nice, it's very pleasant. You're a bullshit artist if you get to the point in your life as a celebrity where being recognized is a bore. It can never be a bore, you know. I play concerts all the time, and the director or the stage manager will come in and ask me, "Listen, can you sign autographs?" and I'm happy to do it. It doesn't take fifteen or twenty minutes, and if those kids can come in and spend their bread and want to hang out in the snow waiting for you or whatever, who am I to tell them to fuck off? If I have to catch a plane or something I'll apologize for having to split, but if I have no place to go, of course I'll sign autographs because that's recognition. They're saying to me, "We really love what you're doing and we want some kind of remembrance," so how do you say no to that?

Sure, there are times when I don't want anybody to fuck with me. You're entitled to your space and I'm entitled to mine. But that's got nothing to do with the overall picture. You know, when you're sitting eating and somebody grabs your arm and you've got a forkful of steak on it, I don't think that's really hip. And that happens, it happens to anybody. But if you don't want to be recognized you shouldn't be in a business where people recognize you. That's as simple as it can be. Or else wear a wig and bullshit yourself that you hate fame. I love it. I don't hate it. What the hell am I doing up in front of hundreds of people tonight if I don't really dig it? I got a real good ego. I've got to feed it all the time.

HOWARD COSELL

Sure, it has its gratifications in petty material ways to which I suppose we're all humanly susceptible. It's a nice thing for my wife and me to know that we're going to get special treatment at the airports and that kind of thing. To know that we can go to any restaurant in this country and we're not going to have to sit and wait. Little things like that. Tiny, vain gratifications. But the price you pay is enormous. And you must either agree to pay that price or as Harry Truman said, get the hell out of the kitchen.

I have reached a point of visibility in this country that is little short of phenomenal. And it's not said arrogantly, it's said factually. The net result is you can't walk down a street. You can't take your grandson to the park. You go to the stadium, you need police protection. Otherwise you're gonna get mangled by people clamoring for your autograph. You can't go to a restaurant and have dinner. "We don't mean to bother you but . . ." They sure as hell do mean to bother you. Now, y'know, you reach a point where you are utterly demolished by this, and my wife and I have reached that point. So you face a judgment. Do you quit now? Well, not if you don't have total financial security you don't. So you have to pay the price.

GEORGE PLIMPTON

Recognition I simply find embarrassing. I'm told that actors actually feast on it and that when Bob Hope went to Moscow and nobody recognized him, it threw him into such acute fits of depression that he cut his trip short and came back to a country where he could walk down the street and people would recognize him, where you could see it in their eyes. But I find being recognized on the street rather embarrassing. Not that it happens that much, but when it does, people yell at you from a bus or something and want to know what you're "up to next," in my case.

But writers don't ever get marked by it the way actors do. People *do* ring an actor's doorbell because part of his success is what he looks like and how he talks . . . all of which is immediately recognizable. The writer is an obscure person who hides behind the pages of his books. What turned me into somebody recognized on the street was not the books but those television shows . . . seven of them, and they pushed me up a step into some sort of public recognition. People come up and ask me, "Gee, what was it like to be on the trapeze?" They say that rather than, "What was it like to be a quarterback for the Detroit Lions?"

But I don't think it changes the pattern of your life in any radical way, other than officials in airlines saying, "Don't sit back there in coach, come on up and sit here." That sort of pleasant and sometimes rather annoying way people try to get you out of lines and waiting for tables in restaurants, all those sort of hierarchical things. In a way, I suppose that the public expects that to happen to you. If you stand in a theater line waiting to go into a motion picture and someone recognizes you there, they say, "What the hell are you standing here for? Why aren't you sitting inside?" It annoys them somehow. They feel that's the way it should be. I don't. But then if they do see you ushered by them, they snarl a bit too. So you get it both ways. It's odd.

REVEREND IKE

If you're going to be in public life there are certain things that you have to accept. If you don't think you can deal with those things you shouldn't be in public life. Sometimes when things get a little bit out of hand and people get a little sticky, following the car and hanging around outside, I say to myself, "Well, listen, I'm glad that people are attracted to me because if they weren't attracted to me, where would I be?" So you just have to learn how to handle the excess.

JERRY DELLA FEMINA

I remember when I wrote my book, I was walking down Fifth Avenue and someone came up to me and said "Hey, Jer, how are you?" I said, "I'm fine. How are you?" I looked at him and realized I didn't recognize him, so I walked along with him for a block, talking with him and trying to place him, and finally I said, "Excuse me. This is embarrassing, but I just don't remember your name." And he said, "Oh, you don't know me. We never met before. But we saw you on the 'David Frost Show.'" And for a second I kind of lost something. I kind of lost a little bit of the private person. That goes. But you could also like that.

I mean, the people who complain, "Gee, I don't want anyone to bug me, call me, see me or talk to me anymore," ought to give it up if they just don't want people to do it. They don't want people to stop doing it, really. No, I like it.

BILL GRAHAM

I'm not an entertainer, I am not a star, but I deal with them and after ten years in the business people will recognize you, especially in New York and San Francisco. Years ago when I walked down the street a lot of it was "Rip-off pig!" and "Capitalist motherfucker!" but now it's "Hey, Bill!" You can't know how good I feel about that. It's a marvelous feeling for two reasons: One, it's a reconfirmation for me, and, two, the guy's admitting he realizes that when he used to call me a rip-off pig he was wrong. He's telling me, "I used to yell at you for charging me five bucks, but then I walked into that place for six and that one for seven and the sound sucked, the act wasn't who they were supposed to be, they only played for forty-five minutes and there was no production. I never realized how good the Fillmore was until you closed it." The line will usually be, "You know something? You're okay."

Sometimes I say thank you and other times when it catches me the wrong way and I remember the scars and the shit that I took I'll look at them and say, "I got to tell you something, mister. Fuck you, you're late." I don't mean to sound like I hate him. I'm really saying, "Okay, okay, shmuck." Because that's uranium, a really wonderful feeling. You know, I'll walk down the sidewalk and a guy's coming toward me who I don't know but he recognizes me, he picks up right away. There isn't any direct thing. All he does is make one contact which is an instant rush, and he goes, "Hey, Bill! What's happenin'?" He's saying that he dug what I did, and that's a very rich thing to have. Many times you get a bunch of kids saying, "Hey, Bill, when's the Who coming?" I say, "March." "Far out!" Whack! It's hard to leave something like that. Even though they wouldn't forget if I went into something else, that's part of the success that's very hard to walk away from.

CLIVE DAVIS

I think it's nice if one is publicly recognized. I don't think it's important, but it's nicer to be recognized as having accomplished something than to have no recognition at all or indifference. I've not really been able to find out the answer. I've done certain things for public exposure where the initial impetus to me, consciously, was a business advantage. For example, when I was at Columbia Records, I hosted Madison Square Garden concerts and MC'd midnight concerts of classical music at Radio City Music Hall. Now that kind of visibility could be attributed to ego gratification, and not having been in analysis, I'm sure that would come out at some point. But I know that each time in my own mind I was doing it because I felt that a point had to be made for classical music and I wanted the institutional benefit to redound to Columbia. I was the president of the company, and therefore I did it. And it seemed to come off well when I tried it in smaller meetings and at conventions at Columbia, and then it became very natural to gravitate to the public forum.

More recently I've been asked to host some television. I hosted a *Midnight Special* television show because they were doing it around all the major artists I had signed. From there I've been asked to appear on many television shows, to some extent in connection with my book and to some extent in connection with my overall career in music. I've done some of it. I don't know, it doesn't enter into my psyche that I'm doing it. I gravitate toward it very naturally. And each one that I consent to do seems to make sense in terms of some business purpose. I turn down three for every one that I do.

I've been asked to host a weekly television show, and I would never do that. If it interferes with business, it would just be an ego trip. I don't need that kind of public exposure. I think it's also a little dangerous to confuse the issue as to who the star is. The record business is similar to movies in the old days in that executives who have built successful track records have greater public visibility than the presidents of the tire companies or industrial product companies, so that one tends to get a public image. And therefore you've got to be more careful to make sure that it does not interfere with your artists because although they're gratified by it if they dig you and if you're friendly with them, I think some of them perhaps could feel threatened by it. I know that from a business point of view it makes the most sense not to forget—and therefore you don't forget—that the real creativity at the source is the artist's. And therefore it becomes something of a dilemma when you get that kind of attention. A lot of the attention you get you don't particularly care for, you know. You don't particularly want it. So it's accepting public exposure when it seems prudent. It's liking more than disliking the recognition. And it's caution that it not reach a state where it really interferes with your handling your artists' careers and their futures.

MILTON GLASER

I don't enjoy the parochializing that occurs by being visible, the fact that people assume from what they've seen that you only do a certain kind of work. Your very visibility becomes a limitation. It's a kind of typecasting that goes on, I'm sure, with anybody who's successful in some way where they have an identifiable product. So a high degree of visibility also entails a perception that you very often want to break down. It becomes increasingly difficult, obviously, the more successful you become. That is an enormous limitation. So I'm very happy that my success doesn't come out of any personal visibility. The burden of being a performer success, being visible in the street or in a restaurant—I can't imagine how anybody can live through that. Literally not being able to walk down the street in privacy is something that is inconceivable to me. I'm sure people react differently to it. Or also alternately. I mean, some people may like it some days and not others. But what is really nice is to be invisible and to have your product take the burden of all that visibility. Because then you can still take it when you want it. You have that choice.

MIKE WALLACE

I would lie to you if I said that recognition is not satisfying. Recognition, however, for what I believe to be a substantial piece of work. Along the way I did broadcasts in which I took no particular pride. I did them professionally, even slickly. They were more or less successful. But I didn't take any particular satisfaction in them. The recognition that comes when you do something like *60 Minutes* or *CBS Reports,* in which your own ideas and capabilities can come into play, is much more satisfying than something which is merely "noticed."

And your visibility does expose you to detractors, there's no doubt about that. The fact that you have achieved a certain height exposes you to criticism, which can sometimes be cruel, sometimes destructive. I find that journalists, who spend so much of their own lives looking into the actions and motives of others, are very thin-skinned themselves, and I do not except myself from that. You try to tell yourself that those are the rules by which the game is played, but that's very little consolation sometimes. I suppose it's one of the prices you pay for prominence.

EDGAR D. MITCHELL

My view of recognition has changed somewhat in the last few years, since I've experienced it. In the beginning, yes, I enjoyed recognition, but it was a recognition for excellence. I guess I have always wanted to be recognized as capable and honest, a man of integrity, and I think I succeeded. But the recognition that came with the space program—public recognition, fame, the glare of the public spotlight—that has many drawbacks. Once you've experienced it, it's kind of heady stuff and you get to liking it, but sometimes the minuses that come with it are very disturbing. Your life is hardly ever your own anymore. Because you're a public figure, people begin to think they own you and that you really owe that to them and they get ticked off when you cannot spread yourself thin enough to satisfy all their demands and still carry on your own life. It becomes detrimental to your business, to your family's well-being, to your own well-being. You lose your center. You can be diverted from your goals, even to the point of putting your own survival in jeopardy. People are that demanding. They become very angry if you don't satisfy them. You're pushed and pulled in a thousand different ways, and that can be very destructive. The trick is to learn to live with recognition and still maintain your own values.

ELIZABETH ASHLEY

Fame is kind of a two-dollar whore. If you're really lonesome and down and busted and low, it's a two-dollar whore with a lot of rhinestones and flash that's gonna make you feel better for a little while. But on the other hand it might have the clap. At its best it's an ego stroke, generally to egos that desperately need the stroking. It makes people act like assholes. It makes me behave ways that I really wish I didn't. It makes you feel real good on a low lonely night, but it might have the clap and quite often does. It's no way to live.

But I'm a performer. I'm not some high-rent artist. I'm a tap dancer. I get out in front with my tutu and do my dance and sometimes the man puts a nickel in the tambourine and sometimes he doesn't, right? But I do it for people. I don't do what I do alone. And I'm into people. I'm just crazy about people. They're the best movie I ever saw. And sometimes people will come up to you after a show and they were really moved by what happened, by what they saw, what they felt, and they will sometimes tell you. And that's a gift, man, that is a gift. And let us not kid ourselves, that's what we do it for. So assholes that get cunty about that one, man, are just low rent, they're just small change.

On the other hand, I am nobody's property. I do not owe the public anything other than I owe my fellow human beings, however I encounter them. So I deal with the public like I deal with individuals. Subjectively. Out of whatever I'm feeling at that particular minute. Get me on a bad day when I'm in a rage, when I want to blow everything up and when I've had it with the whole fucking human race, and little old ladies can come down the street and sometimes they're just gonna get it. And I can't punish myself for that. I'm a human being too. And there are times in a long-run play—and people don't understand what hard work that is—when you just run out of responses. I can no longer hear. I can no longer respond. I have nothing to say. I can't even be polite. I don't have one more how-do-you-do left in me. I do not have an autograph left. The only thing I can do is come in and do the dance and go home. That's it. And people will not take no for an answer sometimes. People assume because you did it last week you need to do it again, and performers are responsible for that because it's that old thing of private reality and public image. Well, with me, I swear to God, there is no private reality and public image. I am who I am as I come. I would be better off if I had a number that I could do. Get me on a good day and you might even get a thrill. Get me on a bad day and you're gonna want to know what hit ya. Just like anybody else, man. And I won't change that because when I'm good, what I give them is something straight from my soul. And the only thing that makes that valid is that they react to it. It's a two-way thing. It's not a hand job. And it's direct. When I'm good I'm not shucking and jiving. And in my life I'm directed the same way. Sometimes the magic works, sometimes it doesn't. Sometimes you're hot, sometimes you've got nothing to say, right? So consequently I don't feel that I ethically owe the public anything other than the way I am. Take me on the come. Like everything else you go up for in your life.

So fame is an inconvenience. What it averages out to is an inconvenience.

ALICE COOPER

It's very important to me when I see an audience leave the theater to be able to sit back there exhausted and think, well, I really made it tonight. You know when you do a good show or don't do a good show. And when you do, you sit back there and go, "Yeah, that one really cooked."

REVEREND IKE

Self-fulfillment is the thing that I'm looking for. Turning other people on is really what turns me on. I gave some examples today at the service. Like when the lady got up in that stormy press conference in Chicago, that was rather remarkable. If you know anything about Chicago you've heard about the gangsters, and it seemed like they were all there in that room. They weren't black militants, they were black revolutionaries: "Why you got all these whities working for you? Let's confront whitey with guns, with guns!" Really. And then here's this little southern black lady who may split a verb or two, and she said to them, "Y'all hush, you've talked enough now. Hush, sit down now." And, you know, for some reason something told them that "Well, this is mama." That's how she was acting, she was mama and they were the naughty children. And then she went on to say, "Well, Reverend Ike helped me to get my nursing home started." And when this guy said, "How much money did Reverend Ike give you?" she said, "He gave me the inner strength." Wow. For me it was like the time back during the summer when this young man gave his testimony at the Forum in Los Angeles. He said, "Reverend Ike, you helped me to find something that I didn't know I had." That was very fulfilling to me.

MARTIN SCORSESE

One of the biggest satisfactions is seeing an audience react to the picture and knowing that you've done something that you can feel good about because you've gotten through to some people, you've made them feel something, you've made them understand something about themselves maybe, about you, I guess about life in general.

BUDDY RICH

With a big band you are not just playing drums, man, you are driving a tank. You're up there, you are a commander of sixteen people and they all have to listen to what you are doing because if you let down, sixteen guys fall right on their asses. That's the function of a big band drummer, just to drive, and that's beautiful, especially when it's cooking right and the band is really smoking. It's just lovely, I can't tell you what goes on up there when everybody's playing right. You're just drowning in sound. It's very unlovely when it doesn't go down right, I'll tell you that much. When it's not like that then it becomes hard to play because you're in a good mood and you might have other people in a bad mood and what you have to do is draw them out of it and sometimes that's very difficult. It can be very difficult to get them to go where you want to go. But when they all say green light, it's dynamite.

So success affords me fun. Success affords a lot of things to a lot of people—money, fame, whatever—but first of all it affords me fun because I enjoy playing, and when I'm playing good music with a good band, as long as my family is taken care of, everything else becomes secondary. People ask me, "What do you think about when you go to work?" I don't think I go to work. I think I go to *play*. You see, it's not a job. I'm playing something, I'm listening, I'm having fun. This is the only business I know of where you do the thing you love, you get paid to do it handsomely, and then you also travel around the world and get to meet every kind of person on the planet. I get to see the whole world every year and I'm doing what I want to do. What's better than that? That is success, isn't it?

JOE EULA

You can't put it on money, that's for sure. You have to put it on what makes you happy. If you're not happy doing it, you're not successful. That's my rule of thumb, but it took me till forty-five to find it. By working toward a certain goal I thought

I could eventually find happiness and peace of mind, but it didn't work that way. It's really a very simple thing to ask yourself what makes you happy in your life. I mean what do you need, what do you really need? Right up front. Do you need the job, do you need to work it that way? Do you need *the* person? Do you need whatever it is? And can you contribute, can you really contribute something to make *it* work? If you can do that, it's really successful. In these terms I consider myself very much a success. I used to be too far all over the lot. I was too nice to everybody, really a good guy. Lately, I'm a prick, the number one prick in the world! They call you a prick, so be one! One day, you know, you just start to grow up. It's that long slow process, not a specific thing, person or incident. Just that time, that time machine.

JOHN DIEBOLD

Most of what I do is what I like to do, and I think I'd probably go up the wall very fast if it were any other way. I'd much rather do what I like even if there were enormously greater financial or other kind of rewards for doing something else. I wouldn't want to do the things you have to do in politics, for example, if you're running for office, even though I've spent a lot of my life on public work. I've been enormously fortunate in being able to structure my life the way I want, but to me that's very important, much more important than money, power, prestige, etc. Given the fact, of course, that one would always like to be able to walk out and spend your days in the country.

QUINCY JONES

When you write for strong musical personalities, people like Toots Thielemans and Ray Brown, Freddie Hubbard, Dizzy, Grady Tate, and all those cats, you have to know what are the right musical environments for them. And I guess love is an important element in it too. When you love the person enough to care, it's like with your old lady. You know what your old lady likes and dislikes, what her shortcomings and strengths are, and in the same way you know what your players will and will not respond to. It's like sex there. And if you dig it, you're both giving and taking. You turn each other on. Toots used to tell me, he'd say, "Man, you really know how to push my button. You put just the right note in there, man. It gets my kneecaps hard." And I'd say, "You do me too, man." And I'd hear it in his playing, man, and that to me is one of the greatest thrills that somehow makes up for all the hassles. It keeps you from the heart attacks and nervous breakdowns and all that bullshit, because I think the people that get those things in many cases don't really like what they're doing.

You can stay up for five nights writing something and if you really dig it at the end somehow it erases all the physical pain and everything else because the reward just makes up for it. There's that glow, man, that glow of fulfillment, and my head feels like I've been to a shrink for twenty years, man. Everything is cool and light and happy. You know, you get to a place where you just say, "God damn! How lucky we are to be doing something we love and making a living at it." We'd be in a lot of trouble if people found out that we'd do the same thing we're doing without a quarter.

BRUNO SANMARTINO

We often get criticized and even ridiculed in professional wrestling. A lot of newspaper people won't even recognize us as athletes. A lot of people make cracks about us. But wrestling has always been my life ever since I was a very young boy. I always loved it. I always wrestled, even when I was a sick kid in the old country. We had a man in our village who had competed for Italy in the Olympic Games in the 1930s and he loved children, he was a good man who had great interest in youth, and I remember being down in his basement playing hooky from school just to learn about it because I so loved the game.

I always knew it was going to be wrestling for me. I tried boxing for a while. Not that I wanted it, but some people in the fight game saw I had fast hands and so forth and I did it, I fought for a while, but my heart was never in it. I loved wrestling so much and everything came so naturally to me. I could do moves that nobody ever taught me. My body and mind just brought them to me. It was natural. You could feel it. You know how when you try to be something you're not, you can work at it, work at it, work at it and maybe capture some of it, but if there's something that's really for you, it flows there, it comes to you.

I don't know if you ever heard of a wrestling bear. I wrestled a few bears when I was young 'cause I'd do anything to get a break. But a bear's an animal, okay? Just an animal, a big huge animal. I don't know the mentality of a bear, yet a bear is a natural wrestler. And when you wrestle a bear it makes moves on you that just amaze you, that bomb your mind out. How does a bear do this? But it does. I wrestled this bear in Toronto one time and just the way it spun behind me, no amateur I ever wrestled when I was an amateur ever did it so cleverly, so smoothly. The way this big ugly bear took me down, the way it would hook your leg and bring you back or shoot its arm out, it was just unreal, it did it so beautifully. It's just such a natural thing.

I'm not saying that I'm like a bear, but in the same way I feel the moves like they came to me that way. And regardless of what people thought of wrestling, it didn't matter. I knew myself that I had this ability and this is what it's going to be regardless of how any newspaper man who doesn't know a damn about my game is going to pick on it. I know that I can do it, I know that I'm a natural for it, and this is my life.

JOAN GANZ COONEY

I don't enjoy it very much. I wish I did. If I should die my last thought would be, "Why didn't you enjoy it more, Joan? Why couldn't you relax and enjoy it?" And I would be surprised if most successful people don't feel the same way, that they're beset with a lot of free-floating anxiety. It's one of the things that probably keeps us moving. We have a very hard time patting ourselves on the back and relaxing.

GEROLD FRANK

Whatever success means, it doesn't mean a damn thing to the person himself unless he feels he's accomplished his utmost. I think in many things I've been extremely lucky but that there is still something I can do beyond what I've done. One of the most poignant lines I ever heard was that the thorn that pricks the breast of the minor poet hurts just as much as that which pricks the breast of the major poet. I mean the pain is there.

I'm still waiting for the fulfillment of something not quite clear. I feel that everything I've done has been done with my left hand. I work very hard with my left hand, but my right hand still hasn't gotten in there. And yet when I read some of the things I've written I think they're pretty good. Since *Judy* has been put in pages I've been doing nothing but reading it, starting at page one and reading to page 703 and then starting back at page one again, just reading it endlessly without ever getting tired. My little granddaughter said to my wife, "Grandma, grandpa is so funny. He sits there all day reading his own book."

HOWARD COSELL

Do I get personal fulfillment out of broadcasting a football game or a fight? No. None at all. It's a job. Do I get personal fulfillment out of taking stands even if they're unpopular when I believe them to be right, like my support of Muhammad Ali when he was unconstitutionally deprived of his title, his duly achieved property right and his license to fight, his right to earn a living? I get personal fulfillment out of that. Do I get personal fulfillment out of trying to get blacks a more equal shot in sports? Yes. Do I get personal fulfillment out of exposing owners in sports when they defy the public interest? Yes, I get personal fulfillment out of that. And I get personal fulfillment out of certain relationships with certain people who would have to be considered exceptional in any stratum of the society. Like Jackie Robinson. Like Vince Lombardi. People like those. That's where the personal fulfillment comes in, not in broadcasting.

GEORGE PLIMPTON

I think the gratifications come in the little things. A man wrote me a letter not very long ago, somebody in the Midwest. He'd read my book *Mad Ducks and Bears* and he said something like this: "Dear Mr. Plimpton: The last time I laughed at a book was Aldous Huxley's *Point Counter Point,* which I read in 1939. Your book has made me laugh for the second time, for which I am extremely grateful. Sincerely yours . . ." You get something like that in the morning mail and you don't give a hoot about the critics who blasted you, the difficulties of the craft. That's the marvelous thing about communications—when you reach somebody and there's some reaction.

I'm interested in humor. Not that I'm a particularly funny person at all, but I try very hard to capture that quality in the people I write about because it seems to me it's not been written about, particularly in sports. We're apt to be rather serious about sports. It's a solemn occupation. But it's pretty obvious when you spend time with athletes that it's not a heavy trip for them at all. They live these absurd lives committing themselves to children's games and the extraordinary discipline that's involved with them, so that one of the few hedges against it really is humor. And I try very hard to capture that. I don't want to hear about how some guy scored a touchdown. I want to hear about what his teammates said to him afterwards that made him laugh in the locker room. The lighthearted areas of it.

When humor works on the printed page and makes somebody laugh on a plane trip or this man out in the Midwest who hadn't laughed since 1939 (I wonder what sort of life he lives out there), it gives one a tremendous sense of power. That really is what success is, I guess: It gives you a sense of power. You write something and somebody a long way from where you've written it is moved to laugh. It's an extraordinary sensation. Bernard Malamud in his recent interview in *The Paris Review* was asked for some sort of final statement about the pleasure of writing, and he said, "I'd be too moved to say." I know what he means.

EDGAR D. MITCHELL

I've had to recognize in my life that the attainment of a goal is not an end point, that the way I'm made up it is the process of achieving the goal that's important. I used to say, "Gee, I'll be happy when I've done this," but when I got to that point I found I never was. I discovered that it is the process of doing it that one has to find fulfilling. That's where the happiness is.

GEOFFREY HOLDER

The most important thing is to be a successful human being. The rest is really work. It's not because people stop me for an autograph or recognize me as the Uncola man or the guy from *The Wiz.* Those are just labels. The success is in being a human being sensitive to other people and being able to communicate to them regardless of the medium. Whether it's painting or dancing or just walking in the street, you're making a statement. You have to be articulate with your body when you walk, when you sit, when you enter into a room. I don't mean being constipated and conscious of how you sit or what have you, but you are a *statement* and an example for other human beings. That's the success; that you can communicate by just being. The rest is work. Because to have a successful art exhibit, does that mean that everything has to be sold or else the paintings are trash? Or is it that you are happy with what you did, you have made a statement? I'm a very successful man because it happened early in my life and I was formed from there. And I don't do things I don't want to do. And I'm a successful human being because I have a lot of friends. That's the key to success, you know. I have friends who I can talk in shorthand to. That dig me for me. That know where my head is at and still allow me my mystery. That is successful to me.

I just want to be more articulate in whatever I do. As a dancer you can say so much with your body and it's nonverbal, and if you can get that message across, bravo. As a painter I'm an impressionist. I would like to be able to draw one line and for the whole world to see it and know what that one line is all about. I like to follow the yellow brick road, and I sound very tacky saying that. The yellow brick road goes in different directions, but it eventually comes to a head. There are all these little side tracks that take you off through heaven and hell, but that's a chance you have to take. And in my life it's all leading to simplicity. We begin very simply like children, and then we have to go through all the stages of life to come back to being like a child, where with one line you've said everything, with one word you've made up a statement. Picasso did it. Martha Graham is doing it. At the age of 105 or whatever, she can stand there and say it all by just standing. That's what it's all about.

MILTON GLASER

I can never understand being a painter the same way as I can understand being an applied artist. There's a sense of utility, and the idea of being useful in the world has always been an extremely important aspect of my life. I want to be well used. You know, people get very resentful about the idea of being used, but that's essentially what we're here for. What you don't want to do is be badly used. You want to be used in the best way and the way you can be most useful. That's one of the things I like about teaching—people can really use you well in that situation.

I really feel that I've been blessed in the world through my talent, through my situation in life, and that people have been enormously good and helpful to me and that you just have to give it back. I find it enormously replenishing. When I was twenty years old I went to Switzerland and I called up every Swiss designer I'd ever read about, all the heroes of my childhood—Hans Erni, Leupin, Jan Tschichold, all these names. I was in Basel, and every one of them invited me to see them, this punk twenty-year-old kid. They all invited me to their homes. Jan Tschichold, who at that time was the greatest typographer in the world, took me in. I stayed in his house, in his son's room. He was incredibly gracious to me, and at that point I decided I had to pay them back. I mean, that was the only way to be in the world, to understand that you've got to give it back once you've got it.

QUINCY JONES

I think there are three trips that every person should go through to get a healthy growth, as long as he doesn't get stuck in the first or second. Especially since damn near dying a year or so ago, I know for sure I'll never get stuck in them. The first one is the quest for wealth and materialism and survival, right? Well, after you've done that, you find that you can't eat but one steak a day and so forth. I don't drive so I don't need a goddam sixty-five-thousand-dollar car, and gold rings and stuff I don't dig. So once you get past that you know that's there and you can move on to the next.

The second thing people get into is to see whether that quest for wealth has any meaning, and so they transmit the same passion into power and influence to test it. This is still very healthy if you get past it. If you get stuck in it, you get fucked up like a lot of people do.

And I think the third phase is when you say, hey, man, I'm a person too, I'm gonna be here my twenty-five thousand days and I want to be very honest with my existence from here on out. That's when you can start doing things for other people without expecting a goddam thing in return except the satisfaction it gives you. I don't mean this to sound like any saccharine shit, but if somebody is deserving of it, man, and you can do it, it's a great feeling. I don't give a shit whether they even know it or not, it feels great. And you only get that feeling when you get a little older. You're very selfish when you're young because you're still in phase one: "Move over, man, let me have some too."

I guess everybody forms their own profound kind of shit as they get older, and for me the main things are the satisfactions of the heart and the satisfactions of the head. It's your gig and your old lady, man, and when you've got those two things together, that's as much as you can ask for. Your old lady and your kids are healthy and happy and when you get out of bed in the morning you go to do something you love for a living—shit, I can't ask for any more than that. I wish everybody could have it, that's all. I also can't enjoy it with any kind of smugness. You've got to stay on the case and spread some of that good fortune around somewhere else, man, because you can't really handle it if it's just you by yourself. It's a nice feeling, but you can't close your eyes and become an ostrich and just say, okay, everybody else should be straight because I am. I'm not trying to paint a picture of total bliss, but I just have a very strong appreciation for all the good things that have happened to me.

The Changes and the Dues

JOAN GANZ COONEY

Success as the world sees it brings its own set of problems. And make no mistake, I would rather have those problems. In fact, I made up an aphorism recently, thinking of Joe E. Lewis, that goes: "I've had success and I've had failure and success is better—in some respects." And the qualification is that "success" brings such tremendous demands on your time that I think no one can foresee. If you were to say to someone before they launch something and they've never lived through it, "Your book or your TV show or your Broadway play is expected to be a huge success. What do you think it will all mean?" they'd all answer, "Gee, I'll drink a glass of champagne and I'll feel so good about it." They don't know that the phone's going to start ringing off the wall, that there will be problems about subsidiary rights and fights over the pieces of the pie.

And that's even a little easier than what goes on in a corporation. In a company like this one, there's almost instant growth and tremendous pressure to do more, which we did right away. Within weeks of *Sesame Street* going on the air we started to do preliminary work on *The Electric Company.* So that makes automatic growth, which makes automatic personnel problems, and before you know it you're into administration, which I didn't understand at all when I was just running a little company with sixty people. I didn't understand that we would be in international rights, we would be in licensing products, that I would in fact be running a large business. It's a whole different set of problems from any that you can imagine. You can imagine creating another television show, but I don't think before the fact you can foresee yourself meeting with lawyers and accountants and renegotiating with the government and that sort of stuff. I didn't think that if we were successful we'd have such a hell of a time keeping going. I never would have foreseen that.

But on the other hand, most of the problems do get resolved and some of them the way you want them to. You do savor those moments, but then it's pretty much a quick handshake and congratulations to us all, and on to the next problem, so that one really never has time to sit back and feel satisfied. Someone once said to me, "You seem to have so much humility," and I said, "I've got a lot to be humble about. I'm the one that knows all the problems here." Success to me, I think, means having all your problems behind you, not having to top yourself anymore. Maybe it's death, I don't know.

HALSTON

I think that one is not so aware of it. Other people are much more aware of your success than you are, you know. I know a lot of star-types and they're all leaders in what they do, but they're just not aware of it.

I can tell you things I don't like about it: being easily recognized. People sitting back with their arms folded and saying, "Okay, show me." Sometimes people expect too much. Sometimes they're unfair. And it's hard to keep the record straight. I sometimes don't like some of the silly business that one has to put up with, because the climate of business in the fashion industry can be a little shallow sometimes.

EILEEN FORD

Yes, there are things that I don't enjoy about it. There are people to whom I talk that I consider cheats and liars. In business that appalls me. I hate people like that. The realities are that I do talk to them. I listen to them and I know they're lying and I know they're being dishonest.

BILL GRAHAM

I've probably been in the entertainment business at the most hypocritical time in the history of entertainment. The successful rock and roll star wants to give such a different view of himself. The entertainment star of ten years ago was proud to show his Rolls-Royce, whereas now he may still have it but he keeps it hidden and will build a tunnel so he can drive it unseen. It's a different kind of success. But deep down the majority of the people I do business with—including myself to some extent, those are my limitations—are all still pretty much the way they were before us. It just hasn't been in to say so. It's so easy to stand on the stage and go "Up against the wall, motherfucker!" or "Do your own thing!" or "I just want to relate to the people." But, really, all you want is the same thing they wanted before you. You want them to like you. You want them to buy your records. You want them to come back again and pay $6.50, $7.50, $8.50 to see you. The rest is just jargon.

And the image that so many of our stars have tried to give to the public about really caring, do they really care that much more than Betty Grable? Anybody can say it. The only difference is that in her day you didn't win your fans by showing them your soul. You won your fans by showing them your talent. The Third World, the I Ching society works so hard at showing the Real Me. They've worked so hard at it. And, you know, a man will stand on the stage and talk to people about doing their own thing and dropping out and how education isn't important and you should just roam the world and not relate to material things but to the wind and the fire and the snow and the rain and the little beaver running across the creek. Well, the cat just landed in his Lear jet and he's gonna be on the stage for about an hour and make a lot of money for it and then he's gonna go back to the city that he owns. I don't want to knock their success, but they should be honest enough to say who they really are.

They're big business. I am big business. I just happen to enjoy what I do.

JOAN GANZ COONEY

I'm not going to kid you, I felt very good after *Sesame* went on the air and met with such acclaim. I almost couldn't believe it. It's hard to imagine the *swish* that happened that year and went on for maybe two years afterwards. It was like reversing a vacuum cleaner. And there was much that was a lot of fun about it. But I was also saddened to some degree because I understood what others here did not understand: that it would not come again, that it was something that happened maybe once in twenty or thirty years. I mean, how many great events in television have there been? They come once every twenty years, and I knew it would not come again quite that way. And it shouldn't. Plus it won't. Even if we did something just as good, it's now really expected. *The Electric Company* was extremely well received, but it was the second. We were *expected* to do something highly original. What we can't do is have anything perceived as failure, and I consider that part of the experimental game. People really expect us to be successful, and that is not a good pressure for our kind of work. It's expected if you are Grant Tinker or Norman Lear because that's the name of their game, numbers and money and stardom and so on. But that shouldn't be our game and yet we're trapped into the same kind of thing.

MIKE WALLACE

Occasionally you feel the pressure that you can't let down. In order to keep the quality of the enterprise high, you feel the need to work as hard at it now as you did seven or eight years ago. And neither the mind nor the psyche nor the motivation are quite as sharp as they used to be.

ALICE COOPER

Being successful, you can afford to experiment more. In the old days we used to sit back there and talk about "Hey, boy, someday we're going to have enough money to build this and do that," and now if I think I need a thirty-thousand-dollar cyclops, well, we call Disneyworld and have them build it. That's one of the nice things about having money. And it's really important for the show.

JERRY DELLA FEMINA

When I was young I remember saying I wanted to be a Republican because I was going to have money some day and my father told me that the Democrats were for the poorer people. Everything I did in my life was saying, "Hey, this is what I want." I think my philosophy has always been pretty consistent. I'm a fairly conservative person who always believed that people should really be totally, totally, completely free. And I try very hard to extend this freedom to those people I work with or live with. I've always wanted to be treated that way. I've wanted to be free. The philosophy's always been there. It's just that now I have more of a chance to use it.

REX REED

Barbra Streisand once told me that all she ever daydreamed about was having a penthouse. She thought that if she ever had a penthouse that would be success. So she got her penthouse, and there was just as much soot and dirt and grime on the twenty-fourth floor as there was down there in the basement. She was never able to use her patio because it was too dirty. And I guess maybe that happens to all of us. You get a certain amount of success and it's not what you thought it would be so you want still more. But I don't really want anything more at this point.

The only things I need now are certain freedoms within myself that only I can provide.

My one major disappointment is that I haven't written a novel yet. But that's my own problem. It doesn't have anything to do with anybody depriving me of anything. It's just that I've not had the time to really work on fiction the way I'd like to. And I also fear that if I become too famous, people will expect a certain kind of fiction from me and then when they don't get it they'll be disappointed. But that's what I want to do with my writing eventually. I don't want to interview any more movie stars. And I don't want to review any more movies after a while either, because you really do get stale and you begin to look at everything as though somebody came in and spat on the floor. I find I'm not having as much fun at the movies anymore. I think anyone can be a movie critic for only so long. So what I want to do is fiction, and I have to free myself from all these pressures to do that. I'm disappointed in myself in that regard because I think there is so much more that I have to give as a writer than I've given, than I've allowed myself to give.

ROCKY AOKI

I don't enjoy success. I've been so busy that I don't know how to enjoy it. But I enjoy working and talking to people. I enjoy participating in the Benihana Grand Prix and all my other company promotions. I enjoy these things. I'm really quite an unhappy guy. I'm not a happy person. That's why I stay so busy. I have a lot of friends who come up to my office at nighttime. I take them out for dinner. We play backgammon. When I go on a boat race, I take maybe ten or twenty people along. I pay for them. But I cannot be alone. When I'm alone, I'm very lonesome and very unhappy.

BRUNO SANMARTINO

If you are a realist about life you know that it's hard. When I didn't have a dime I used to think that if I had enough money not to have to worry about the hospital bills, not to worry about the house payments, not to worry about the food bills that all my problems would be over. At that point finances were very important. A lot of the people who say money means nothing never knew what it was like not to have any. And finally you get some money—and I have money, okay?—but what happens now? Well, my wife has bad problems. She had discs removed from her back and her gallbladder removed. We have three children, and always something happens when you have kids. They're always coming down with something.

What I'm getting at is that there's always things in life to make you worry, that make you unhappy. There's no such thing as a success that is going to complete your life. You're not going to have a perfect life of happiness and joy because you're a successful wrestler or a successful movie star or writer. There's always problems that will take away from that fulfillment. There's always things happening. Maybe your mother becomes ill, your father gets sick, whatever, so you're constantly worrying. I go overseas a lot, and I always have this tremendous fear that I'll be in Japan or Australia or someplace like that, where you can't catch a plane and be home in an hour, and something will happen to my dad or my mom, because I think of their great age. Don't misunderstand me, I'm not trying to paint you a picture of a miserable life, but you can't be happy when you have something like this on your mind.

You know what I have to laugh at? Sometimes you watch Johnny Carson or Mike Douglas and they'll be interviewing somebody who'll be going on and on about what a terrific marriage he's got and the people who are watching the program will say, "Wow, why can't it be like this for us?" It's so artificial. If people are going to be real and honest they have to admit that there is no marriage in this world that is so 100 percent perfect, complete joy twenty-four hours around the clock. There's always that up and down, whether it's emotional or health or whatever. I have a good wife. I can't complain about my wife, but

I'd be the biggest fool in the world if I say I've been married sixteen years and it's been one honeymoon. There's unhappiness when I'm on the road because she'd like me to be home. There's unhappiness for me when she's in the hospital and I have commitments to be someplace else. And there are just plain misunderstandings when she and I will have an argument. It doesn't happen often, that's the truth, but it does happen now and then, and then you are apart for a few days and that makes you feel bad. Do you know what I mean? There's just no such thing as complete serenity and happiness in this life, there just isn't.

HOWARD COSELL

I don't think I've changed because my standards have never changed. I wouldn't think I ever gave up one shred of anything. That's why it took me fifteen, sixteen years to really make it. I don't take myself that seriously. I take my work seriously, but I know that my every value is lodged in my family. I watch everybody around me in Hollywood, in New York—broken homes, messed-up children. Never gonna happen to me, my friend.

ALICE COOPER

I went through a bunch of different crazy things because that's part of living, going through all those changes. But even so, I stayed pretty much straight ahead. I'm glad I never got into drugs. I think the people who really got into them were afraid, just a little bit afraid of their talent, you know. I do drink a lot of beer and whiskey, but it's not to escape the image of Alice. No, it's just because I like to drink. I like the taste of whiskey and beer.

EDGAR D. MITCHELL

The perspective of the Earth from space was a real mind-blowing experience. It was sufficiently profound and provocative to make me set out in search of other things. As a result, I retired and started delving into consciousness research and future research. I started reexamining my own life and becoming far more interested in sociology and the problems of world peace, and how this whole social evolution scene takes place. I became even more introspective than I had been in the past. I've been interested in the apparent dualism of science and religion ever since I was a small boy and I could never accept it. I was always looking for a key to resolve the differences. I went into the space program as a test pilot and engineer, but underneath all that was my avocation of being a student of philosophy and wanting to sort that out. It all came together on the way back from the moon with the perception of Earth. It finally all came together in a nice neat package.

Unfortunately, it wasn't all that nice and neat at the time. It took me several years of soul searching and sorting through all those perceptions and data to make the picture emerge where I was comfortable with it. What happened was a perception on the gut level that the religious point of view is basically correct in spite of it being crapped up over several thousand years due to human self-serving. I recognized that the universe is a harmonious and intelligent place and not the result of a random stochastic process. In that sense the metaphysical point of view has a great deal to offer. From that point, I was able to bring science and religion together in my own mind and find points of view that made them fit very nicely. But it took a reexamination of all the knowledge I had ever acquired. I had to start asking questions about universal value systems and cosmic consciousness and these sorts of things and to try to get them resolved in a language that was compatible with my science so I could develop a total cosmology. I feel I've done it fairly successfully, but as I say, it took a while. The recognition of what this meant was very traumatic.

JOAN GANZ COONEY

How it changes you life is an interesting question. I think it's an evolutionary process in which one does gain more confidence. One is, after all, aging. Norman Mailer once said psychoanalysis does not so much change you as age you. The same way, I don't think you so much change in success as age in it.

JACK HALEY JR.

I think you just become more responsible. I would stay and party when I was younger, and I won't do that now. You know, enough days behind the desk with a hangover and you say, "If you can't do that and have what you want, then don't do that." Sammy Davis Jr. and I had a conversation about that the other night. We realized we've been friends for over twenty years. I originally met Sam in Vegas. We were chasing the same girls. And we sat the other night and talked and talked and talked about how when you get older you just can't do it, you can't shake off the effects of the night before. And by the time we finished the conversation, the birds were twittering. It was seven o'clock in the morning already, and his wife Altovise was asleep on one couch and my wife Liza was asleep on the other. I said, "Look at this, we've just been talkin' about how we can't do it, and here we just did it." But that's truly what you *can't* do. He can't do it anymore. I can't do it. Age and responsibility catch up to you, and you can't play games with yourself.

F. LEE BAILEY

Experience in this business is like a huge bank account. You get to the point where you very seldom see a situation you haven't encountered before, in principle, and although as a youngster it's a terrible mistake, you get to where cross-examination becomes instinctive and instead of spending days in preparation for a witness, a couple of hours is enough and you are much more relaxed. It's just a matter of acquiring experience.

QUINCY JONES

Experience and I guess age give you a focus after a while. You still get very concerned and uptight about the more important things, things that are really challenges, but after a while you are able to filter out the bullshit because experience lets you know what you really have to worry about. You have had personal one-to-one conversations with so many different trips that you know where you have been bruised and you've learned how to avoid that, how to go straight past it. But we still all get our follies and our crazy things that we worry about even though we shouldn't. And I don't know, man, I think if we ever stopped worrying about it, it would be a bore. If I ever got my confidence so together that it was all "Man, I can handle that, it's a breeze," I think that would bore the shit out of me. You always have to be in the water a little deeper than you think you can handle. You always have to have that little fear of failure somewhere behind you to give you the adrenaline you need to get your energy together.

AL GOLDSTEIN

Being successful with *Screw* makes me feel I'm capable of being right about other areas. In fact, it probably impeded my analysis a lot because I hold on to my patterns as neurotic as they may be. I say, well, as crazy as they are, they're working in the business area. My analyst feels I should be doing serious writing, fiction, that I really have capabilities beyond what I do. But I'm not hungry enough. I'm not driven enough because when I come to this office I can make eight hundred dollars a day. I get such easy gratification from the staff. I walk into a massage studio and I'm made to feel like King Farouk. I'm not willing to pay the discipline required for serious writing because it's too lonely. I'd rather just stay here and take it easy. I think I can do more, but it's hard to shift gears. I fantasize that before I'm forty-five I maybe will be doing the things I really believe I'm capable of but I'm afraid to engage in now, such as serious writing dealing with some of my craziness, some of the pains. Meaningful, transcending stuff.

But at this point just being the publisher of *Screw* is sufficiently rewarding and nourishing that I don't feel the drive to go on to the next step. I'm moving, I'm not dormant, but I have the arrogance of my success to confront my analyst and tell him, "Well, who's to say you're right that being this serious writer is any more valuable than what I'm doing now?" I mean, you really should go on a diet when you're totally down and you should go into analysis when you're ready to try anything. I go with all the accoutrements of success, and so I'm not ready to drop my life style to adopt someone else's.

The danger is that you start thinking you're hot stuff, that you mean something and you're too important. For me being in the hospital was a good experience 'cause it humbled me. Even though certain aspects have made me more relaxed and self-accepting, I'd become very arrogant and really cocky and obnoxious. So there I am—Al Goldstein, makin' a lot of money, to me a lot, close to two hundred thousand a year. I mean it's huge money, I can have anything, any toy I want I buy. And I'm in this hospital and a Puerto Rican guy who's making $2.50 an hour comes over to me and shaves me from my chest right down to my balls. He shaves me and emasculates me, and I say, "Goldstein, you're not such hot shit. You're like a naked little chicken." And I was afraid I was gonna die on the table. But it was good for me because in the trappings, in the context of success, you start getting insulated from the real world.

I understand how Nixon got into that cocoon mentality because sometimes my secretary is mean to people who are maybe from a high school paper who want to interview me because she wants to protect me. People become overeager to protect you. And on one level you want it, but you sort of lose a certain truthful experience. I'll take the subway uptown to a screening because it's so fast, and it jars me because it's not the limousine that I'm using more and more frequently. I realize that in two or three years I will probably have lost touch. And I see the seductive abilities of success. There are times I'd rather be in this office than anyplace else. At home, my wife and I are still fighting for power. I have it most of the time, but she doesn't feel she's my slave. She'll say, "I don't work for you, Al. You dial the phone." And I'll say, "Worship me." And here in the office I can get it because I can command it. I may not deserve it, but money is tremendous leverage.

BILL GRAHAM

I consider myself something of an expert on successes and what they're all about. I'm fascinated by them. I find that what a person wants to put out to show you who he is is an extension of what he thinks his success is. For example, we'll have three groups on a show: the headliner, an up-and-coming group in the second position and then a brand-new group who nobody ever heard of who'll open the show for the exposure, the group that plays while everybody is fixing their heads and getting a little stoned in the lobby, the sacrificial Claudette Colbert in the Coliseum. Now the road manager for this opening act will come up to me and he says, "Hi, Mr. Graham! God, I always wanted to meet you! Wow! *Wssh!* Bill Graham! Far out! Is everything all right, sir?" Like a busboy. "Did you like the band? Will you have us back?" I'll be nice to him: "I found it quite interesting. I think the bass line should be a little more up front," whatever it is. The guy: "Gee! Gee!" A very nonsuccess word. People who say "gee" usually aren't successful. "Gee! God damn! Hey, man! That was far out!"

Okay, the opening group has a good record and the next time they come in town they may be the second-line act. I see the same guy and he's not a corporal anymore. He's sort of a master sergeant. He's now the road manager for an up-and-coming group that's getting some recognition, and it's no longer "sir" or "Bill Graham, gee!" Now it's loose: "What's shakin', Bill? Anything good?" But not in a friendly way. It's like: "See these stripes? I ain't no shithead anymore." Now nobody ever called him a shithead, but he treated himself like one because he was only the road manager for the lowly opening group, and now by talking to you in a particular way he's telling you how much more successful he is: "My group is number twenty-two on the charts with a bullet. Don't I look like twenty-two with a bullet?"

All right, maybe a year later they're back for the third time and now they're headlining, and it's "Hey-y-y, Bill-ly." I look at this guy. I say, "Why does he treat me differently, why can't the respect just be there the same as it was before?" And I don't have the secret of knowing how to treat people at their level of success. I know who I am and I'll just say, "Hey, come on. Get your stuff ready."

I'll say the same thing to a headline act. In fact, I usually get uglier as somebody gets more successful to counteract who he thinks he's becoming. When they finally get to the headline position you've got to take them and somehow remind them that you know who they are. They go: "Hey, Bill! You call that food in the dressing room? Man, I mean, hey!" And then I go like this: "*Shmuck!* Remember I knew you from four years ago when you were the opening act. You got that? Now go play!" Well, that's a daily occurrence with me.

ALBERT ELLIS

I don't really know, but my success has probably helped me get to a certain point where I can give up that ego rating. When you don't achieve something you frequently think, "When I achieve it, I will be a better person, I will be ennobled, I will be godlike." And then you see empirically, when you get to that spot, that you're really still you. You're not ennobled. There are no gods or anything like that. So maybe succeeding has helped me to see through what we call ego, or what I call self-rating: deifying and devilifying yourself. So I probably give myself, my totality, less of a report card than most people, partly because of my success. But I might have gotten rid of my ego crap without that because, as I teach in rational-emotive therapy, unsuccessful people can get rid of it too.

MARTIN SCORSESE

I've had to learn how to accept praise. Yeah, that's hard. Being an ex-Catholic? Sure, that's hard. The way I am, I'm more open to accept criticism than praise, though to an extent that's also something I've had to learn.

MILTON GLASER

I think that success has helped me. The feeling addressed around the idea of having to prove and defend your position in life is self-justified. There's nothing left to prove on that score. In some ways, it just makes everything much easier, internally.

REX REED

I feel that I am more anxious, more irritable and less tolerant than I used to be. That requires a lot of elaboration, but I think it's mainly because I go from A to B to C and back to A again without branching out to X and Y, and it's all a matter of time. It's all a matter of how to program yourself and how to control your time and make it count for something. I'm not a good organizer. I'm not good at organizing my time so that I spend a certain amount of time doing this and then I'm free to do whatever I want. So it all goes back to feeling hemmed in. I'm anxious about all of the things that are going on in society, but I don't have time to go out and get involved in them and make them better. I would like to get involved in politics. I would like to go to the presidential conventions. I would like to get involved in the mental health programs, the animal programs, the ecology programs, but I'm just sliced up into forty pieces now and it's difficult for me to devote myself to those things when I have so many screenings every day that I have to go to. It's hard to keep a private life going too because work never stops. My assistant goes home at six o'clock, but that doesn't mean the phones stop ringing. People are calling me at night. They call me early in the morning. They call me on Sundays. I don't have a nine-to-five five-day-a-week job. My leisure time has suffered greatly because of my success.

JOHN DIEBOLD

The first thing you give up is sleep. Another thing is the sort of random steps in everyday life which are less and less possible the more active you are. To do the things I want to do I have to be highly scheduled, so I'm not able to do all sorts of random things that would also be fun. You go by the window of a shop or you go by a museum and you'd really like to spend the next two hours in there. Well, sure, you can do it, but you'd inconvenience a lot of people. Your life is too confined, too limited for those sort of things. And I think that's unfortunate because they're also important.

F. LEE BAILEY

I've had to travel a good deal to give lectures to bar associations and other things because it would have been inexpedient not to do so and yet turn up the next day and ask to be specially admitted to practice in the state. I've had to, I won't say do favors for judges, because that's not what I mean at all, but certainly to be very attentive to a request to help a charity or things like that. On the other hand, I can't say that it's been terribly burdensome. I'm very flexible and usually have tremendous transportation capability, so tooling around the country really isn't so bad. But there are times when the whirlwind is exhausting, and if you think of a boat sitting out in the moorings that hasn't had any use for the better part of the summer, you do begin to resent a little bit getting caught up in the flywheel.

CLIVE DAVIS

The business is narrowing. In order to do well, you have to give it your constant attention. So you have to give up other things that interest you, other aspects of yourself. Certainly you have to give up reading on a breadth of topics. You can read on airplanes and at night, but you tend to read about music then —the trade papers, *Rolling Stone, Variety.* You do all your reading at night. You can't do it during the day because of unanswered phone calls, if you're compulsive like I am about returning them. I think it's polite, and I think it's right to do so. So you can be an informed citizen, which I think I am, but not a terribly well-read person on subjects other than your immediate sphere of interest. At best, as a holding measure I can keep informed by reading the *New York Times* and some magazines, but to do reading in any kind of depth for pure pleasure is impossible.

AL GOLDSTEIN

I think you become very pragmatic. I sold insurance years ago during my first marriage, about ten years ago. I was a success because, of 7000 salesmen, I was thirteenth nationwide. I wasn't dealing with big policies, but I sold a lot of them. I learned to see everybody as a prospect. I'd go to a party, instead of saying, there's a girl with lovely cleavage, I'd like to suck her pussy or fuck her, I'd begin: Well, she's a single girl, I can probably sell her a $5000-a-year endowment. Or some guy with three kids, not much money, I'd figure I'd sell him term insurance. I mean, it wasn't totally ruthless because I believed in insurance. I still do. I have a million dollars in insurance myself.

But you begin focusing. If I worked on Seventh Avenue, I'd be looking at what the people were wearing and saying, "Well, who cut this cloth?" Here at *Screw* I really have very few nonwriting relationships. My friends tend to be people in the business. It's always shop talk. I realize I'm as boring as a hardware salesman. I'm bored when people talk about things that do not occupy me fully. In other words, I think I've let die some good friendships.

BUDDY RICH

Give *up* anything? I've *gotten* everything. What is there to give up? I don't starve for my art. I never gave up anything for my art. I'm a lucky guy. I'm good and am recognized as being good and I get paid very well and there are no outside influences to keep me from doing other things. I do what I want. I think that I can really say that ninety, ninety-five percent of the time at least, I do exactly as I want to do. I'm my own man, totally, and I don't know if that's a very bad thing. I think it's a very good thing. My opinions are my own. I say what I want. And I'm ready to stand by what I say no matter what the repercussions may be. If you listen to what I say and you don't like it, you have the option of saying, "Bullshit," and I have a certain option too. I can say, "Well, that's my feeling about it and that's it, my man." I haven't suffered any great defeats in anything in my life.

If I have made you think that all I'm interested in is my music, then you have a completely wrong impression of me. The only time I involve myself with my music is the three or four hours a night that I play. The other twenty hours I'm involved in everything from karate to UFOs. I have many, many, many outside interests. I listen to music, but the music I listen to would probably surprise you. I listen to things like the old Jackie Gleason records with Bobby Hackett and strings. I love sentimental music. The only kind of jazz I really like to listen to is the old big band stuff or the present big band stuff, the Basie things and all the new guys who are playing today. I really dig that, but I'm not that kind of jazz musician that excludes everything in his life but jazz. That's bullshit. There's a whole world out there. When I leave here tonight, when I get through at one-thirty or two o'clock, good-night, that's the end of my music career, man. If you walk into my house you wouldn't find anything that is representative of a drummer. There are no sticks. There are no pads. There are no extra drums. You wouldn't even find a picture of me in my house. Buddy Rich of the drums is Buddy Rich on the job. Buddy Rich at home is a father and a husband and a playboy. I like to have a good time. I really do like to have a good time.

REVEREND IKE

I've had to give up my personal life. Frankly, to tell you the truth, I've almost had none. It wasn't a question of choice. Sometimes when people give things up they have to consider it —well, it's either this career or my personal life. But it was never that for me. It was never a choice between the two. It was never a decision to make a sacrifice. I don't consider myself a sacrificing person because whatever I really want I get. But I've just been so involved in this ministry and in wanting to be and to do and to have this that I didn't really consider what I was leaving out.

HALSTON

Basically, I haven't changed. I've maybe become more careful with my time. I think the time factor is always a problem for anybody who does something. I'm very sympathetic with friends who just don't have time. My friend Liza Minnelli is in town now, and she's standing in for Gwen Verdon in the show *Chicago*. It just turns her on to do a Broadway show with Bob Fosse and Chita Rivera, and she has six days to learn the whole thing. I called her a couple of times. Now, most friends would call her and say, "But she didn't call back." She's only been in town for two days. "She didn't call back. Well, you know, she doesn't want to see me." I know she's busy. She's working night and day, and I'm sympathetic with her. So I probably won't see her till the opening night. But if you don't do that same kind of work or make the same effort, you don't ever know what it is to be under that kind of pressure. And many of your friends don't do it. They're nine-to-fivers and fudge a little here and there, and they're just very unsympathetic with your problems of your work program.

GEOFFREY HOLDER

There are a lot of distractions. The phone keeps ringing, and I have to go through it like a fine-tooth comb, you know, only because it interrupts my energy, my direction. My friends understand me, and when I talk in shorthand if I'm busy, they are not offended. On the street it disturbs me when I'm in a hurry. I will stop for any man or woman if they want to talk with me unless I am in a great hurry and the rain is falling and I have two shopping bags in my hands. I have a great respect for the public because they put me there. And I know that I am a public servant.

REX REED

When you have a lot of deadlines, as I do, and a lot of commitments and a lot of responsibilities, you certainly don't have the kind of time you used to have to spend with your friends or to do fun things or go to the country on weekends or go to picnics or just walk around in Central Park, talking about life and politics. I mean, you just don't have the kind of social freedom you used to have. So people think you're a snob because you can't see them all the time. People arrive in New York from out of town and they don't even tell me they are coming and they call me up and say, "I'm here for three days, let's do something!" and I say, "Well, listen, you don't know what my schedule is like. I have to go to Toronto this afternoon to do a television show and I won't be back till tomorrow morning at which time I have a screening at noon and then I've got an interview." They say, "Wait a minute, wait a minute, you don't *have* to see me." They become very defensive. This sort of thing happens to me all the time, and it has nothing to do with any change that has taken place in me. It's simply that I don't have that kind of time any more.

ALBERT ELLIS

The hazard of my profession is that I don't allow myself to get intimately involved with my clients, even though some of them are quite charming. By the same token, although I meet many more people than most individuals meet, I haven't the time to get together with them intimately. So if I were less successful and had less to do, I'd probably spend more time relating to people, because I do enjoy that to some degree. People sometimes view me as cold and unwarm when they don't realize that I'm really very efficient. I could be warmer to them, but I'm thinking of the next thing to do, you see. Right after my Friday night workshops at the Institute for Rational Living in New York, people come up to me and want to talk for awhile. But within five or ten minutes after the workshops are over, I have a scheduled appointment with a client. So I can talk with my questioners for a short while, but then I just say, "I'm sorry, but I do have an appointment." And they may think I'm deliberately putting them off. They may feel hurt. But there's just not enough time. So the more successful you are, the less time you have for certain, you might say, more relaxed kinds of things.

GEROLD FRANK

If you do something that's successful I think it puts you in a difficult position vis-à-vis many other people in the same field unless they are more successful than you. There seems to be an assumption that if you write a book that's a best seller you must in some way have given a hostage to fate, you must have in some way betrayed your talent. One would wish to be a best selling author like Nabokov: quality and everybody reading your book. I have never tried to write a book to be a success, and I have never tried to write a book to be a movie, and I've never tried to write a book to make money. I try to write a book to be a creation, to be something which will give me reassurance and will make others deeply touched. I want to move them. I want to read the book and feel hot and cold all over. I don't know what else to say. And if somebody else does it, then I am immensely respectful. I don't think I'm kidding myself. I don't think anybody can write a best seller deliberately. I mean, with all the money they have in Hollywood, they don't know. They put out a film and it flops, and they're sure they know all the ingredients it takes. We don't know.

F. LEE BAILEY

When I was a young lawyer, there was a good deal of resentment both at the bar and at the bench mainly, I think, from people whose wives were saying, "How come your name isn't in the paper, and this kid's only twenty-six?" I have seen that subside because my colleagues are now on the bench and no longer feel so resentful. You know, they accept the fact that they are not going to be recorded in the annals of history except on a very professional level, if at all. Other than that, I haven't seen a great deal of change, nothing really adverse. There are times when you have to exercise a degree of patience when it's raining and you're trying to crowd into the back of a taxicab and somebody runs up with a piece of paper and wants an autograph or photograph or something like that. But I think that's one of the obligations of drawing any part of your success from the remote public.

The only other disadvantage is being a walking target. There are times that I'm rather convinced that prosecutors who know damn well that they ought to fold their tent and leave or dismiss a case or take a lesser plea will say, "Well, I know I'm going to lose it, but I'm going to go in and try this case because it will certainly get my name in the papers and I won't be the bully boy in the picture." And there are certain groups that would gladly prosecute any defense lawyer that's been in the hair of the prosecution. As a matter of fact, most defense lawyers—Ed Williams is a notable exception—get chased down somewhere along the way because all the grand juries are owned by the other side. I see my good friend Percy Foreman just got indicted. I thought he was going to escape it. He's about seventy years old. Didn't quite make it.

MURRAY KEMPTON

Emerson talked about the Party of Hope and the Party of Memory, but I think in every society there is a party that he never mentioned that is larger than either, and that's the Party of Envy. People are incredibly envious of success. I remember once many years ago when I lived in Princeton and was doing interviews with people at the Institute about Robert Oppenheimer, how I kept running into this incredible envy of the man. I was talking to a very great Hungarian physicist who had won the Nobel Prize, and I said, "You know, it's sort of odd that the London tailors picked Oppenheimer as one of the ten best dressed men in America," and this physicist who in dress, manner and everything else was a central casting European scholar—abstract, wearing glasses down at the end of his nose, little bit of hair over his eyes—he says to me, "Zat is ridiculous. He is var-ry sloppy." And you understood immediately how in some curious way it was the envy for Oppenheimer that generated that response. A friend of mine used to say that he would like to read one piece by somebody about Adam Clayton Powell that wasn't full of penis envy.

JOAN GANZ COONEY

I recognize that there are a lot of people around who would love to see us really fail. A lot of people didn't mind the *Feeling Good* show not being perfect. I don't think that many people wish me ill personally. I have not made a lot of personal enemies, I think, which was partly due to luck. I mean, everything fell into place and we really weren't in competition with anyone else. No one else was doing our kind of work. so I don't think people sit around the way they did with maybe some of the former network entertainment presidents just holding their breath until the top executives got theirs, because some of them weren't very nice people.

But I do find a phenomenon that is absolutely fascinating, and that is a *bad story*. I know that phone's going to start ringing with a lot of solicitous acquaintances saying they are so terribly sorry about a bad story, people you haven't heard from in three years. No one ever calls after a good story, ever. My mother maybe. So there *is* something in people. Now maybe they're being friends and saying, "I hope you don't feel bad." I mean, there are a number of calls to pep you up from people who really want to pep you up, who have a stake in it with you or who are fellow professionals. They say, "I got mine last year and you'll live through it," and that's nice. But I'm just talking about those funny people you haven't heard from in years who call you up on a bad story to congratulate you or something. I don't know what it is. You never hear from them on a good story.

I'll bet that most successful people have a tiny little streak of paranoia in them, and part of it is because you are used, to some degree. It isn't paranoia exactly, it's more leeriness. I mean, you are always listening with an inner ear to find out what the bottom line is when somebody is being awfully nice, and it's a terrifically nice surprise when they are just being nice, they just like you. But part of it I think is my own personality. I'm not very close to many people. And part of it is in the nature of one's work.

REX REED

I try not to even think about success. I just do what I want to do. I think it's a very sad thing for anyone to live his life by the criteria of other people. It's very important to do the things that are fun and that make you happy. So I go on talk shows and get things off my chest, and I do game shows on TV, and I appeared in a movie because I've always wanted to be in a movie. And I did a stage play in Chicago that was sold out for five weeks because I wanted to do a play. I mean, I do the things that I want to do, and I don't care what anybody thinks. So success to me has simply given me the financial freedom to do the things I want to do. That's what success is to me, financial freedom.

But there are a lot of people who sit around and judge you because of what you're doing. I think this is insane. I don't hate authors who write best sellers, even if they stink. I don't hate or envy anyone else's luck. Some people just want to stab you to death because of this success. All the criticism I've ever had has been from other writers. It's never been from the people I've interviewed or from the people whose movies I've reviewed. It's always from other members of the press. They are really out there with scalpels, waiting to tear you to shreds for no other reason than because you're successful. There are people who don't know me, who would probably like me if they did, some of whom have nothing against me personally. It's just the idea that you've become successful and they want to kill you for it. And the same thing happens even in your own circle of friends. So it's not so much what success means to you or does to you. It's what it does to others. It's how your success is reflected in the eyes of other people. This is what I find so maddening.

AL GOLDSTEIN

When I get a call from somebody who knew me in high school or public school, I'm really happy. They don't know it, but they're giving me a chance to go back to a period of my life when I was a failure. I was left back in public school. And I want to go back to find out why, why was I not able to have it together then and now I do. Maybe because of then I'm able to do what I do now. Was it my mother hated me? Did my father kick me in the balls? And I want to see where I was. I see photos of myself as a kid, and I thought I was a fat slob then. I wasn't. I was a little chubby. And so any time I meet somebody who knew me then, I really want to see them and pick their brains and get their perceptions. And then I realize that most of the people who come here who knew me really wish me ill. My success makes them more contemptuous of themselves, for the obvious reason: If I could do it, if a shit like Al Goldstein could be successful, why aren't they? And I realize that there's an envy and a jealousy and a very encompassing kind of puzzlement. "How could this person have made it? We knew him. That was Alvin, that was Fat Alvin." And it's a problem. I only see them once or twice because they're looking for the key as if I found a pill or something.

JACK HALEY JR.

I've always maintained friendships from childhood, but it does put a distance between you and some of your less success-ful friends. They obviously feel it a great deal more than you do. That's always painful in a way: "I haven't changed, what's wrong with them?" But in their minds I have. I've always been kind of a loner in the family, and that's just heightened by working hard and not seeing them too often. Some of my cousins and my other relatives tend to mistake that as some sort of snobbery, which it really isn't, but you don't even have time to worry about it if you're doing your job.

MARTIN SCORSESE

Things have changed substantially, yeah. Relationships with people. There's a period where there's a weeding-out process when things explode, and then you hang on with certain people and with others you don't. I try to hang on with old friends, but sometimes those people change, y'know? It's kind of a cliché, but I didn't realize it until it actually happened to me, until *Mean Streets* was shown in the New York Film Festival and there was considerable change in some people who were very, very close to me. It was difficult. I got more and more busy and couldn't see them so much. Even the woman I was with, it was a very difficult situation and we split up recently. Now I'm getting married to another lady I met, but the breaking-up process began that early.

You see, basically what it is, all those years you're waiting to get recognized and waiting to get your work acknowledged and waiting to express yourself the way you want to express yourself, and waiting for people to understand it, some of them anyhow, and all of a sudden there's this flurry of activity going on and you're at the center of it. And this is my nature, y'know, I like very much people saying, "Hey, I liked your picture. . . . Hey, I want to have a dinner in your honor. . . . I want to do this for you. . . . Come to a party," etc. And after a while that began to get on the nerves of the people who knew me before then. Even though you used to be doing the same things, now it's different. As I say, I didn't realize it was happening and before I knew it that's the way it was. That's what my new film is about, in a sense. *Mean Streets* was maybe about that too, setting it all up right before it happens.

And new relationships you never quite trust. You have to be very careful unless the person's a peer, doing the same work in the same way. You try to deal with it in a very warm way, but you also try to keep them at a distance in a sense because a lot of people need things. I would love to do what everybody wants, you know, but you just can't spread yourself that thin. So you try to keep yourself at a distance and then after you get to trust them a little more you let them in a little more and then a little more. But you find yourself much more cautious. There was a whole period where I never answered the telephone. I just stopped answering the phone, and at times you do feel that sort of thing as a loss. But now things are getting a little more interesting for me because a lot of my director friends are out here and we're gathering around together a lot. Everybody's at the same level, just different shades and variations of that level. There's a free flow of ideas, and if we can help people we help them.

MILTON GLASER

I would say that self-elevation and thinking of yourself as special can produce a kind of combination of arrogance and detachment from the other areas of your life. It may, in fact, reduce your capacity to deal with certain levels of humanity. That's certainly one of the potential dangers of any kind of internal isolation. I mean, it can be used for that. You know, there's a funny thing about people who are successful. It's like this extraordinary aptitude people have when coupling. You see the exact level of attractiveness between them so that you always see two people together who are on the same attractiveness level. I mean, it's very rare that you see an ugly woman and a handsome man. And we're so conditioned to that that when we do see it, we don't believe it. We say, "Oh, well, it's for the money." We always think that there's an external reason for it. And that kind of sense of commodity value, which occurs on a level like that, also occurs, I think, in success. Successful people like to be with other successful people. You tend to move more in the area of other people of comparable accomplishment. Inevitably, you're sought out and you also seek out.

One of the things about teaching is, in fact, that it changes that a little bit. You're introduced to people who don't have that. I have deep friendships out of my teaching experience that tend to dissipate some of that exclusiveness. Sometimes with people you've just met, their expectation produces an immediate distortion in the relationship. So there are several issues there. One is that it's highly advantageous in terms of making certain connections that you otherwise wouldn't make. Two, it puts you, I suppose, in an ego-feeding relationship with certain kinds of people. And three, it distorts the possibilities for other relationships from the very beginning. I mean, it's really a mixed bag.

REX REED

I'm not one of those vertically motivated social moths. I only care about the people who interest me. Some of them happen to be very famous and some of them are not famous. My closest friends are probably people I've known since college, but on the other hand I've become very close to a lot of very famous and powerful people too. You can't help it. You start going to parties as part of your job and then you start knowing these people. It's one of the things that happens to you. Let's face it, when you become successful, when you become a celebrity, you're not just Joe Smith from Baton Rouge anymore. You are mingling with people who are also successful. It's just the nature of my profession. I don't see any reason to become paranoid about it. Avoiding famous people because they're famous is just as dangerous a trap as avoiding your old friends because they aren't famous. I've been to so many Group A parties, you know, and a lot of those people are quite nice. Beneath the facade of success, they're just people.

GEOFFREY HOLDER

I'm not changed. Everything I was I am. Some people call in a defensive manner, "Oh, you are so successful. Now you won't speak to us." But that's their insecurity, their inferiority complex, not mine. I still shop at the supermarket. *I* want to pick out the meat that *I* want to cook.

HALSTON

You lose some friends because they become too competitive, and then perhaps they weren't real friends. I don't know, it just freaks people sometimes. It's a harder job socially, or maybe in your personal life, to overcome the problems of success. People look at you in a totally different way. You know, they think you're sort of special and you're not. You're just a person. You have to extend yourself much more.

MARIO ANDRETTI

Even in your own neighborhood, one person may want to talk with you and associate with you, and someone else just flat-ass doesn't want to know you, maybe out of a certain envy or maybe for no particular reason. Sometimes I don't have the easy bullshit it takes to walk up to a stranger and start talking. Like even in an airplane, I can sit next to someone and feel I should introduce myself and say, "Hi, we're neighbors for a couple of hours. How are you doing?" But I don't know, a lot of times I just don't want to bother, and some people might say that I'm a snob or something. There's one particular man in my town who I've known since we were both teen-agers. We used to go to the same dances and both go for the best-looking girls. And we'd say hello, but I really hated the hell out of the guy—he was one of the playboy types in town—and I thought he felt the same about me. Well, just in the last year and a half we became really good buddies because for some reason or other we decided to give each other a chance.

You try to credit yourself with being a good judge of character, but you're not, you know, not in all cases, and it's strange how it sometimes works. And a lot of people just don't know how to approach certain people. You know: "He doesn't want to be bothered." But we're all human beings. The guy who's a big-time newsman on television, Christ, all he's doing is his job, just like the man who works in an office. But people have a tendency, just because they hear your name, all of a sudden to put you way up there.

ALICE COOPER

Everybody expects me to be wearing black eye makeup and black leather and chasing people around the house with a bullwhip, whereas I'm the total opposite of that. You know, I'm Fred MacMurray offstage. A lot of people are disappointed about that. Not the kids, but the parents. They'll see me maybe at some old Jewish Miami Beach resort or something, and they'll say, "You mean *you're* that guy up there with all the . . . ?" I go, "Yeah, I'm the guy," and they're actually disappointed.

F. LEE BAILEY

People have a perception, an image in their minds, before they ever meet you, and it's usually generated by the news media. If the news media say you're flamboyant, they expect someone who's flamboyant. If they said gruff, they expect someone who's gruff. The news media really aren't a very good way to get to know a person, because a reporter who has a dull story on his hands will liven it up a bit. Very frequently, people will say to you after a meeting, when they have some basis for individual judgment, "Gee, you aren't what I expected at all." And frequently people who are telling their neighbors, "That guy's an SOB. He's going to come down here and turn that murderer loose in our community," and be really resentful, even to the point where some of them make threatening phone calls saying, "Don't come in here," they will be the first ones at the head of the line when you are receiving, with a long story of BS. So you do have to weed them out a little bit.

JERRY DELLA FEMINA

People want to like you. It sounds strange. Why is it that a guy who is a messenger—a bright, nice, good man with a sense of humor—why couldn't he be considered a success with people? But the fact is that they judge you on what you've achieved in one area, and it does carry over. And so when I walk into a room I have an advantage with the people there because I feel they really, genuinely would like to know me and like me, and are predisposed towards liking me. It's just kind of an automatic thing that I've got a step ahead. I don't stop and try to figure out why, but the fact is they would prefer to like me, prefer me to be what they think I am, whatever that is. I've always felt comfortable with people, but now I feel they're comfortable with me. I've always felt good. I've never said, "Gee, that person doesn't like me and that person I'm not hitting it off with." I've never had that feeling, but I never had the vibes that made people automatically say, "Hey, this is a person I like." Now I do, and that has something to do with being a success.

JOAN GANZ COONEY

It's increasingly difficult to relax with people because I am invited even by close friends—and it really does make me angry —to a lot of small dinner parties for a reason: Someone's asked to be introduced to me. Well, that's very off-putting to me even if they warn me in advance and I say, "Sure, sure." So you're constantly guarding against being used, getting into a trap where you are going to be working on your free time rather than playing. It becomes increasingly easy to be alone and read or to be with just some old pal. One becomes very close to family, at least I do. They become the only people you can trust finally not to try to use you. That's a little bit harsh, and it's certainly not always true. I mean, there are many people here in New York who consider themselves close friends and I think I would consider some of them friends, but I use that word far less than I do "warm acquaintances," which are really what I have.

But in terms of opening up to people, there would be very few outside of my sister, who lives in Arizona, that I really feel I could be absolutely myself with. Ninety percent of the people I see socially I've met since *Sesame Street.* They have only known me in this incarnation and many of them would not be my friends, believe me, if I weren't "somebody." I can relax and enjoy them, I like going to their dinner parties, I like knowing famous and glamorous people, but I don't kid myself about it. If I start going downhill, baby, I will not get asked to those dinner parties anymore. I understand that very well and still take the pleasure of it and enjoy it, but it does not for intimacy make. It makes for a warm evening, a pleasant evening, some bons mots, some laughs. But in a situation where you *can* hire people and you *can* do business with outside companies, it's very hard to have close friends, and it's quite a disappointment to find that out. Of course, part of it is just a personal problem. I'm not a very open person. I seem to be very open and I have no problems talking about myself personally, but I'm still not open about my feelings.

DON KING

I don't feel alienated from people by success because I'm a part of the people. I feel that my magic lies in my ghetto ties. Yes. And as long as I can remember those less fortunate than myself and can keep my sensitivity connected to theirs and recognize the plight that they're suffering, then I feel I can be a conduit to something that has positive motivations towards change. But the day I feel that Don King did it, that it was all I, I, I, and not us and we, and that no one played a practical part in it because I was the conceiver, the initiator and the performer, then that will be the day that the star I have that was extending to the heavens will begin to cascade precipitously down and there will be no more Don King.

Now, though my physical being is out of the hard-core ghetto, my mind, heart and soul remain there until all those who are shackled and fettered are out or have a better means to get out. That's my commitment. I have to be a part of it. And I feel that I can speak to that now because through their encouragement and assistance they've allowed me to become a spokesman from the position that I hold. So therefore it's kind of hard for any businessman or any man, period, to refuse to listen to what I have to say. He doesn't have to agree with what I say, but he must give me his attention to hear it. This means that I have a platform.

Now how I utilize this platform is what's gonna tell what kind of man I am. I feel I must contribute back to this community of the underprivileged, and that means white Appalachia as well as Harlem. Blacks have no exclusivity on poverty, on privation, on want and hurt and pain. So what I want is something that will be beneficial for all the people. You dig? All right, now if I can by my efforts create atmospheres that are conducive to coexistence, then I think I'll be contributing something. But I won't be if I withdraw into myself and become a recluse or feel, Why do they all bother me with these hundreds of calls and letters every day asking me for this and that and the other? It's my obligation to receive these calls and help where I can and pacify where I can't, you understand? This is what it's all about. It's not about that I got so big that I don't need them no more. The people you pass on the road up the ladder are the same ones you pass on the way down, you dig? So sometimes when you're slipping and you miss a few rungs, those under you will boost you and put you back up. But if you been a bad fellow, they jump away from the ladder and let you fall without no net.

CLIVE DAVIS

Being involved with creative people who are affecting youth and then eventually the rest of society—seeing a lot of this talent, working with them—has certainly broadened my perspective and changed my life-style to some extent. I was very much affected by the Monterey Pop festival in 1967 and the culture that came in afterwards. Seeing the way it questioned tradition, not accepting tradition for its own sake but questioning it and making it justify itself each time, which is, I think, the crux of what youth is doing. Finding out that a lot of tradition does justify itself, a lot is difficult to question meaningfully, or reasonably, or comfortably. And yet having tradition change as we all see it change: life-styles, attitudes toward people and sex and mores and behavior . . . I mean, all of this is certainly very much in the forefront of what one has to deal with if you're involved with the creative minds in the music business, people like a Bob Dylan and a Paul Simon and a Gil Scott-Heron. If you're involved with contemporary culture to a great extent, you're necessarily exposed to a lot of that. And I am, and I find it challenging and unsettling and gratifying. It forced me to question certain things that I might not have looked at closely. It's encouraged a greater liberality of approach towards people. I grew up in a melting-pot atmosphere in Brooklyn, so there was not any great rigidity that one had to be eye-opened to, but I think it's given me greater respect for different ways of life, different thought processes, different approaches, a greater familiarity and ease with different kinds of people.

Old friendships don't seem to change. Real relationships don't seem to be affected. Being in music and everyone thinking that they're talented, you're constantly inundated with tapes and with people who think they're great players or singers or writers. I mean, there are demands on you that you wouldn't have if you were running a company that made cornflakes. But I try to divorce personal life from business as much as I can. Your children probably have to make a much stronger adjustment. My two older children are much more visible in their school because music is obviously the life blood of their classmates. They more than anyone else are reading *Rolling Stone* and the other magazines and watching the music shows. Not that I'm a star, but it does make them a little more visible. But they don't seem any the worse for wear. If they were, I'd be more concerned. I keep it low-key. Otherwise, my friends have remained the same, and it hasn't affected things too much.

JERRY DELLA FEMINA

My daughter Donna grew up through some of the real lousy times when we didn't have anything at all. And my older son grew up at the same time when it was just beginning. Jodi is a child of success. I think that they've related to it beautifully. They are three very nice kids who seem to be having a lot of fun. They also have developed a style. They feel, I think, successful as people. My daughter's off trying to be an actress at age sixteen. She's living in Rhode Island for the summer as an apprentice. She told everybody she was twenty-one. She's doing it. She's got that drive. Whatever it is that you need for success, I think that she's got it. I see them as often as I can. We don't have a "normal" family life. I mean, it's not: "It's five o'clock, daddy's coming home." It could be Michael will wake up and say, "Hey, you haven't been around for a couple of days. Were you in California?" But I don't think that they've been hurt by it at all. I think that my wife and I are probably closer now than we've ever been. Heck, we've been married seventeen years. You know, I was born and then I got married.

MIKE WALLACE

Over the last twenty years I've had a good companion, my wife. Most of the satisfying things that have happened professionally have happened within the last twenty years, and I think she has a great deal to do with it. Helping me sort out what it is that I'm after in my professional life. Discarding what is unimportant. So I think that she, plus timing, plus luck, plus a certain preparation that preceded it have succeeded in focusing my mind, my ambition, my understanding of myself. I think there had been a pattern of doing a good many things simply because they were there and paid well, without any professional focus, and she helped me understand the direction that I wanted to go.

WILLIAM GAINES

I became successful while I was married to my second wife, and the marriage broke up. One of the main reasons was money. My wife and I had two entirely different ideas about what standard of living we should have. Had I never been successful, who knows how that might have ended up? We did get along tolerably well before I was successful, but I don't know.

QUINCY JONES

I'm not concerned with leaving my kids a whole stack of money. They're going to get through school and get some advice, you know, and after that fuck 'em. I think that's the worst thing you can do to a kid, taking his purpose in life away from him. It's very hard to finish school and hit the streets and everything else, man, knowing you've got a couple of million dollars in a trust fund. It's very, very hard. I think that one of the big problems that a lot of the people who go through the *nouveau riche* trip get into is that they come from the streets, man, and have the drive that's motivated by the streets and pay those kind of dues. And then they build up a whole fucking platform for the kids, so it's just the opposite and they take all of that away from them. Like they say, "The one thing you can't buy with money is poverty." There's a disease out here called the Beverly Hills blues. You know, this poor kid, his father makes fifteen million a year and he still is fucked up. I never saw that one before, man. I come from the South Side of Chicago. So I try to find ways so that it all takes its natural course for my kids, with a little taste of reality and the streets so it isn't all Disneyland for them. I don't want it to be.

MARIO ANDRETTI

They say about Italian people that we're very emotional, but even with my parents, I'll go away to race in Europe or South America or South Africa and I'll say goodbye to them the same way as when I go down the street to the store. I mean, I just don't want to make a big thing about it. I want to keep it on an even keel. And I want the same welcome when I come home a winner or a loser. That's important. It's not something you say. I never said to them, "Hey, that's what I want." But that's the way it has worked out and subconsciously it has really helped me keep the continuity going. I'll come home and I'll get the same welcome from my wife whether I win or lose. What I've done, the success or failure, is secondary. What's important is just the fact that we're together. And that's what I like. I don't like this mourning because I had a bad weekend, and I don't like to be raised up and have my head banged on the ceiling because I won one. I used to drive for Ferrari, and there, if you won one, Jesus! Champagne and everything. But if you lost it was just like going to a funeral. After a while that could really get to you. Those things are important to a man, you know, just to be able to handle those things properly. I've discussed this with different people, but never at home. I don't have to.

BUDDY RICH

The people who are close to me like my family, my friends . . . they all think that I'm absolutely nuts, but I wouldn't have it any other way. They think I'm nuts in a nice way, they don't think that I'm nuts nuts. They just know that I'm not a very settled man. And I would think that the people who like me or love me understand that. All of my crazy idiosyncrasies, you know, they're there. And sometimes my old lady goes *wshh!* and my daughter goes, "I'll see ya," or my friends don't call. That's all right, because I'm going through one of my days or one of my weeks or months. That's cool. Why not? Why shouldn't I be allowed to say things suck? You say it. Everybody says it. I'm entitled to say it. But when I say it I mean it. It *really* sucks. That's the difference.

MILTON GLASER

I think to a large extent my success is a source of pride to my family. I think its family meaning has been very positive. It's certainly easier to live with than failure of any substantial kind. At least you don't have to deal with the internal bitterness and self-punishment that comes out of that kind of situation.

AL GOLDSTEIN

My father always thought I was a loser and a fuckup and a shithead. Suddenly he shifted to whatever I say becomes golden. He's changed. I wish he had supported me when I needed it, when I was ten and eleven. Now I don't need it. I had him working for me until he retired a few months ago and he loved it. I mean, he really loved telling everyone he was my father. He's in Miami now. And he's very proud of me, and that makes me feel good. It's a nice feeling. I'm sure so many people have had success too late in life. The teachers who told them that they would never make it, the parents who rejected them, the women who put them down will never know. 'Cause all successful people are really trying to prove something. I really believe that. They're trying to prove that all the voices within them that said they're a failure and a piece of shit are not true. They're trying to silence those voices that they deep down still believe.

ALICE COOPER

My family certainly didn't understand what I was doing at all. My dad's a minister, you know, and we're best of friends. He just came in from Phoenix yesterday, and I'm teaching him how to play golf. But when I first started, he was reading all these crazy things about me and getting really upset. I mean, I never killed any chickens on stage. My folks finally understand that, "Listen, no matter what you read about me, I'm still a pretty good kid. And don't pay attention to Alice because that's a character on stage and I'm still okay." You know how parents worry. My mom still hears about things I'm supposed to have done in Germany that never happened.

HOWARD COSELL

I think it's been a problem for my two girls, and for my wife to a lesser degree. My wife's an extraordinarily stable and balanced lady, and I think she's imparted that magnificently to my two girls. But it's not easy to read that your father is a scoundrel and your father is an idiot, and it's being written by people who are probably on average the most limited element of the human species I have ever known. Sportswriters. Somebody who is not even a college graduate, whose whole life and whole horizon is dedicated to whether or not Yogi Berra puts in a certain pinch hitter, whose line of vision extends to the left field fence, somebody like that will write that Howard Cosell—who edited one of the three or four major law reviews in this country—is an idiot: "Now he's going to do the Kentucky Derby? He won't even know which end of the horse eats." And you get this day in, day out. Does it have an impact upon your children? Yes, it's caused my daughter Hillary to question whether or not she should have pursued her master's in journalism. Of course it has an impact.

You are now on the air. It's the Kentucky Derby. You've got forty-five million people watching you. You're on with a little ex-jockey of whom you're very fond, John Rotz. By the format set up by the producer, because producers are bound by format, you are allotted something like a minute and a half to talk to this man. And you go in saying, in the presence of the president of Churchill Downs, "John, I don't agree with this format, and it will be written by at least fifty papers that I was rude to you and cut you off in my bigshot way. I want you to know that going in. I want you to try to make your answers as succinct as possible, yet convey your knowledgeability as a jockey. I will give you the lead questions." We went on the air that way and the poor man, he couldn't express himself. He's not trained in journalism. And then came the word which he heard from the truck: "You've got twenty seconds." Well, the poor man fell completely apart. And it was immediately written, even in *Variety,* our trade publication, "Cosell, who knows nothing about thoroughbred racing, cut off the distinguished ex-jockey Johnny Rotz so he could bumble on with his views." No matter my brilliance or absence thereof, except that I could recite by heart Peter Chew's *The Kentucky Derby: The First 100 Years* and no one else in America could. No matter, there it is, there it is written and your children pick it up. Does it have an impact on them? Of course. It's got to, even though they know the total falsity of it and that it's animosity, bitterness and envy which are exceeded only by the respect for writer's anonymity.

You know that no man can possibly talk like me who wasn't an educated man with a high degree of intelligence. Well, the one thing you learn about communications that's terrifying is the lowness of the mass intelligence quotient. I mean there are a lot of people out there still lovin' and believin' Richard Nixon. You understand? And most of them don't want the truth about sports deep inside. It takes away that tiny little last vestige of a dream world. I say "most of them," but that's no longer true because we have a new society and the principal audience is now the young adult, both male and female, and my daughters are right in that group.

The young adult—that's where I have had my greatest response. The young people of this country buy me lock, stock and barrel. So do the blacks. So does every disadvantaged group because of every cause I've stood for. But the establishment, people over forty-five, fifty: "Why's he knocking baseball?" Because they're still living with those names that sounded like music: Robinson, Reese, Campanella, Snyder, Hodges, Furillo. "We're witcha, Duke. We're witcha." In those days the society was relatively leisurely. Baseball, somehow, people had been convinced, *was* America, *was* motherhood, *was* apple pie. And along comes a guy now and tells them, "C'mon. They're a bunch of cheap carpetbaggers who've been rendered above the law.

They take their franchises from city to city wherever the quick buck presents itself." I tell the truth. And then a writer writes that I'm a goddamn shill, while he gets paid $3,500 a year for writing the Mets' promotion film. The impact upon my family? Sure. They're aware.

EDGAR D. MITCHELL

To the extent that my work has taken time from my family, I have found problems. In the astronaut program you had to be dedicated and goal oriented or you wouldn't make it. As was fairly typical, your family suffered. My former wife was really unable to take that kind of high-powered life. It scared her to death. She needed more stability and security around her than my type of goal orientation could provide, and this was our main problem. But I'm learning to handle that much better. I don't like to make the same mistake twice, so I try to give much more time to my family than before and be much more relaxed with them. I'm working very hard to learn how to turn off business when I'm with them. I'm not very successful with that yet, but that's what I'm trying to do.

GEROLD FRANK

There's no question that I could have been a better parent. Although I wrote with children climbing all over me, it was always understood that daddy was working and I regret the fact that the books might have appeared almost more important than they were. But writing is what I do. I don't do anything else. I don't play tennis. I don't have a boat. I have no car and I have no summer place. I just live here, and if I don't work I'm impossible. And if I work, I work because it's the only thing I want to do.

ROCKY AOKI

I'm getting away little by little from my family. From my brothers. From my mother and father. I want to keep them close, but my business won't let me stay with them that much. I want to be here fourteen, sixteen hours a day. I go back home sometimes three o'clock, four o'clock in the morning. Everyone's sleeping. I don't want to wake anyone up, so I just go to sleep and come back here at ten o'clock. My kids are gone from the house before I leave. Sometimes I'll travel for two or three weeks. Every three or four months I'll go to Japan because my father retired there and I'm helping with all his assets and business. I don't know, I have no guarantee of my family staying with me in the future. I love them, you know, but the business gets bigger and bigger and the family gets further and further away.

MARIO ANDRETTI

What you give up is your family life, there's no question about that. So you just have to work that much harder to keep that together if it means anything to you. And it does. I have three wonderful kids. I was married quite young. I wasn't yet twenty-two. That's damn young, I'll tell you, to get married and begin your life in so many different ways. So kids come along. And naturally I appreciated my kids, but I could much more easily break away and say, "Well, I'll see you kids next month," because that's what I was involved with—I had to go away. And not really missing them that much because I had, you know, just one thing on my mind and that was more important than anything else. Obviously, as you mature things change. Other things become important too. And as life goes on and as you travel, you just broaden your scope and you see how other people live. Yes, you do begin to appreciate other things, appreciate maybe what you have even more, and that's where the sacrifice comes in.

As of the last two or three years, I'm giving up more of the things that I like now than ever before, and I still have to give them up. Before, I didn't realize they even existed. Now I do, and I hate like hell to leave home. I hate to leave the kids. I hate to go away for a week or two weeks. I do it, naturally, but I hate it. And that's my sacrifice. You know, I just love to spend time with my kids. The two boys I have, man, we just do everything. I'm just their pal. We do a lot of physical things together. I have a place up in the Poconos, a lake, and Christ, I have racing boats, we ski, we do all the things. And I really, truly enjoy playing around with them. We play hard. And I miss it when I can't. That's where I come from today. That's where I'll be Monday right after the race.

And, again, these are the things that I appreciate and I miss because of what I have to do. I'm not complaining. I'm just stating what it takes. I don't have to run as many races, but I'm the one that committed myself. I'm doing it. It's like the old saying that you can't have your cake and eat it too. It just seems like there's always gotta be something that you've got to give up.

BRUNO SANMARTINO

I feel like I've given up an awful lot, yeah. For example, I have a wife and three children and I don't get to be with them nearly as much as I want to, especially my oldest boy. He's sixteen now, and all the time he was growing up I'd only come home every two or three weeks and I'd see him for maybe one day. I felt so damn bad about it because my poor wife had to be both mother and father to him, and as this kid was getting older he got used to seeing this guy coming home on a Sunday and leaving the next day and it became so easy for him to say, "Well, see you in a couple of weeks." Which wasn't nice for me, you know, but he couldn't help it because he was just a kid and this is what he was used to. Yes, that bothered the heck out of me. But then I always look at it this way: No matter what you do, it's going to have its pluses and minuses. So even though I'm not home all the time, at least I'm able to give them this, this and this. I know guys, friends of mine, who are home all the time and they're frustrated because they can't give their families anything. So that's life.

The good thing about it for a man like me is that I'm married to a woman who can at least cope and understand and try. When the wives in my profession can't, that's when you have real trouble. There are many divorces because the wife couldn't cope with the situation. This is where I feel extremely lucky. My wife coped with me when we were starving, she was with me all the way, and now that I've prospered she's still with me. I'm extremely grateful about that because there are many people who can't deal with a bad situation but only with the healthy part of it. I come from the old country and I guess I still think old-fashioned, but I do believe that a woman who can stay with me when I'm starving is a hell of a woman, a great woman. So my wife has a lot of problems with her health, but I'll always be with her in her problems because she's always with me in mine.

AL GOLDSTEIN

I haven't had to give up as much as most people. Because the driven corporate salesman, the disparity between what he is deeply and what he appears to be, is, I think, very great. With me, not really. I mean, *Screw* started with a hundred and fifty dollars from me and a hundred and fifty dollars from my partner. It wasn't started to be successful. I had been turned down for a salary increase from a hundred twenty-five to a hundred forty dollars a week, and my dream was to make enough money in my own business to make a hundred fifty dollars a week. So I never thought I'd be making what I make now. I had not had to change my dress or my appearance. I was always sexually compulsive and sexually open. So for me the price was minimal. But there was a price in terms of the hours, the weekends.

I still see my ex-wife, my second wife, and I love her very much because she stood by me then, she knew me when I was on welfare. I was on welfare for a year and a half, but she stood behind me and supported me in terms of the hours I didn't spend with her. My present wife doesn't realize it. We sometimes talk about it, but she has a maid. Now I'm making a lot of money and we go away on weekends, but when a business starts you can't afford those kinds of luxuries. So time is your big thing. I was lucky when I started out. I didn't have a family, I didn't have a structured marriage. My second wife was an airline stewardess, so she was always flying. I didn't have children. I'm very late. At thirty-eight I had my first child. So I think there is a price you pay, but in my case, it wasn't really ruthless. I mean, I was not the classic Madison Avenue killer.

JACK HALEY, JR.

For a long time I was reluctant to get married because I was really throwing myself into the job. I remained single until I was forty, and it was a pretty conscious decision. The timing was not right. I think I was wise to do so, especially in Hollywood, in that environment. I think I was pretty smart when I look back because I look at some of the girls I was seriously involved with and I see them today and I say, "God, that would have lasted twenty minutes." So that's probably the only sacrifice I can truly think of because, boy, I had a lot of fun. I worked my ass off, but, boy, I had a lot of fun.

ALBERT ELLIS

I'm sure my success has affected my relationship with women, because some of the women I would otherwise have been closer to, I just haven't been. Or I have been for a while and then parted from because their way of life interfered with mine. One of the main women in my life, whom I probably would have married years ago, wanted to keep me doing a nine-to-five job and then come home and mainly be with her. We broke on that issue. Not me! I won't do that kind of thing. I will always work way beyond 5 P.M. at something or other, and certainly will not just go to dinner parties or sit at home reading a newspaper with my mate or anything like that. Not by a long shot! So largely for that reason I've broken with several of the women with whom I had deep emotional attachments. I've also avoided some attachments because I could see from the beginning that they just wouldn't work. On the other hand, it hasn't been that serious because I always find at least one woman who is willing to go along with my way of life. I still have problems there, because I am so busy that she will get deprived. Even though she agrees not to feel deprived, at times she will feel it. But I've managed by a highly selective process to live with one woman for eleven years now who is able to take this kind of thing, so my business really hasn't interfered that much. But it would have if I went mating with an average woman. It just wouldn't work!

So the main things I've given up for success, ironically enough, are probably sex and emotional relationships. Not that I've really refrained in those areas! I've done as much as anybody sexually and amatively, but I could have done ten times as much. I could screw new people all the time. I could enter many more emotional relationships. I don't have trouble getting involved. I never have. I fell in love first at the age of five. But I know that if I give in too much to my natural sex-love propensities, I just won't do other things. So I deliberately limit myself in those respects.

When I was analyzed years ago, the one thing I got out of my analysis (or perhaps from thinking things through myself at the time) was the conclusion—"Shit, when I die there'll be scores of enjoyable and important things I still will not have done. Too bad. My life is limited. I'm only going to live my seventy-five years or so, and the day only has twenty-four hours. Now I'd better make choices within those limits. It's impossible to get in all the things I want. But I can at least choose among pleasures, including the pleasures of working and of accomplishing what I want. If something has to go, tough shit!" I still abide by this philosophy.

EILEEN FORD

Of course you give things up. You give up a lot. I guess you give up a lot. The thing is, you know, I used to think that I wished I had stayed home and raised my children and been a better wife and a more feminine creature. I used to be very sorry that I hadn't done that. Yet as time goes by I find that—well, I knock on wood when I say it—my children are wonderful, they're growing up really nicely, and I'm happy and I hope my husband is happy. But many of my friends who stayed home aren't happy. Facing all the emptiness that's in their lives.

JOAN GANZ COONEY

I don't think I've had to give anything up. Others looking at my life might think so, but I don't. You can only have so many experiences, you only have so many hours in a day, and I've really spent my life the way I wanted to and am very glad I did. It was happenstance to a degree. I wanted children, there was not a plan not to have children, and had I had children I doubt that I would be doing this particular job. I would have worked, but I don't think I would have been able to work at this kind of job. So I would have been having another kind of experience which might have been just as satisfying. But I didn't have children and I did this and it's been super. I mean, how can I complain?

MARIO ANDRETTI

I wouldn't do anything different, I'll tell you. I have no regrets. I know that I've made a lot of mistakes. Hindsight is always twenty-twenty as they say, but in terms of the overall trend of how I went about things, I have no regrets, I really don't.

Walking Away and Moving On Up

HOWARD COSELL

When you face the kind of written vilification I've faced in my career you think about walking away all the time. All the time. It took all my strength to beat that back when I started *Monday Night Football.* I probably had the worst day-in, day-out press of anybody with the possible exception of Frank Sinatra, and it took a great deal of strength to surmount it.

You see, if you expose the frailties of sports as a business, they say you're biting the hand that feeds you. And if you don't, automatically you're a shill. There's no way to combat the failures of sports journalism. No way. It goes in an unending circle leading to nowhere. One of my major disappointments is the failure to get this country and all its media to treat sports the same way you would treat anything else in life journalistically. You go on the air on a Monday night football game and you say the game is dull, it's a field-goal stereotype, and then a guy writes that you're a company pimp while the owners of the NFL are screaming to ABC, "Get this sonofabitch—what's he doing to us?" I've actually been blacklisted from the air in my time, and every day I'm on the precipice of professional peril. And yet when you get into the full sweep of the society, the television critics will say, "Who cares? Who cares? It's the toy department of life. Who cares about the games?" Well, in the full sweep of life they're right, but they're the same ones who are always crying, "Where's the truth? Where is the truth on television?"

REX REED

I think about walking away from it every minute of the day. I would give anything to give it all up and get out of this whole mess and get myself a farmhouse somewhere by the sea. I'd like the freedom to think for a while. I'd really like to be free from all these pressures. I really do admire Pete Hamill, for example, for just giving it all up. He said, "I want to write better and think about life. There are too many important things that I'm not participating in. I don't know what people are thinking any more." And he did, he gave up his column and moved to California and he's writing screenplays and an occasional column about some political idea of his. I think it's marvelous. I don't think he has as much fame as he used to have. But Pete Hamill also was never an industry. I'm almost an industry at this point.

It's just incredible how many people depend on me. I don't just go to a movie and review it and the review appears. I have all this newspaper syndication and a whole magazine-writing career. I have all these television shows I do and a radio show that's being prepared right now for syndication. I have constant demands and invitations and things to mull over and think about turning down. I'm incorporated now. It's put me into a ridiculous tax structure. When I stop and think about all of that, it just gets to be too much sometimes and I'd like to simplify my life and prune away the clutter. I had no idea all of this would happen when I started writing.

So I probably will put the brakes on one of these days. But right now I'm just trying to save enough money to make myself really financially comfortable. I'd like to have enough to not ever have to work again if I don't want to. I don't want to take what I have now and go off to Tahiti and then be desperately ringing everybody's phone in two years, after I've spent everything. You can't even be a hippy today without money. It costs a lot of money to run one of those communes. Apple crops were bad this year in Vermont. All these hippies are out mugging old ladies again. I don't want to have to do that.

BRUNO SANMARTINO

As grateful as I am to my profession and as good as it's done for me, I have to admit there are times when I get very depressed about it because I miss my family so much. Sometimes I just feel like I want to be home with them and the hell with it all. But, you know, this is in your mind, a mood that you go through, and when you stop and think about it, you say, "Hey, before long you'll have no choice but to get out of it. Age is catching up, so let it run out. Be in it as long as you're capable, so when you do get out you'll have no regrets." So you kind of reason with yourself that way and you usually come out of it thinking straighter, I think.

BUDDY RICH

Walking away from it is bullshit. I love it when actors say, "This is my last picture! I've *had it* with Hollywood!" and then they're back six months later. You know, that grand *I'm retiring* bullshit. When I retire, man, I won't be coming back. When I finally decide to hang them up, I'm going someplace and lay down, you know, out on a beach somewhere and get some sun. But even then, even in full, total retirement, I think I'll be looking for someplace to sit in. Because I like to play, I really do like to play.

HALSTON

I wouldn't know what to do if I quit working, I really wouldn't. I feel that much of life is a bit like an anthill and we each have our little roles. Certain people produce this and others produce that, and if you don't produce you're sort of eliminated, programed out. And it's much better for life and mankind to produce. I just feel that the more you produce the better off you are. It's hard to convince other people of that sometimes. You know, some people think you should have lots of leisure hours with nothing to do but sit around the barbecue pit and drink beer. Well, that just doesn't interest me at all.

WILLIAM GAINES

I enjoy what I do very much and I'm not at all hobby oriented, so without a business I think I'd go out of my mind. That's what's happening today to everyone who has to retire. I think the biggest tragedy of a working person's life is when he suddenly finds out for one reason or another he can't work anymore. And, Lord, I think that would be the worst, most terrible thing that could happen to me.

JERRY DELLA FEMINA

I would think that someone would have to be disturbed to walk away from something he truly loves. And I truly love it. When people walk away, it's I-can't-stand-this-anymore. I feel very lucky. I can wake up in the morning and know I like what I do for a living. I like advertising. I like business. I like to work. I like to write. And I feel like I'm living a couple of extra lives. You know, it's not that humdrum, dull, dead, dead life. It's more. There's an excitement to it. There was a line about Jack Kennedy I always loved. A man who went to school with him said, "When we got out of school, we all stopped and he kept going." And that's what success is—somebody who keeps going, keeps trying more and getting more and enjoying more when everybody else has stopped.

MARIO ANDRETTI

Damn right I want to keep topping myself. That's what I've always done. Every year I itemize my previous season's work, and I say, "Well, how we doing? Where the hell have I been? What have I done? Are we wasting time? Is it time to improve in certain areas? Or maybe time to pass on to something else?"

ALICE COOPER

I don't like to keep doing the same show. That's why every time I go out on tour I do something different. Like I did the hanging first, then I did the electric chair, and then I did something else. I always go out of my way to come up with something more exciting. It would be so boring to keep doing those same bits again. I think the scariest thing in the world is boredom. When I start getting bored then I know I better get back to work because that really does frighten me. That's why I travel so much. Even when I'm not working I'll be in Mexico or some other place just 'cause I like to keep moving and doing my thing. I hate boredom worse than anything. Almost as much as liver.

CLIVE DAVIS

I've never operated on the philosophy that you should keep moving on to bigger and better achievements. I don't think of it that way. If there were dissatisfaction, perhaps one would. I've got the excitement of the growing Arista Records and it's doing well and I'm gratified by it, so I don't think about, Well, should I move on to something else? I've always been somewhat wary of people who do well and are happy in what they do well but change for the sake of change. I don't believe in that. I never did. When I went from public school to high school they'd say, "Well, go to Erasmus Hall, it's a good school. It will prepare you for college." And then it was, "What college are you going to go to to prepare you for law school?" And law school was supposed to prepare you for this firm, and that firm should prepare you for the next. And I'd always say, "At what stage do you stop preparing and end up?" Not necessarily for the rest of your life, but you know what I mean.

To me, the desire for change should creep in only when you're badly dissatisfied either with the economics of what you're doing or with the work, and not necessarily in that order. And if you like the work and you're happy with the economics, don't leave. I'm satisfied, so I wouldn't change what I'm doing.

EILEEN FORD

I'm not superambitious. I'm happy with what I'm doing now, I really am. What else can I do? The only thing I could do would be to stop this and go do something completely different because there is no time in my life for anything else. I leave the house at eight in the morning and come home around six-thirty every night. I work on weekends writing books. I'm perfectly occupied, you know, twenty-four hours a day.

JACK HALEY JR.

I feel I'm just halfway in the middle of a terrific life, but I don't have the drive for that next pinnacle: "I want to own my own network, I want to own my own studio." Not in a million years would I want to have that kind of thing. It pulls you too far away from the line where you want to be. I want to be creative. I want to entertain people. I want to direct and I want to write and I want to produce, and that's what I'm doing . . . and that's what I'm going to stay doing.

MIKE WALLACE

I have had a certain pattern in my life of working at something, trying to make it successful and then walking away. For fifteen to twenty years I lived in thirteen-week cycles, whether I was doing news broadcasts, or interview shows, or the *Biography* series, or whatever. And that was a very wearing pattern, not one calculated to let you work persistently on a given body of work. It seemed I was always moving from one place to the other. I became a kind of juggler, and there was a good deal of anxiety along the way. I have never worked at a single enterprise in my life as long as I have worked at *60 Minutes.* We're ending our eighth year, and I wonder if it might not be renewing for me now to move on to some other enterprise.

Yes, I do feel the need to keep topping myself, and I deplore it. For a long time that was an interesting challenge. No longer. And I say to myself, "Why? Why is it necessary to keep topping yourself, to keep searching for something more successful than the last, more challenging? Why is it necessary to keep going beyond what you've done? Why not just enjoy what you do as you go, as much as you can?" It's difficult for me to find answers to those questions. I suppose I've established a pattern for myself that is difficult to break.

AL GOLDSTEIN

The sad thing about success is that it's never enough. I'm insatiable. I think successful people are driven people, compulsive people, crazy people. I'm in analysis, and I think some of my drives for success are insane, I really do. Now that I'm Al Goldstein, I want to be Clay Felker of *New York* magazine. I want to be Jann Wenner of *Rolling Stone.* I'm known in more places, but I feel that they have more impact. I wish I had *The Village Voice* with its one hundred fifty thousand readership. So it's never enough, and I do feel that it's neurotic. Analytically, hopefully, one would change it, yet whenever I'm at my shrink's and I talk about why I'm at *Screw* and not an editor at *Time* magazine, I tell him that my neuroses permit me to pay his high fees, one hundred dollars an hour.

It's a contradiction. It's very complicated because I don't fully understand my motives. And I'm afraid to take the defensive position of saying, "Well, everything I do is healthy." I really want to view myself as objectively as possible. And I think the price you pay for success is very high. Long hours. Preoccupation with business. Up until the birth of my son, nothing else mattered. My wife is, in fact, still second choice to my business. If I had to make a choice between my son and *Screw* I have a feeling my son would win, but this is the first change. You are a true believer when you have a business. You're captive to whatever god that business represents.

BILL GRAHAM

I closed the Fillmores in 1971 because I wasn't enjoying it any more. It wasn't because rock was dead. I never said that. I said that it was getting to be such big business that it was no longer fun for me the way it had been before. Before, it took four or five conversations to make a deal for a headliner, but now it was taking twenty because the food rider was this long, and you had to go through it about the limos, and the pink sheets, and all the rest of it. I doubt very much in the history of entertainment that places of that size ever made more money. They were money machines to the end. Of course, *Rolling Stone* and all the others could never believe that a capitalist would close his business just because he wasn't enjoying it, but that's what it was. The real beauty and joy of creating shows was beginning to diminish. The people were changing too. They no longer said at the end of a show, "Hey, can we hear some more?" Now it was, "MORE! MORE! MORE! I paid $6.50, you cocksucker!" Also, because Woodstock told America how big rock had become, the agencies started to say, "Well, we'll tell you who the support acts are." Then the headliner would have a friend with a group and he'd say, "You want my group? You gotta take his group." So the real producer—and I consider myself a real producer—no longer had the right to create his own art form. So for these various reasons I left, I walked away.

After many years of work I wanted to do nothing for a while and then maybe write a book, maybe do a film, anything other than what I had been doing. So I took a couple of months off and went to the Mediterranean, but then that which I wanted to have happen, gradually did not happen. Not being a writer, I couldn't say, "Well, today I think I'll get up and write. John Steinbeck writes four hours a day. I read where Algren does two in the morning, six in the afternoon. Let's go!" Here I am, you know, off of Corfu, and it ain't happenin'. And then only a few months after I closed I received a call from the Who and they said, "Bill, we're coming to America. Will you do us?" That was the first sign. All of a sudden I realized, Man, I want to get back to that. I said to myself, "How could it say 'Sam Schwartz presents the Who in San Francisco'? It can't say that. I'm the producer in San Francisco for the Who. Yes, I'll do it." So there was that show and then another show and then a big outdoor show and then another management contract and then another publishing deal, and within the next six months I got back into doing that at which I am very good.

I know some people say I'm rather vain and egomaniacal, but I've always felt that as a producer I am very good, and if I didn't think so at least the public told me that I was and so did the groups by the way they accepted me. So it is now 1976, and the volume of business we're doing is even bigger than it was in 1969. We're doing a lot of outdoor shows and managing a couple of groups. I have an eighty-man staff, a warehouse with a million dollars' worth of sound equipment, lights, trucks. And that's where the failure comes in.

You see, since I've come back I keep saying to myself that I really do want to get into films, I really would like to write a book, I would like to take another vacation, but I'm still here, I'm not doing any of these things. Now when a man's a success he's supposed to be able to do what he wants unless his success is based on a job that requires him to be there. If a guy makes eighty thousand a year flying the President of the United States, he can't hire anybody else. He has to be at the gig to earn the bread. So I tell myself that I have to be where I am to run my company because I want to run it in a particular way, which is my way. I don't have partners. I don't have a little guy doing my work for me. It's my personality that relates to this particular situation. If I do a Grateful Dead show somewhere and it's a festival scene and people get there early and are crowding around the building, to this day I will go to my car, get a football and say, "Hey, how about six guys from the Bronx and six guys from Queens," and we'll go out and play touch football and divert the attention away from the building. I'm not saying I'm a genius, but I'm gonna get you with that: "What do you mean, no? Come *on!*" Well, the next guy can't do that. You know, the best he can do is, "Please don't break down the fourth floor windows."

But what I've been doing over the past four years is something I've already proven myself at. The only gain now is an occasional get-off on a show. And sure, there are great Stones dates, great Who dates, great Dylan dates, but deep down I've had sex with these situations before. The only thing that's left is knowing that I'm good at what I do, but there's also a great feeling of failure that I haven't the guts to leave what I know I'm good at to try something else. So success to me is that I've had the chance to do what I've done, and the failure is that I'm still doing it.

Whatever it is in me that is necessary to pull me out just hasn't come along yet. I know I'm not the kind of guy I tried to be in '71: "I'll quit and I'll do it. I'll just stand under the apple tree of life and wait for it to fall." No, the way that has to happen is that you reach up and grab that apple. Well, that hasn't happened yet, and I've spent a great deal of time thinking about it. I know I'm only a failure unto myself, just as the guy who played Marshall Dillon on *Gunsmoke* for eighteen years, if he has anything inside him, must also question himself even though he maybe owns San Fernando Valley, unless when he's not shooting for four months he *does* deep-sea fish, he *does* meditate, he *does* paint, he *does* relate to his community, he does get off that way. I don't because my thing is twelve months a year.

I've made something of a study of other people more famous than I am outside of the rock business. I'm not in Willy Mays's world or Gordie Howe's world, but I think they're still doing what they've done for so long for the same reason that I am: This is what I'm so good at. This is what the world has told me I'm good at. This is my El Rey brand that I'm wearing and, God, how tough it is to leave it. I'm willing to fail at something. *Am* I? I've thought about leaving many, many times. I admit that I'm a prisoner of my own Frankenstein. So why don't I leave? Well, why did Willy Mays play till he was forty-one? Why does Bette Davis do small parts? The roar of the crowd. Willie Mays didn't make the catches the way he used to. He didn't still go from first to third on a single to right field. I still do, that's another thing. The shows are still good. We still do brilliant productions. We still make a lot of money. So even though I know there are other abilities in me, I don't leave. That's the failure.

I've visualized an analogy. I've thought of Muhammad Ali, not now at thirty-one or thirty-two, but at the age of twenty-six or twenty-seven, holding a press conference at the peak of his career and saying, "I've fought everyone there is to fight. I've proven myself. I'm world champion, and I'm proud to be the world champion, but deep within me I've taken this part of success as far as I can in my life. I am at the peak of my career, unchallenged heavyweight champion of the world, but I'm going to retire because just repeating that particular success is not a get-off for me, and I consider myself a *mench* inside. I'm going to retire from boxing and attempt something I've never done before because most of my life's been fighting." Most of my life has been producing shows. And Ali would say, "I'm going to attempt to become a professional surfer." Now my question to me is, What kind of a man does it take to do that? For the time being, someone bigger or deeper within than I am. Okay, *who?*

Can you tell me about someone who was a tremendous success within his field of endeavor who left voluntarily when he wasn't forced to leave? Don't tell me about a grocer who closed after thirty years. Tell me about Richard Avedon. Tell me about Tony Curtis. Tell me about Willie Shoemaker. How come they ain't leaving? You see, it's such a problem to get away from the heroin. I'm a junkie the same way Gordie Howe is a junkie, the way Willie Shoemaker is a junkie. At the age of forty-seven he just goes on and on, on those fucking tracks. And he cannot tell anybody he loves to ride horses. He's ridden seven million winners. He's got roses coming down his throat. So we're all in the same boat. The only difference is maybe they don't think about doing anything else. Maybe Willie Shoemaker says, "This is all I can do, man. All I can do is ten percent of eight million dollars a year. Shit. Fuck."

So I'm gonna keep doing what I do until there are enough inner forces that make me want to do something else, until it's "God, I read this book and I think I can get this guy to make it into a script and then I'll give it to that guy and, what did you say, the Stones are coming? And I don't care? That's great!" Because deep down I just wish something would happen that would let me stand up and say what I really want to say—fuck it. I must get to that point myself because nobody can do it for me. The most famous person in films today has offered me a three-film contract and I should say, "This is it!" but I'm very well aware that it's an outer force that has created this situation. It didn't come from me, and I have a fear of doing anything that isn't from within because I closed a business before and waited for something to happen from within and when it didn't I came back. So I'm waiting for Bill, is what it amounts to, and meanwhile I'll have to live with that inner failing until my makeup can handle the two things of leaving what you know you're good at and taking a stab at failing at something else that you want to try.

Index